Anders' Army

This work is dedicated to the memory of Franciszek Hałuszczak (1920–1967)

Born in Poland – served in 'Children of Lwow' 6th Armoured Regiment as Liaison Officer to 10th Indian Division. Wounded at Piedimonte, 18 May 1944.

Died in Leeds, 1967.

Anders' Army

General Władysław Anders and the Polish Second Corps 1941-46

Evan McGilvray

Pen & Sword
MILITARY

First published in Great Britain in 2018 by
Pen & Sword Military
an imprint of
Pen & Sword Books Ltd
47 Church Street
Barnsley
South Yorkshire
S70 2AS

ISBN 978 1 47383 411 8

A CIP catalogue record for this book is
available from the British Library.

Printed and bound in England by TJ International Ltd, Padstow, Cornwall

Pen & Sword Books Limited incorporates the imprints of Atlas, Archaeology,
Aviation, Discovery, Family History, Fiction, History, Maritime, Military,
Military Classics, Politics, Select, Transport, True Crime, Air World,
Frontline Publishing, Leo Cooper, Remember When, Seaforth Publishing,
The Praetorian Press, Wharncliffe Local History, Wharncliffe Transport,
Wharncliffe True Crime and White Owl.

For a complete list of Pen & Sword titles please contact
PEN & SWORD BOOKS LIMITED
47 Church Street, Barnsley, South Yorkshire, S70 2AS, England
E-mail: enquiries@pen-and-sword.co.uk
Website: www.pen-and-sword.co.uk

Contents

Acknowledgments and Thanks

I owe a great debt of thanks to Janusz Jarzembowski as not only has he proved to be a great friend but has contributed so much to this work. Janusz has waived the copyright of images reproduced here taken from his late father's archive now known as the Armoured Hussars Archive. In addition Janusz had freely given advice in correspondence regarding the images and my work in general. I am also grateful for Janusz's input in providing captions for the images as well as the provision of the map used to illustrate the book.

I also wish to thank Roman Hałuszczak for allowing me to use his late father's book as well as providing other material concerning the Italian Campaign, especially the Battle for Monte Cassino.

Further thanks go to Andrzej Suchcitz and Jadwiga Kowalska at PISM for their help and cooperation in this work. Their knowledge remains unsurpassed.

Thank you to George Anderson for his swift turnaround of the map and at such a good price. And of course my family, who help me in my daily struggles with IT and tend to keep me on track.

Evan McGilvray
Pudsey
Palm Sunday 2017.

Maps

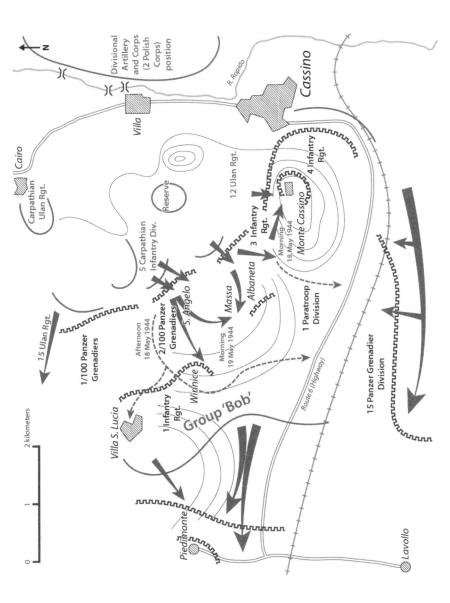

Polish Second Corps' Operations, Monte Cassino, May 1944.

Chapter 1

General Władysław Anders, Origins and the Polish Army, 1892–1939

The future General Anders was born on 11 August 1892 near Warsaw. Anders, like a number of twentieth-century Polish military heroes actually had little Polish blood in him and, in his case, originated from German stock; hence his rather un-Polish family name. Furthermore, unlike most Poles he was born into a Protestant family rather than Catholic, as many Poles were and remain so. At the time of Anders' birth there was no Polish state as it had been wiped from the world map in 1795, a result of annexation and division by the three east-central European empires of Austria, Prussia (after 1870 Germany) and Russia. Anders was born in the Russian sector of Poland. His family were unassuming people and there was nothing in his background which may have pointed towards the leader he became, or the controversy which he was to provoke. As Anders and Poland grew together, they were both shaped by the events of the twentieth century.

Anders' father, Albert, was an estate manager and at the time of Anders' birth was running an estate near Warsaw. He later moved to manage a large estate for Prince Vasilchikov at Taurogi, north of the river Niemen, today in Lithuania. During this period the young Władysław Anders remained in Warsaw where he was educated in a local grammar school. In 1909 at the age of 17 Anders had completed his secondary education. There was a slight shadow cast over the early years of Anders however, as under Imperial Russian rule, most young men who were subjects of the Russian Emperor, the Tsar (in 1909, the ruler was Tsar Nicholas II), were required to serve in the Russian Army once they reached the age of 21 years. Young men were conscripted to serve for a period of three years' compulsory military service in the army, however this could be reduced by volunteering to serve immediately after leaving secondary education. If a youngster volunteered to serve the three-year compulsory term was reduced to a single year of military service. This meant that after completing their year of voluntary service young men were free to attend university without any interruption, having already completed their obligations regarding military service. Many young men from Polish families took this step and Anders was no exception.

At the end of September 1910 Anders, as a volunteer, joined a cavalry regiment, the 3rd Novorossiysk Dragoons in Kownie, close to where his father was working. Anders was quickly sent to the regimental school for the training of non-commissioned officers (NCO). In April 1911 he was promoted to the rank of corporal and by June 1911 he had finished his training at the school. During September 1911 Anders passed the examinations necessary to qualify as a reserve cadet officer in the 3rd Cavalry Division. On 1 October 1911 he was released from his obligations to serve in the Russian military and was placed on the army reserve list as a cadet officer. After this and for the next three years, Anders studied mechanical engineering at Riga Technical University. In 1912 however, an incident occurred which was to have a profound effect on the remainder of Anders' life: he saved the lives of two generals when the horses pulling their coach bolted. As panic set in Anders stepped up to the plate and was able to get to the horses and bring them back under control. One of the generals in the coach, General Pavel Rennenkampf, a Russian general despite his clearly German surname, told Anders that if he was ever in any difficulty he was to get in touch with him.

When it became likely that Russia might go to war during the summer of 1914 Anders took Rennenkampf at his word. Anders was recalled to serve in the Russian Army on 23 July 1914, but instead of a chance of action he was told to report to a horse-drawn supply unit which brought provisions to Rennenkampf's Army. Anders immediately telegraphed Rennenkampf about his posting. Rennenkampf changed the order and Anders got what he desired: a posting to a front-line cavalry regiment, the 3rd Dragoon Regiment, IV Cavalry Corps of the Russian First Army which Anders joined on 23 September 1914. Very soon Anders was in the thick of the fighting of the 1914 Eastern Front and perhaps like many young men and soldiers, seeking glory.

Anders was wounded for the first time on 20 November 1914 when he received a head wound while on patrol at Szelnihem. He seems to have recovered quickly as by the beginning of 1915 he was back with his regiment on the Baltic coast operating on the northern flank of the eastern Front. However, from the middle of February 1915 until the beginning of May 1915, Anders was hospitalised. It is not clear why but as he had not been wounded again it can be assumed that he was ill.

Anders was wounded once more during an enemy artillery attack in the area of the village of Litowież. The exploding shells threw up earth and wrecked houses which showered Anders with debris including bricks; he suffered wounds to his head, chest and right leg. This time Anders was in hospital until the end of August 1915. During the period of May to August 1915 Anders was decorated three times for his services. This was the beginning of a rapid rise in his military career. In addition to being thrice decorated, Anders received further kudos when he captured the German general, Generalmajor Siegfried Fabarius (1853–1915) who was the Commander of 82nd Reserve Division, Imperial German Army. Anders' capture of Fabarius was recognised and he was awarded the Order of Saint George. He was also yet again wounded. Fabarius died while in Russian captivity; clearly he was an elderly man for a soldier and should not have been at the Front at the age of 62 years, but during the First World War such elderly men were indeed serving as senior officers on both sides.

While Anders was away from the Front a combined Austrian–German offensive had begun in the east and by August 1915, much of what is today Poland, had fallen into the hands of the Germans and Austrians. The Polish towns and cities of Warsaw, Lublin and Brześć had been captured in August; in September both Grodno and Wilno (today Vilnius, capital of Lithuania) had fallen. After these losses the Eastern Front became more static and Anders became part of an operation that held a line which ran from Riga along the Dzwiny River to Dyneburg, crossing Lake Narocz around Baranowicz and Pińsk along the Styr River and finishing around Czerniowiec. This represented the Eastern Front until February 1918. However life and events were about to prove more fruitful and interesting for Anders who, after three wounds and being promoted to the rank of captain, left the frontline to attend staff college in St Petersburg, or Petrograd as it was known by 1916.

It was rare for a Pole to be allowed to attend staff college while serving in the Russian Army as there were certain discriminations practised within the Russian Army and Russian society in general. As we have seen however, Anders was hardly a Pole and was Protestant not Catholic, so he could attend staff college. The Russian Empire itself was in turmoil owing to the War and in March 1917 the monarchy collapsed with the abdication of Nicholas II; the first revolution in Russia of 1917 served both Anders and Poland well as separate Polish units were formed within the Russian Army at that time. As a result, Anders joined First Polish Corps in Bobruisk and was given the command of 1st Krechowicki Lancers. Following the second Russian revolution of 1917, the Bolshevik revolution during November, and the subsequent peace treaty signed between the new Russian state and Germany in March 1918, which saw Russia leave the war, First Polish Corps was disbanded. Anders, as with other officers, now more or less unemployed, made their way to Warsaw (which was still in German hands) during Spring 1918.[1]

Luckily Polish historiography puts some flesh on the bare bones of Anders' career between 1918 and 1920. Anders, as we have seen, joined First Polish Corps which had actually grown out of the Dowbór-Muśnicki Corps which was basically a formation of Polish troops serving in the Russian Army even before the February 1917 Revolution in Russia. Its founder, a Pole but a senior commander of the Russian Army, General Józef Dowbór-Muśnicki, took full advantage of the weaknesses of the Russian state as war and revolution took their toll, and gathered Polish troops around him in preparation to strike a blow for Polish independence. On 23 August 1917 this formation had developed and was established and named as First Polish Corps. By January 1918 it had evolved into three divisions based in modern Belarus.[2]

1918 was a pivotal year for Poland as it led to the creation of the modern Polish state. Once Russia had withdrawn from the war however, it seemed unlikely that this would actually happen. The Russian withdrawal allowed the Germans to move troops from the Eastern Front and commence operations on the western Front in France. The timely arrival of American forces in France prevented a German breakthrough, while in both Germany and Austria domestic discontent blew into full-blown revolts and mutinies. The Bolsheviks may have been put out of the war during Spring 1918, but as winter beckoned that year, cold and hungry people in Germany and Austria threatened the perceived stability in those two lands while the spectre of Bolshevik revolution was never far away. During late autumn 1918 both the Austrian and German monarchies collapsed and on 11 November 1918 fighting on the Western Front stopped. Out of the shambles of the First World War emerged new east-central European states including Poland, which declared its independence on 11 November 1918.

A consequence of the rapid collapse of traditional authority in east-central Europe was a free-for-all as the newly emerging nations began to make land grabs as they tried to establish their frontiers before peace treaties dictated where new boundaries might actually lie. Poland was no exception and fought a war against Ukraine, which was also trying to establish its own western borders at the expense of Poland. During the period of late 1918 and early 1919, Poland, as with most east-central European states, did not have a formal army but instead relied on local militias as well as troops returning from the various fronts of the 1914–1918 War.

On the whole Polish forces were quite successful and during 1920 advanced into Ukraine as far as the capital, Kiev. Then the Soviets or Bolsheviks, sensing danger to their revolution as well as seeking an opportunity to spread their doctrine following the concept of 'world revolution', counter-attacked the invading Polish Army. The Soviet counter-offensive was so effective that by August 1920, the Red Army was at the gates of Warsaw itself. It seemed that the fledgling Polish state was doomed to return to Russian or Soviet rule once more. It is at Warsaw that once more we can pick up the traces of Anders' career because he was seriously wounded in his legs while leading an attack against a Bolshevik offensive on 29 July 1920. For his actions on that day Anders was awarded the *Virtuti Militari*.[3]

The *Virtuti Militari* is often touted by some Poles as the 'Polish Victoria Cross' – it is not and is far from it, it has five classes of award with the top award often granted to senior officers for service rather than bravery. It was awarded so often in the Second World War that its value is of little meaning when compared to the Victoria Cross. Indeed the illustrious Polish general, General Stanisław Maczek, was very critical of the devaluation of the decoration.[4] Given that Anders was to win the *Virtuti Militari* (5th Class) once more in 1920, as well as twice receiving the *Krzyż Waleczyna* (Military Cross) for his actions on 29 July 1920, medal inflation in the Polish Army and later during that period is obvious.[5]

The Soviet counter-attack and the resulting Battle of Warsaw, against the expectations of the world, saw a Polish victory in August 1920. Soviet forces withdrew from Poland and returned to their own territories. The spread of Bolshevikism had been postponed for a generation. However the Polish victory at Warsaw had consequences which were to be disastrous for Poland and would be felt to at least 1989. But to return to the Anders' story, by 1921, Anders, now a lieutenant-colonel, was sent on a two-year course at the *Ecole de Guerre* in Paris. This French military academy was considered to have been the best in the world at the time. The Polish Army had also re-organised along the lines of the French Army and trained under French guidance, so it was a natural step for the Polish High Command to send some of its more able officers to France to become fully conversant with French military doctrine.

Even though on the surface Poland looked as if it was at peace with itself and enjoying democracy, there was a simmering resentment among some of its officer corps who sympathised with Marshal Piłsudski, considered to be the founder of the resurrected Polish state. The consequences alluded to earlier in connection to the Polish victory at Warsaw finally flared up in May 1926 and are the roots of how the modern Polish state was established. The popular Polish myth is that the re-independence of Poland centres on a single figure: Marshal Józef Piłsudski. The title of 'Marshal' was honorific, as Piłsudski never received any military training. Indeed the historian, Adam Zamoyski observed that Piłsudski had led an interesting life, having been born a Lithuanian nobleman; he was to become by twists and chances of fate, a terrorist, a Socialist, a train robber and finally a self-appointed military commander.[6] John Coutouvidis adds to this assessment of Piłsudski in writing, 'Józef Piłsudski had personified independent Poland. Successively convicted terrorist, Socialist agitator, cavalry officer, Commander-in-Chief and vanquisher of Trotsky's Red Army, democratic president and dictator, he became the embodiment of Polish statehood.'[7] This was the problem with the post-1918 Polish state; it was founded on a myth.

It is true that Piłsudski, taking advantage of the relatively lax conditions of the Austrian sector of Poland between 1908 and 1914, did establish a para-military formation: the 'riflemen' or '*Strzelcy*'. However in many ways they were military clowns, poorly armed with out-dated weapons and drilling in the evenings and at weekends. When war broke out in 1914 they went on some farcical adventures worthy of Don Quixote before retreating back into Austrian held Poland. In 1917 Piłsudski was imprisoned by the Germans for refusing to swear an oath of allegiance to them and their allies. Therefore, when Poland achieved independence owing to the collapse of the east-central European imperial system Piłsudski had played very little part in it as he had been in prison in Magdeburg, Germany for the previous eighteen months. It was actually professional soldiers such as Anders and his comrades, who had played a larger part in fighting for Polish independence in 1918, who were responsible for the resurrection of the Polish state, but Piłsudski had charisma and that was what counted.

Piłsudski had schemed and plotted since the turn of the twentieth century to bring about Polish independence and it was only he who could bring the various factions in the re-born Poland together and then override them all. It was through him and the victory at Warsaw, with the belief that the Polish Army had established Polish frontiers, that the Polish Army managed to become the primary political force in Poland by the beginning of 1921. Many in the Polish Army considered that they were owed by the Polish people. Piłsudski and his most loyal supporters, his original comrades from the *Strzelcy* or the First Brigade, thought that their time had come, but they were to be disappointed.

A source of the disappointment of the First Brigade and for Piłsudski was the 1921 Polish Constitution which called for a democratic Poland, including democratic oversight of the Polish military as well as some restraints on presidential powers. It had been widely considered that Piłsudski would stand for election to the Polish presidency and if he had, without doubt he would have won. However Piłsudski did not like the restrictions imposed on the presidential office, refused to stand, and retreated from public life.

Within the Polish Army with French influence and training, the Polish officer corps began to become more professional. This meant that officers such as Anders, for example, were to have a more prominent role owing to their professional training, while those who had served in Piłsudski's Brigades felt slighted as they lacked professional qualifications and training which were becoming increasingly important to the professional Polish soldier. A major problem was that a majority of Polish officers had come from the former Imperial Austrian Army and some considered that these ex-Austrian Army veterans had formed a clique within the Polish Army. Those who felt they had forfeited the most since independence were the amateurs from the *Strzelcy*, or the First Brigade, who had collaborated with Piłsudski. These veterans nursed a sense of loss and a lack of gratitude from the Polish people. Finally, on 12 May 1926, Piłsudski struck and launched a military coup.

During the May 1926 coup, Anders showed some of his spirit and ability to do what he considered to be right even if he risked his career and possibly his head. Anders continued to make his mark in his career; always a difficult thing to do within a peacetime army, but he was an educated man and a veteran of several wars and carried the scars to prove it. By May 1926 he was the Chief of Staff to General Tadeusz Rozwadowski, Military Commander in Warsaw.[8] Anders was certainly on the side of the new Poland and democracy, even if he had sympathy for Piłsudski and his motivation; Anders refused to break his oath to the legitimate Polish government and eventually led the defence of the Presidential Palace and in the last incident led President Wojciechowski and his ministers to safety.[9]

After three days of fighting in Warsaw, Piłsudski prevailed and he took over the country. Piłsudski was a dictator without doubt, but not in the model of Hitler or Stalin who were yet to come. He was not even a Mussolini or a Franco; he merely wanted to control Poland using the military. Even then he did not really trust the Polish Army entirely and so used the veterans from the First Brigade as the bedrock of his dictatorship. What should be recognised however is that with each passing year, the military dictatorship in Poland hardened.

In the immediate aftermath of the May 1926 coup, Anders was interned for a short spell owing to his refusal to support Piłsudski. Then he was sent on 'holiday'.[10] This is a Polish euphemism for 'suspended from duties', perhaps indefinitely as in the case of Władysław Sikorski, who had enjoyed high office during the period of Polish democracy, 1921–26, including having been Prime Minister as well as Minister for War and later was to be the Polish leader in exile, 1939–43. In 1926 he was commander of the regiments in Lwów, and Sikorski kept them firmly in barracks during the three days of fighting in May 1926. This action was more-or-less the end of his career in the inter-war Polish military, as Sikorski had denied Piłsudski the symbolism of perhaps being right by refusing to support his coup. In retaliation Piłsudski and his successors did not have Sikorski arrested or imprisoned, but instead placed him in limbo; Sikorski did not receive any further military or political offices until he was in exile after September 1939. Sikorski was even denied a passport until the late 1930s.

Anders was more fortunate than Sikorski in some ways; he enjoyed a modest career and did not pose a political threat to Piłsudski. During the second half of July 1926 he and eighteen other officers were personally interviewed by Piłsudski regarding their future careers. The result of Anders' interview was that he received command of 2nd Independent Cavalry Brigade, also known as the Wołyń Brigade which was based in Brody in Równe County, Wołyń Province and out of the way on the very eastern border with the Soviet Union and well away from Warsaw.[11]

The British historian, Andrzej Suchcitz, suggests that after the 1926 coup Piłsudski was anxious to heal the rift in the Polish Army, which may explain why Anders was treated so sympathetically.[12] Following the success of their coup, Piłsudski and his supporters set about purging the Polish officer corps of those who had served in the Austrian Army before 1918. Anders was lucky as he had previously served in the Imperial Russian Army and was more-or-less without political ambition at that time. Simply, unlike Sikorski, Anders did not pose a political threat to Piłsudski and could be retained even if at arm's length. All the same, Anders was fortunate in Piłsudski's treatment of him as many officers, especially ex-imperial Austrian army officers, had seen their careers wrecked by not supporting the coup and afterwards would be passed over for promotion. This led to a new adjective being coined which described their plight: '*Zmajowany*' or 'May-ed', because Piłsudski's coup happened in May and these officers considered that this was when their problems began.[13]

Piłsudski personally interviewing officers in 1926 in order to determine their future employment with the Polish Army or otherwise became the norm by 1930. From then on Piłsudski decided on all promotions and postings with the Polish officer corps following question and answer sessions held by Piłsudski at war games. The Polish Army became more politicised after 1926 and after 1930 became even more amateur than it had been after the May 1926 coup, with Piłsudski loyalists being promoted over the heads of more able officers. Meanwhile, fewer and fewer Polish military officers were graduates from staff colleges.[14]

The effect of Anders being moved to the eastern frontiers of Poland was that one of the most experienced and able officers of the Polish Army was kept away from central matters which were always dealt with in Warsaw. This continued even when Anders was promoted to the rank of general.[15] Piłsudski, who died in 1935, must have decided on Anders' promotion. While Anders was away from the hub of things he may not have noticed that the Polish military was not modernising and that defensive plans were not being made. By this time two very dangerous enemies threatened Poland. They were of course the Soviet Union which, since Joseph Stalin became its ruler after 1929, had become a genuine threat to Poland. This danger was compounded after 1933 when Adolf Hitler and the Nazi Party took over Germany. Both the Soviet Union and Germany had foreign policies which were totally against the concept of the Polish state, but meanwhile bided their time until it was possible to re-annex Poland. Furthermore, ideologically the Nazis were totally opposed to the freedom of the Slavic lands and considered Slavs to be sub-human. This should have prevented the Soviet Union and Germany from ever being allies. Even so, the Polish government had to deal with the situation with which it was confronted. Polish foreign policy during the 1930s therefore became one of balance and correctness towards its two potential enemies, even if at times it seemed that the Polish government or more correctly, the Polish Foreign Minister, Colonel Józef Beck, seemed more favourably disposed towards Germany. An interesting development for the Anders' story was that according to the historian Michael Zurowski, after 1936 Anders became 'a man of distinctly right-wing views' and flirted between the right wing of the ruling Polish military junta, 'Sanacja', and the near fascists of the Polish Right.[16] This was quite a turnaround for the man who had defended the lawfully elected government and the legal 1921 Polish Constitution and risked himself and his career when he had defied Piłsudski and his mutineers back in 1926.

Poland had another problem connected to defence; it was a very poor country and even if it wanted to modernise its armed forces it could not afford to do so. Furthermore there was an overarching attitude in the higher echelons of the Polish Army which resisted modernity and considered that mounted cavalry would always be able to defend Poland. The legend of 1920 lived on. Anders noted this attitude when he received the command of the Nowogródska Cavalry Brigade in 1937. He quickly reported that the Brigade lacked the ability to fight armoured units. He also considered that its officers were 'hidebound' in their attitudes. He also reported that in war games his officers were always too quick to charge forward without any reconnaissance.[17] Clearly, in seventeen years, nothing had been learned by some Polish officers as this was an observation made by the commander of the British Military Mission to Poland in 1920.[18] Quite simply, in 1920, many Polish officers never bothered to check what might be around the next corner or further ahead while out in the field or taking up a position for the night. Anders was not a lazy or negligent officer and took his duties seriously.[19] As a product of two prestigious military academies as well as being an experienced combat veteran, Anders must have been dismayed at the Polish Army's lack of preparation for war, which was definitely coming. War came to Poland on 1 September 1939 when Germany invaded and it is from there that the story of Anders' Army can really begin.

Chapter 2

1939–1941: The Division of Poland and Relations with the Soviet Union

War came to Poland on 1 September 1939 with the Germans and their Slovak allies invading from the north, south and west. An attack by Germany on Poland had not been long anticipated, Germany had only revealed beyond doubt its intentions in the Spring of 1939. More astute followers of current affairs noticed much earlier, notably Winston Churchill, but he was considered to have been a warmonger and so was ignored. Simply, the western powers tried to accommodate Germany – or more realistically Hitler – as far as possible to avoid war. The example of Munich in 1938, when a large part of Czechoslovakia was given away to Germany by the western powers, notably the UK and France, is a good example. It was only when Hitler returned for the rest of Czechoslovakia in March 1939 that the scales began to fall from many peoples' eyes and it was finally realised that a stand had to be made against Germany. This was much of the thinking behind the French and British guarantees to Poland and Polish independence. These guarantees were also the reason why Germany turned against Poland or were at least the excuse to turn against Poland.

In fairness, since the death of Piłsudski the Polish government had tried to address the shortfalls of the Polish Army, they attempted to develop viable defensive plans to be followed in the event of invasions by either Germany or the Soviet Union, as well as trying to overhaul the equipment of the Polish Army and modernise it. In their wildest nightmares the Polish General Staff had never considered invasions by *both* Germany and the Soviet Union. Nobody had until late August 1939.

Plans to defend Poland began with those anticipating an attack by the Soviet Union which were not complete until 20 March 1939, while plans against a German attack did not begin until 4 March 1939. The Polish defence plan against a German attack was flawed as it suited the Germans, allowing them to choose the timing, place and methodology. By then Poland was surrounded on three sides by Germany.[1] Owing to history, Poles had anticipated a Soviet invasion as being more likely than a German invasion. The Rippentrop–Molotov Pact of August 1939, which formally concluded an alliance between the Soviet Union and Germany came as a bolt out of the blue to most of the world and Poland was dished. Poland was hamstrung when it came to improving its lot in the world. The major stumbling block was the lack of money; Germany could outspend Poland every time on its military. Jan Karski noted that Poland actually had fewer military plans in 1939 than it had in 1925, a year before Piłsudski's coup, and even though Poland spent fifty per cent of its national budget on defence between 1935 and 1939, it was not enough. German figures reveal that during the same period it spent thirty times more on the *Wehrmacht* alone.[2]

Furthermore, the Polish military was actually ruling Poland even though Poland still had a Prime Minister and a President. General Edmund Ironside, who led a British Military Mission to Warsaw during July 1939 reported, 'the President is a figurehead and knows it. The Prime Minister never appeared. The two men who have all the power in their hands are the Foreign Minister, Colonel Beck, and the Marshal Smigly-Ridz' [sic].[3] Even if the Polish military were in effect ruling Poland, especially after 1935, the top commanders on the whole were not reformers and Anders noted that even those officers under his command were quite hidebound and, rather like many of their commanders, unwilling to see change. Anders was one of the few senior commanders who saw the need for modernity. A trawl through the BI files held at the Polish Institute and Sikorski Museum in Kensington, London, which contain dispositions concerning the Polish 1939 Campaign, reveals that many Polish officers who actually took part in the fighting complained that the Polish military was under prepared for war with Germany. Many considered Marshal Edward Śmigły-Rydz as the main culprit for not allowing the Polish military to be modernised, while the policies of Beck had left Poland fairly isolated once war began.[4] Even though some of these reports and questionnaires were completed years, if not decades, after 1939, the evidence given between September 1939 and January 1940 is quite compelling.

As war approached and the Polish authorities began to prepare plans for defence they were careful not to provoke Germany. As part of these preparations four infantry divisions and two cavalry were secretly mobilised and moved to various points near the Polish–German frontier in case of any sudden German attack. It was considered to have been an 'astute' move. One of the cavalry brigades called up was Anders' brigade, the Nowogródska Brigade. Anders' brigade was transported from the Baranowicz area to Sierpc, north-west of Warsaw. Its purpose was to cover any potential German thrust southwards from the western area of East Prussia. As the Polish government had no intention of angering Germany, it kept the formation back from its planned concentration area. It was July 1939 before the brigade could take up its planned defensive positions near Lidzbark and begin to carry out defensive field-work.

Anders described Lidzbark as being a 'quiet little Polish town' which had a lake and forest nearby, but he also described the countryside as being flat and 'stretched uninterruptedly south-west to Warsaw'.[5] Anders' words provide a clue to Polish defensive problems in 1939. Poland has largely flat terrain and after two years of near drought conditions was bone dry and ideal for armour to run unchecked by natural obstacles until the river Vistula was finally encountered, by then about fifty per cent of Polish territory could be overrun. Of course enemy forces issuing out from mountain passes in southern Poland did have a much more difficult campaign than those of their number sweeping across the central Polish plains.

Lidzbark was Anders' HQ for his brigade which consisted of four regiments of cavalry reinforced by artillery, an infantry battalion and 'some armoured cars'. Anders was critical of the weak defences that he had to manage and it was not until August 1939 that his brigade was permitted to 'dig in' and erect barbed wire entanglements.[6] Later, in a response to a questionnaire concerning the conduct of the September Campaign, Anders answered that in fact his division had been mobilised in March 1939 and moved to the Sierpc area, where it remained until August 1939.[7]

Anders' brigade was part of Army Modlin which was charged with the defence of the northern approaches to Warsaw. The brigade was positioned on the left-hand flank of Army Modlin and covered a front of some thirty-two kilometres based around Lidzbark and Działdowo. Anders' brigade also covered the flank of their neighbour on the right, 20th Infantry Division in addition to the approaches of the Polish city of Płock. In August 1939, prior to the outbreak of war, Anders had organised a system for the possible withdrawal of his brigade towards Płock which lay south-east of their position. Anders met with General Bortnowski as well as having several meetings with General Bołtc. The meetings with Bołtc were to agree on the necessary actions to cover the direction from Włocławek in case Anders' brigade was forced to withdraw towards Płock. This plan was inspired as it was eventually adopted by Army Modlin once the Germans invaded Poland and the Poles were indeed obliged to retreat from their primary positions.

The first few days of the war were relatively quiet for the brigade as the German thrust from East Prussia concentrated on Anders' neighbours on the Mława defences. Anders and his men had to deal only with small probing thrusts by the German 217th Infantry Division. The enemy was easily dealt with and thrown back. Anders even sent patrols into East Prussia but on 3 September 1939, after heavy fighting on the Mława defences, the two Polish infantry divisions bearing the brunt of the German attack were forced to retreat.[8] War had come once more to Anders.

Anders was appointed General Officer Commanding (GOC) of Operational Group 'Tadeusz'. This group consisted of two divisions, 8th Infantry Division and 20th Infantry, as well as Anders' own brigade. The task allotted to Anders was to hold the bridgeheads over the river Vistula on the left banks at Płock and at Wyszogród. After checking the positions of the two divisions, Anders returned to his brigade to order a withdrawal to Płock. In his memoir Anders recalled that when he went to see the two infantry divisions, he also saw the chaos and destruction caused by the German invasion. He was obviously dismayed and distressed, especially when he saw the bodies of children killed by enemy aerial bombardment.

When Anders finally encountered 20th Infantry Division he found that it was already retreating and had begun to do so in an orderly fashion. However continuous enemy aerial attacks had reduced this withdrawal to near chaos. Anders found a similar situation when he chanced upon the Commander of 8th Infantry Division, which had not only been subject to relentless air attacks, but also fire from a German armoured formation.[9] The troops and officers of both divisions were doing their best but were outgunned at every level. Anders ordered a withdrawal to Płock as it gave a definite position to move to and a chance for regrouping after the severe mauling the Polish troops had received in the opening days of the war. While Anders was motoring back to Płock his car was strafed by enemy aircraft. The vehicle was riddled with bullets and Anders was wounded in the back. Somehow his car was 'patched up' and he was able to continue on his way along roads teeming with retreating Polish troops. Much of the time Anders was forced to travel on country roads but eventually he and his entourage reached Płock during the night of 4 September 1939. It was only then Anders' wounds received proper medical treatment and he felt able to continue to command his men.[10]

There is a slight discrepancy in the account of how Anders came to command 8th and 20th Infantry Divisions because Siemaszko asserts that after heavy fighting and aerial bombardment, the two divisions fell back onto Płock, where Anders assumed command of the two divisions.[11] It is a similar account to that of Anders, except Anders, in his official report to the Polish Historical Commission, was very clear that he had received orders to take command of the two divisions and had not assumed command of them. In his report Anders put more flesh onto the skeleton available in his memoirs concerning the events of 4 September 1939. Anders was quite clear that between 09:00 hours and 11:00 hours, 4 September 1939, he was given command of the two divisions which were to be combined with his cavalry brigade.

At that time Anders was preparing for his brigade to withdraw from their present positions and had set out with three officers to Raciąż via Sierpc. The Sierpc–Raciąż road had been bombed by enemy aircraft and it was along this route that Anders met with units from both 8th and 20th Infantry Divisions, which were totally disorganised as a result of heavy enemy aerial attacks. Once Anders reached Raciąż, Colonel Dudziński, commanding officer of 20th Infantry Division reported to him, as did the commanding officer of 8th Infantry Division's artillery. Anders gave Dudziński orders for 20th Infantry to withdraw to Płock and to the artillery commander, orders for 8th Infantry Division to withdraw to Wyszogród. Colonel Furgalski had already moved there in order secure a bridge in the Wyszogród area. At Raciąż, Anders sent orders to his Second-in-command (2ic) Colonel Kazimierz Zelisławski, 13th Ulans, ordering him to leave with the Nowogórdska Cavalry Division and move to Płock, but to reconnoitre the area in front of the city and then, using intelligence gained through reconnaissance, prepare for battle. The cavalry division, having set out on 4 September, finally reached the Płock area during the evening of 5 September. Their route had been bombarded from the air for much of the way especially the Brigade's artillery. The same evening, 4th Mounted Rifle Regiment took up defensive positions in anticipation of battle in Płock.[12]

On reaching Wyszogród, having moved there travelling via Płock, Colonel Furgalski learned that the bridge over the river Vistula at Wyszogród had been blown up prematurely. This meant that units from 8th Infantry Division had to cross the Vistula at Płock or at Modlin. Meanwhile, Anders was relieved to learn that his order to Nowogródska Cavalry Brigade to withdraw to Płock had reached them and that they were in the town carrying out his orders to take up defensive positions and sending out reconnaissance patrols which clashed with the enemy. Even so, it proved impossible to prevent the German advance southwards heading ever more steadily towards Warsaw.

Almost as soon as Anders arrived in Płock he received an order from Warsaw to blow up bridges in Płock, move with his brigade through the Kampinowski Forest to the right bank of the Vistula and cross the bridge there to the south of Modlin. At dusk, 8 September, Anders ordered the destruction of the two bridges remaining in Płock.[13] Anders makes no mention of the following detail but, according to Siemaszko, both of Anders' legs were in plaster casts while he was in Płock as a result of his wounds when his car had been attacked earlier. Therefore not only had he been wounded in his back, but apparently in his legs too, and despite being hardly able to stand, Anders remained in command.[14] Anders makes no mention of the treatment of his wounds, or the extent of them, but it seems unlikely that he was in plaster because he never refers to it and seems to have been too mobile for someone in plaster.

What Anders does mention is just how difficult it was to carry out the move to Modlin. As part of this move he had left some of his force at Płock to await the arrival of Army Pomorze. Conditions for moving the remainder of his force were not ideal because not only were the roads choked with the confusion of war as civilians tried to flee away from the fighting fronts, but the primitive conditions of Polish roads made for slow going, while the lack of water for the horses caused further problems. Once Anders drew close to Modlin he received an order which cancelled the previous one and he was directed to report in person to Rembertów near Warsaw. Another nightmare journey loomed before him, but by cutting across country, at dawn 10 September, Anders arrived at his destination. It was here that Anders learnt that the defence of Poland was not going well and that on all fronts Polish armed forces were falling back eastwards.

The Polish commander-in-chief, Marshal Śmigły-Rydz had already left Warsaw with his Staff for Brest-nad-Bug. General Juliusz Rómmel (not to be confused with the illustrious German commander, General Erwin Rommel) had been appointed GOC Warsaw. Via telephone Śmigły-Rydz placed Anders under Rómmel's command.[15] It should be noted that by this time, 9 September 1939, General Kazimierz Sosnkowski considered that the campaign was already lost and that the Polish Army should disengage from the enemy and withdraw towards the south-east and perhaps even to Romania. Even so Sosnkowski thought that it was already too late and that the armies (Bortnowski and Kutrzeba) had already remained too long fighting in the north-west. Beck admits that by this time he had already advocated that the Polish government and other high officials of state should leave Warsaw and transfer the Polish capital to Lwów in eastern Poland.[16] As Harvey Sarner observes, the defence of Poland deserved better in September 1939. The major flaw to the Polish campaign was that the Polish High Command tried to defend every square inch of Polish territory, when it might have been better if the Polish Army had withdrawn behind a natural obstacle such as the river Vistula, and from there consolidated its forces and shortened the line of defence. Sarner asserts that Śmigły-Rydz was 'too small' for the job.[17] Sarner's remarks may be true, but this would not have prevented the overrunning of Poland in 1939 once the Red Army crossed into eastern Poland and helped their German allies vanquish Poland.

Anders was to take command of a group which was to defend the Vistula to the south of Warsaw. Due to a lack of communications, Anders was forced to return to the Kampinowski Forest where his troops remained, and from there organise their move to the new defensive positions as ordered by Rómmel. This was not the easiest task to undertake as the Polish positions were being infiltrated by enemy forces, while at the same time Polish civilians trying to flee the fighting became entangled with Anders' force, as well as becoming ensnared with other Polish troops trying to manoeuvre in order to complete their orders as well. It was a scene of chaos, but eventually Anders and his men got to their designated position. From their position on the Vistula, Anders' troops began to engage the enemy who were already crossing the river Vistula. The Vistula was not the obstacle that it should have been as owing to two years of drought or near drought, German troops could wade across the river. Anders noted that fighting had already begun in the suburbs of Warsaw while confusion and disorder flourished, and contradictory orders concerning the defence of the Polish capital were issued.

Anders learned that German troops had bypassed Warsaw in the Minsk Mazowiecki area and had cut the road between Garwolin and the south-eastern city of Lublin, which had been under heavy aerial bombardment. Anders was ordered to attack Minsk Mazowiecki and at the same time to secure the defence of the Vistula to the south of Warsaw. He attended to both matters, leaving enough troops to defend the Vistula and then moving the Nowogródska and Wołyń Brigades in preparation to attack Minsk Mazowiecki. The 10th Infantry Division also fell under Anders' command and took part in the attack against Minsk Mazowiecki.[18]

Initially the Germans were taken by surprise by the Polish counter-offensive and the Poles were able to inflict heavy casualties on them as well as taking prisoners. Once the Germans recovered from their initial shock, their resistance became stiffer and their artillery fire heavier. Even so Anders' men continued to advance steadily on the German positions, albeit slower than previously. Owing to a misunderstanding, the group to the north of Anders' sector did not take part in the fighting, which left the Wołyń Brigade advancing but with its northern flank totally unprotected leading to heavy casualties among their number. As the fighting reached its climax, Anders received by radio an order from the Polish commander-in-chief to break off from the engagement and withdraw with his reserves to the Parczew area beyond the river Wieprz. It had been already decided that Warsaw was to fight to the bitter end. Much later Anders discovered that Rómmel had sat on these orders for three days. Ruefully, Anders concluded that this delay had had 'fatal consequences for my group'.

At dusk, Anders' group disengaged from the enemy. This was a tricky operation owing to the widespread dispersal of his force, while an inadequate signalling system made communication between the various units difficult if not impossible. Anders realised that he and his group were encircled by the Germans and that in order to escape they would have to break through enemy lines. Anders decided to concentrate his troops in the woods south-west of

Garwolin. Again this was difficult, owing to the chaos on the roads due to fleeing civilians as well as Polish military vehicles getting in the way.

Most of the civilians had no idea of where to go and were from time-to-time bombed or machine-gunned by enemy aircraft. As Anders and his men moved south they were often forced to leave the road and move across country as well as having to ford rivers because bridges had been frequently destroyed by Germans living in Poland. These 'German-Poles', referred to as Volksdeutcher were ethnic Germans who had ended up in independent Poland after 1918 and bitterly resented their situation: they considered Poland and the Poles to be inferior and longed for reunification with Germany. From early 1939 until the end of the war in Poland, Volksdeutcher shamelessly collaborated with the occupying Germans against their fellow Polish citizens. Once Poland was annexed by the Soviet Union after July 1944 many Volksdeutcher fled towards Germany, but many were to reap a bitter harvest for their wartime collaboration.[19]

Anders began to find the travelling, with the hope of breaking out of the German encirclement, tiring, as his wounds were beginning to trouble him. As he and his group continued their way, they passed through the town of Garwolin. The entire town had been destroyed in a German aerial attack and there was plenty of evidence of the future of Poland under German occupation as the corpses of both humans and horses lay everywhere. German aircraft in numerous formations, reinforcements for German land forces were also seen. The land forces were trying to cut off Anders' retreat. However Anders outwitted his foe and made a feint against the enemy along the Garwolin–Lublin highway and then the entire Polish formation cut across country towards their destination. Anders' deception worked, he and his men were able to cross the river Wieprz intact, along with armoured cars and most of their ammunition and supplies. Anders counted himself lucky to have been able to complete this manoeuvre as there was only a single bridge left intact over the Wieprz.

Anders, his men and their horses were all exhausted: they had been unable to sleep due to the continual fighting, as well as the gradual withdrawal southwards having taken its toll. Even after crossing the Wieprz there was to be no let up, despite their exhaustion. Anders took a car and drove towards Lublin, which was largely in ruins. He found a few Polish troops still in the city, but most had already abandoned Lublin and moved towards Chełm; there were still munitions dumps, food and petrol in Lublin however. Anders arranged for these supplies to be transferred to his force but he had already realised that the end was coming. Poland could not hold out for much longer.

Anders returned to his HQ at Kozlowka and realised that he needed to stay there for another twenty-four hours in order to reorganise his forces. The supplies arrived from Lublin as arranged which put good heart into Anders' troops, but almost at once the enemy began to attack. Lublin fell to the Germans and so Anders and his men made for Chełm. During the night 16–17 September 1939, Anders ordered a march in the direction of Rejowiec. As they ate their last meal together before moving out Anders and his men reviewed the progress of the war. A major question which never ceased to baffle them was what were the French and British doing on the Western Front? When were they going to begin their offensive? Then the Poles were hit with a major shock – that night the Soviet Union had invaded Poland and was marching westward deeper into Poland. Anders and his men were truly stunned. They had nowhere to go and no orders. What were they to do?[20]

When they stood-to in the morning of 18 September 1939, Anders and his men spent the daylight hours in the Kozłówski Forest evading detection by the enemy. Once dusk fell they set out towards the river Wieprz via the Łęczna–Puchaczów route. On 19 September, in either Łęszna or Puchaczów, Anders met with General Plisowski, who appraised him on German activities in Brześć to the south of their position. Throughout the day Anders had been in receipt of various reports concerning German activity in the Zamość region. Anders' force left their position at dusk and moved to the Rejowiec area. The march was without incident with the exception of 10th Infantry Division which was fighting the Germans along the Chełm–Lublin Highway: while some of his units were in the Rejowiec Forest area they came under aerial bombardment. The Polish losses were light owing to the efforts of units engaged in reconnaissance patrols outside the forest.

Another night move was made beginning on the evening of 20 September with a march towards Grabowiec. Along the way Anders and his men came across units from 1st Infantry Division as well as General Dęb-Biernacki, who appeared to have recovered his composure since his previous encounter with Anders only a few days earlier. This time he seemed quite agreeable that Anders should serve as his second-in-command and to accept Anders' operational planning. Anders also learned of the Soviet entries into Włodzimierz Wołyński and at Łuck.

General Dęb-Biernacki had also considered an offensive which might have a chance of breaking the German lines between Zamość and Tomaszow Lubelski, and head towards the direction of Zamość. The operation was devised as follows:

Either General Olbrycht's or General Kruszewski's group was to move in the direction of Zamość, the route Komarów–Majdan–Krasnobród was to be dealt with by Anders' Group while 1st Infantry Division, operating with General Wołkowicki, was to head towards Tarnawatka. The attacks were to begin at dawn 22 September 1939. Anders was unimpressed with the planning and considered the entire operation indulgent and almost lazy, believing that his group were being put in unnecessary risk in order to break the German Front. Dąb-Biernacki refused to back down.

10th Infantry Division was taken from Anders and placed under the command of General Kruszewski and were to head towards Zamość. At the time Anders was holding Mazowiecki Cavalry Brigade in reserve, they were covering the rear of the group, in addition, Anders also had in his group a combination of Colonel Zakrzewski's brigade as well as, in reserve, Wileński Regiment Cavalry Brigade and the Warsaw Ulan Regiment. Colonel Karcz was given command of a unit from 7th Ulans Regiment which had been with Anders' group, as well as a cavalry regiment from the Border Defence Regiment. The 1st Jozef Piłsudski Lancers remained with Anders.

The Polish offensive was to begin at the Polish settlement at Polany and move via the Zamość–Tomaszów highway, from where the group was to move in the direction of Suchowola-Krasnobród. It was thought that the Warsaw Ulan Regiment was at Komarów but there seemed to be have been precious little evidence of their presence in the area. During the period of preparation for the offensive Dęb-Biernacki, under a flag of truce, tried to parley with the Germans and convince them to surrender or leave, but was unsuccessful in his endeavours.

Fighting along Zamość-Tomaszów Highway began between 23:00 hours and midnight: the German opposition was about a company. The Poles captured seven or eight machineguns and took large numbers of prisoners. From the edge of the road Anders could see many dead. The Germans were replying with light artillery. After receiving orders to capture the road, Anders received a radio message from Dęb-Biernacki informing him that the route was clear. Even so, from the north side of the highway on the route towards the Wołyń Cavalry Brigade's position in the Polany region, the Germans, again about a company in strength, attempted a counter-attack. The fight was one of close combat with much hand-to-hand fighting.

The march to Suchowola passed without incident. At Suchowola; Anders met Colonel Filipowicz who was bringing horse and reserve units with him. Anders was aware that he had to get his own brigade to Krasnobród which was under heavy enemy pressure. Anders thought about his orders – 4th Mounted Rifle Regiment was at Suchowola holding the position for the passage of the brigade under Colonels Zakrzewski and Karcz, who had told Anders via radio that they were moving towards his position. At Krasnobród, 25th Ulan Regiment had met with German opposition which had quickly broken the Polish ranks especially among the officers, with 1st Squadron under Lieutenant Gierlewski receiving the highest casualties.

At Krasnobród it seemed to Anders that the battle was not going well, even if a number of prisoners had been taken; the Polish hospital there was told a tale of heavy Polish casualties while through Krasnobród came the following: Nowogórdska Cavalry Brigade with 25th, 26th, and 27th Ulan regiments with the divisional artillery, but all with reduced supplies. They were followed by the Wołyń Cavalry Brigade supported by 19th Ulan Regiment with minimal supplies; 1st Lancers minus two squadrons with 1st battery divisional artillery, as well as the remainder of 22nd Ulan Regiment as well as Major Perucki's battalion.

The problem for the Poles was that Polish supply vehicles had been cut off by German action from Rudki and Tarnawatka. The sound of heavy fighting on the northern banks of the river Wieprz could be clearly heard by Polish units on the river's southern bank. The Germans were pressing aggressively from the west to the southern banks of the Wieprz, in reply a Polish defensive position was established during the late afternoon in order to deny the German advance from the west.

From the Józefów-Ciotusza region Anders decided to move his group to Puszczy Solskiej. Anders and his men took up a position on the Oleszyce-Belzec Highroad until dusk on 24 September and then during the night 24–25 September moved on. During that night many Polish units moving from the east were able to slip past German lines. On 25 September in the forests of the Lubaczów region, Anders and his troops met up with the remnants of 6th Infantry Division. There was also a link up with General Piskor's group which had been badly mauled in the campaign thus far. At dusk on 26 September, Anders and his men set out once more, heading southwards along the Radymno-Lwów Highway between Kraków and Jaworów. The group marched in two columns and skirmished in the rear against marauding German units. Even more frustrating, if not bizarre was that not only did the Poles have to beat off these attacks, but also Germans kept trying to surrender to them. Obviously the Poles were in no position to accept these surrenders and detain enemy 'prisoners'. Orders had already been issued to Anders and his men that forced them to release all German prisoners.

At dawn on 26 September, Nowogórdska Cavalry Brigade massed in the west and then its column weaving in and out of German lines headed northwards towards the outskirts of Broszki. As the Poles made their move they frequently got into fire-fights with the Germans and acquitted themselves well. For example, 26th and 27th Ulans were very successful, killing many Germans, and one assumes disobeying previous orders, took 100 Germans prisoners undoubtly the Polish position had changed for the better. After capturing and occupying the outlaying area of Broszki, 27th Ulans moved into the suburbs of Morańce. It was here that fighting was renewed as the Poles launched an assault against a German battalion, some of whom they had already fought at Broszki.

During this time Anders linked, via Broszki, the remainder of Nowogródska Cavalry Brigade and 9th Horse Artillery Battery which at that time had not been involved in the fighting. This group was massed into a column east of the Grobicki Brigade's position and struck mainly, and evenly, along the length of the road. The sound of this fighting reached the ears of the Poles some distance away, such was its ferocity. The fighting was at its most fierce at Morańce and this is where Anders parleyed with the CO of 20th (German) Infantry Division in hope that the Poles would be able to surrender their arms and leave the fighting.

Amazingly, a truce was agreed and the Poles were given free passage to the south under the condition that they did not attack any German units that they might encounter en route (one can only assume that the German commander allowed Anders and his men to retain a certain measure of arms), as well as return all prisoners they were holding. Anders agreed to what can only be described as generous terms. There was also an exchange of officers as a form of guarantee of good behaviour on both sides – Colonel Szweicer went over to the German lines as the Polish 'hostage' – as Anders noted in 1958, a single shot would have ruined the entire arrangement, which was being orchestrated to prevent a mass slaughter on both sides. If Anders' negotiations had failed, the Poles were quite willing to fight on no matter what.

After the Germans had withdrawn from their positions, Anders and his formation moved to the Dernak region where it was thought that other units of the Polish group were located. From the Dernak area Anders had to decide in which direction he should lead his troops. The problem was that he lacked sufficient information concerning the whereabouts of the Germans and the territory they held. Anders knew that the Germans had withdrawn westwards and so he concluded that it was possible that they were close to Lwów. However, as Anders and his group reached Dernak, they soon learned that the Red Army had already occupied the area. Indeed Colonel Grobicki, who had gone ahead with his units, was taken prisoner by Soviet troops.[21]

Anders moved his force southwards with the idea of moving to either Hungary or Romania. This decision was based on the consideration that there were treaties between these two countries and Poland as well as an existing good relationship between them. Anders no doubt appreciated that Romania had become dominated by Germany with the consequence that Poles could no longer expect a sympathetic reception there, but he was correct about Hungary as General (in September 1939 Colonel) Stanisław Maczek was to find out when he led his men, complete with arms, vehicles, and colours flying from Poland into Hungary and of course internment.[22] The Hungarians bent over backwards to accommodate the Poles who fetched up in Hungary however, as most Polish troops were hell-bent on escaping to France in order to rejoin the Polish Army and continue to fight. Therefore it suited the Hungarian government to turn a blind eye to Polish escapes out of Hungary before the Germans took too close an interest in the Polish presence on Hungarian soil and began to bully the Hungarians into being less than helpful towards Polish endeavours to escape to the west.[23]

It should be noted that during the September Campaign the Hungarian government denied Germany permission to transfer troops across Hungarian territory, as well as mining strategic positions such as the Koszyce Tunnel and railway bridges. The Hungarians told the Polish government on 11 September 1939 that the reason for their actions was that it was a 'matter of honour for the Hungarian Nation'.[24] During the Warsaw Uprising in 1944, when the Polish Underground Army (the AK), rose up against the occupying Germans, the Germans realised that Hungarian Army units close to Warsaw were actually aiding the Poles and so had to be withdrawn from the area. Ironically the Red Army, sitting across the river Vistula which bisects the Polish capital, looked on as the German Army destroyed the Polish rebellion. By the summer of 1944 the Hungarians, then allies of Germany, were aiding the Poles, while the Soviets, allies in theory to the Poles, did nothing until it was too late to aid the Polish uprising. They did, however, ensure the destruction of the AK which they feared would oppose the Red Army as it began to annexe Poland in its drive towards Germany.[25]

The situation unfolding in Warsaw during the Polish uprising was known by the British Government; both Churchill and his Information Minister, Brendan Bracken, were horrified to learn that the Red Army was held back thus allowing the Germans to slaughter the population of Warsaw during August 1944. Bracken stood up to Soviet demands that the BBC should not publicise the Warsaw Uprising, complaining bitterly to Bruce Lockhart 'whenever they complain there is no satisfying them; they're a bunch of savages.'[26] The matter of the fact was that by 1944, militarily, the UK was totally dependent on Soviet goodwill in relation to events in eastern Europe and the relentless advance of the Red Army into Poland and towards Germany. British policies and propaganda therefore had to be tailored to this, no matter what senior British ministers knew or thought of Soviet actions in east-central Europe, especially Poland.[27] This was the very problem that faced Anders in 1944 – he may have been right about Soviet actions and atrocities against Poles in Poland, but there was nothing he could do about it.

To return to 1939, in his memoirs Anders recorded that every effort was made to reach the south. He and his troops crossed the Lublin-Chełm Highway although 10th Infantry Division was engaged in heavy fighting with the Germans who were attempting to cut off the Poles and isolate them. The Luftwaffe was relentless in their attacks but still Anders and his men pressed on. Eventually Anders caught up with General Dąb-Biernacki and placed himself and his force under Dąb-Biernacki's overall command. Dąb-Biernacki's forces were exhausted. Anders proposed that Nowogródska

Cavalry Brigade should try to make a breach in the enemy lines in an attempt to find a passage for the remainder of the Polish force to pass through. Anders warned Dąb-Biernacki that he might not be able to hold any such breach open for long as it was obvious that the enemy would do their level best to prevent Polish troops from escaping.

During the afternoon of 22 September, Anders put his plan into action. He and his troops did well and by 23.00 hours the enemy had been defeated; the breach opened thus allowing exhausted Polish troops to make their way through this passage. By this point most motorised vehicles had been lost, but there was no fuel available for them in any case. Artillery guns were hitched to four pairs of horses who were just as tired as the men, but they did their best and progress was made. Even though the Germans counter-attacked and tried to close the gap in their line, Anders was able to hold it open long enough for many Polish units to pass through, although Polish casualties were very heavy.

Anders and the other Polish troops learned that Lwów had fallen to the German Army while the Red Army was thrusting ever deeper into Poland from the east. Therefore it became obvious to the Polish commanders that Polish units had to move to the south as fast as they could. Anders remarked that 'speed' became their guiding word. However the men were shattered and were sleeping in their saddles while officers had to keeping riding along the columns waking their men up. To call a halt to the march was unthinkable because if one was called, the troops were so tired they would never arise again to continue. Furthermore, even the Polish terrain was against them owing to the flatness which favoured German armour as we have already noted, while there was no forest cover which, yet again, favoured the enemy as their aircraft could easily seek out the Polish formation.

At dawn on 26 September, Anders' column suddenly stopped. Reconnaissance patrols had reported that the Germans had been seen dug-in in the village of Broszki on the Jaworów-Krakowiec Highway. When a single German shot rang out it was realised that there was no chance of by-passing the village. Anders launched a cavalry charge against the village using two regiments of cavalry. The Germans were taken totally by surprise and many were killed in the ensuing fighting; nearly an entire enemy battalion was captured.

The Germans sent messengers from the HQ of 28th Infantry Division (German) to Anders with the suggestion that his forces should surrender as they had no way of escape as Poland had been overrun by German armed forces and the Red Army was advancing ever westward into Poland. Anders refused to surrender but agreed to return captured German soldiers providing the Germans did not fire on the Poles when they withdrew from the area. Anders and his force decided to press on and concentrate themselves at Dernaki but discovered that the Soviets, or 'Bolsheviks' as many Poles would have it, had already taken and occupied Dernaki: Anders decided to try and slip his men unnoticed between German and Soviet positions but this proved to be impossible as, for the first time, they met Soviet troops in large numbers.

Anders once more tried his parleying skills with the Soviets and sent one of his best officers, Captain Stanisław Kuczynski to the Soviet HQ to try to persuade them to allow the Polish force to continue on its way to Hungary. The Soviets refused and indeed robbed Kuczynski of everything he had; he was very lucky to have been sent back alive. Then suddenly the Soviets began to shell the Polish position; this was followed up with machinegun fire and the appearance of Soviet tanks and so battle was joined. Anders wrote of 9th Battery Horse Artillery that they were always at their best when they were in a tight spot as they were on this day. The Polish artillery fired accurately at the approaching Soviet armour and destroyed a large number of tanks. Even so, as Anders recorded, such was the density and numbers of Soviet troops and weaponry that the Poles had little chance. The Polish passage was entirely blocked.

At the time Anders could not understand why no bridgehead had been established in a suitable area to allow Polish troops to escape westward. He later learnt that such work had begun but the Soviet invasion had prevented its completion and so the escape of 200,000–300,000 Polish troops was prevented. These men could have been of great value later in the war but alas, it was never to be. Anders and his men fired their last shell and rifle round, at least on Polish territory, on 27 September. As a large group, Anders concluded that there was little chance of a breakout and that it would be better if they split into small groups and try to reach Hungary, taking advantage of night and forested shelter. Even so, their chances looked slim given the preparations made by the Soviets in their invasion and annexation of Polish territory.

Anders, with a group of officers and men, began to weave his way through Soviet encampments, sometimes passing within 100 metres of Soviet positions.

It was only then that Anders realised the enormity of the Soviet invasion. He saw that every village, and even farms, were full of Red Army troops. Even so, Anders and his little group continued on their way passing through Sambor and, with the help of loyal and skilled guides, made their way over the steep and wooded hills to the heights near Turka. During the morning of 29 September 1939 they halted in woods to rest their horses and planned to continue their journey at dusk. Very quickly however, the group discovered that they were surrounded by Soviet detachments which Anders guessed had been detailed to capture Polish troops trying to escape from Poland. Leaving their horses the Poles hid in the depths of the thick woods. From their position they heard shooting and at times Soviet troops passed within a few paces of Anders and his party. At dusk they moved on, always in a southerly direction. After dark they were passing near the village of Zastowka where they were ambushed by Soviets. This led to a shoot-out at almost point blank range as well as some vicious hand-to-hand fighting. Once more Anders was wounded, but he was about to discover how loyal his men were to him.

Anders had been wounded in the back and hip. He begged his men to leave him as he would only hinder their progress and chances of getting away to Hungary. His group tried to carry him away but eventually Anders had to order them to leave him and make their way to Hungary; then he lapsed into unconsciousness. The next morning Anders felt well enough to move on with Captain Kuczynski and Trooper Tomczyk, who had both defied his orders and had remained with him. The trio reached the village of Jesionka Stasniowa and decided to take their chances but as soon as they entered the village one of its inhabitants, a Ukrainian, betrayed their existence to the Soviet authorities and they were taken into custody. In vehicles escorted by armoured cars they were driven via Turka to Stary Sambor which was serving as the Soviet HQ in the area.[28] Anders life was about to take its most important turn.

The Soviet invasion and occupation of Poland was actually quite well thought out and structured but hell bent on destroying Polish culture, as a Polish document dated 28 November 1939 records. It was estimated that 400,000 Red Army troops were used in 1939 to subdue the Polish lands annexed by the Red Army in 1939. Immediately, strong propaganda to spread the message of communism began with the use of the press, posters, cinema, mass meetings as well as leafleting. This was reinforced by the confiscation of all private farms, factories, quarries, shops or any form of private enterprise and replacing them with the establishment of various committees for workers, peasants and the police. But as the report suggested, it was only 'the scum of the streets' that followed the Soviet directives, and it seemed to have been only the incompetent who could be entrusted (but no doubt politically reliable) against private enterprises. Polish morale was swiftly cut down owing to the Soviet actions which were relentless as the Soviet political police, the GPU, attacked society with continuous activities such as registrations, confiscations, evictions, day and night searches, arrests, imprisonment and executions. There were also attacks on the priesthood and religion as well as against education, especially history. Intellectuals (which in Poland could be as something as humble as a clerk) and workers were offered employment in the Soviet Union. These led to mass deportations of Poles, especially military officers, doctors, engineers and clerks, as well as their deputies and assistants to the Soviet interior, often to the most far flung parts such as Soviet Asia. The Soviet authorities further looted eastern Poland for industrial materials, especially those used in the manufacture of military hardware. Then they took food, which led to destitution and famine among those Poles still in Soviet occupied Poland; effectively, they broke Polish life in that part of the world.[29] This report does not mention how entire families, including children, were deported to the Soviet Union to be used as slave labour. The Soviet rape of Poland between September and December 1939 was complete and unrelenting: it should have been no surprise that Anders was to become the natural leader of those Poles who had undergone this collective humiliation at the hands of the Soviets. The big surprise is that the London Poles, especially Sikorski, made no effort to try to understand what their compatriots had been through and it was to lead to grief and disaster for both: Poland and the Poles.

Initially, Anders was not treated badly and was detained in hospital in Lwów. He had a bullet lodged close to his spine which remained there for the rest of his life. To begin with he was allowed visits from his wife and family who came to his hospital bed, but this all changed during December 1939. Anders' status was changed by the Soviet security police, the NKVD, and he was no longer considered to be a prisoner of war, but instead, a civilian detainee. The Soviet authorities wanted Anders to join the Red Army with the rank of general but he refused. As a consequence he was thrown into a small dungeon with a tiny window which lacked glazing. The winter of 1939–40 was severe and, in addition to the open window, Anders received no warm clothing, little food and no medical care. At the time he doubted whether he would survive such inhumane treatment.

At the end of February 1940 Anders was suddenly transferred to the Central NKVD prison in Moscow, the Lubianka. For the first time in three months he was allowed a shower, but he still refused to cooperate with the Soviet authorities. As a result of his lack of cooperation Anders was transferred to the more severe regime found at the Butyrki Prison, again in Moscow. For five long months, until the end of August 1940, Anders was kept in solitary confinement. During that time he saw nobody except his prison warders; he received no medical care for his wounds and could only walk on crutches. At the end of August 1940 he was returned to the Lubianka.

Anders was in such poor physical condition that the governor at the Lubianka ordered that, in addition to his daily ration of food, he was to receive 300 grams of white bread, 25 grams of butter and a glass of yoghurt (kiffar) with a dinner. The implication being that normally, prisoners did not receive a dinner or evening meal. At the Lubianka Anders was interrogated further and at the end of November 1940 he agreed to sign the interrogation protocol which seemed to relieve his situation somewhat. The NKVD seemed very interested in the relationship between Anders and Sikorski before the war. This relationship had been quite friendly. Another point of interest was that while he was in hospital in Lwów, Anders had tried to make contact with Sikorski who, by then, was Polish Prime Minister in exile as well as being Commander-in-chief, Polish armed forces. The NKVD seemed to know all about the event as they had captured those who had been carrying messages either on the way to Paris, where the exiled Polish government was seated, or on the way back to Lwów. It seemed that they may have been fishing for further information, but it was clear that they were satisfied with the intelligence that they already had. After signing the 'protocol', *prisoner* Anders was granted several privileges, which was unusual and suggests that he was, to a point, cooperating with the Soviet authorities at that time. Indeed Jan Romanowski, a future aide-de-camp to Anders, asserted that Anders did not collaborate with the Soviets, but he was sure that some Polish officers did. Romanowski certainly made sure that Colonel Zygmunt Berling (future commander of the Soviet dominated Polish Army) and Captain

Klimkowski, whose career will be detailed later in this work, were specifically mentioned in his testimony. Later, gossip was to spread in London regarding Anders' loyalty and whether he was a Communist or not.[30] His subsequent actions certainly prove that he was never convinced by the Soviets, and that his instinct at the time was one of survival – assuming that there was any measure of collaboration.

From December 1940 he was granted a packet of cigarettes every other day (Anders was a heavy smoker) at the expense of the NKVD. During February 1941 Anders was lent two books by the NKVD, of which one was a Russian–English textbook and then in March the security service, perhaps in their haste to convince Anders of the supposed values of the Soviet system, granted him not only an extra mattress but also the use of the prison library. The mattress no doubt provided Anders some relief from his wounds, especially the bullet which remained lodged in him, but the library was of course well supplied with the works of Lenin, the mastermind behind the Bolshevik revolution, and those of Stalin. Anders had a perfect command of the Russian language and from these works gained a deep insight into Communist ideological principles. His experience of Soviet captivity led him to conclude that the NKVD was dominant in the running of the Soviet Union.[31] Furthermore Anders' experience and knowledge of Leninist–Stalinist principles and ideology coloured his views of the Soviet Union. Once free from Soviet captivity and enjoying British patronage, he made embarrassing (yet true) observations of the Soviet government which, in reality, was bound up with the wishes and whims of the Soviet dictator, Stalin. It should be noted that Anders was not the only student of political texts as Stalin had read Hitler's *Mein Kampf*, marking the passages in which Hitler had written that Germany needed to acquire new lands in the east at the expense of Russia.[32] This suggests that the Rippentrop-Molotov Pact of August 1939 was Stalin buying time, but equally does not explain why he was so surprised when Germany invaded the Soviet Union in June 1941.

In his autobiography Anders give an account of the early days of his capture by the Red Army and his subsequent captivity on Soviet territory. Initially Anders was struck by the large numbers of troops and equipment which the Red Army possessed. However on closer inspection he realised that Red Army troops were actually poorly clothed and quite shabby in appearance, while their horses were in equally poor shape. Even so, these troops were an improvement on those of the Red Army that Anders fought in 1920 because discipline had improved and officers were obeyed. At the time of his capture Anders encountered officers of the NKVD for the first time. He observed their blue and red caps and noticed how everybody was in awe of them. Anders had to be told who they were.

After being taken prisoner, Anders had been taken to the Soviet commander-in-chief for the area, General Tuleniev, who reprimanded Anders for 'resisting' the Red Army. Tuleniev trotted out the usual Bolshevik claptrap about the invasion being 'liberation' from landlords and capitalists. Anders realised that there was to be no meeting of minds here. In fairness, Anders commented that Tuleniev was one of the few 'kind-hearted men' that he met among senior Soviet officials. Indeed it was Tuleniev who sent Anders to hospital in Lwów to receive treatment for his wounds. At that time Anders could hardly walk and his wounds kept bleeding. It was during his time in hospital that Anders learned of the reality and horrors of the Soviet occupation of Poland from the Polish medical staff who were still working there.

While in hospital Anders was visited by various Soviet officials. At first he was slightly bemused but then became apprehensive because these visits, which were polite and proper yet seemed to be pointless, were relentless. Eventually Anders was visited by the Soviet Town Mayor of Lwów, General Ivanov who was accompanied by NKVD officers. After a lengthy political preamble Ivanov finally cut to the chase and told Anders that there was a proposal that a Polish government should be established on Soviet territory and under Soviet protection or supervision. Then Anders was asked if he was interested in being part of this government. Initially Anders was rather perplexed by this offer and tried to work out what was actually going on and what the Soviet intention was behind the establishment of an exiled Polish government.

Anders worked on the assumption that the Soviet plan was to try to counter the establishment of the Polish Government-in-Exile established by Sikorski in Paris during October 1939. This government had been recognised by most of the world as the official Polish government but of course the Soviet government and German government both did not recognise it. At the time Anders was still ignorant of the secret clause in the Nazi-Soviet Treaty signed in August 1939. This most unlikely treaty established friendly and cooperative relations between Nazi Germany and the Soviet Union and contained a secret clause which allowed for Poland to be annexed and divided up between the Soviet Union and Germany. The Soviet Union had been allocated Polish territory as far west as the river Vistula.

There were further conversations with Ivanov and each time Anders refused his entreaties to be part of a proposed Polish government. Of course this would have been a Soviet-dominated puppet government, as was the case in Poland between 1944 and 1989. The Soviet authorities were relentless in their courtship of Anders and tried to seduce him with various attractive offers of high office within the puppet government. If Anders had agreed to serve in the Red Army he would have been awarded the post of Commander or 'Army Commander'. Anders refused as ever, but with each refusal he began to sense an air of menace and felt threatened.

Anders had an idea of escaping from his present captivity to either Hungary or Romania; clearly at that time he was unaware that he would have been interned if he sought sanctuary in Romania. Even so, his wounds would not allow for any escape attempt, while life on the run in Anders' case would not have been practical. Therefore the only realistic route left open to Anders was to try to get transferred to the German area of occupied Poland and then to disappear, with the intention of reaching Hungary via Slovakia once his wounds had sufficiently healed. Anders was influenced by the news that all badly wounded Polish troops who were born in those Polish territories now occupied by Germany would be allowed to return from Soviet captivity back to Poland. To this end, convoys were being prepared in Soviet occupied Poland ready for such a transfer of Polish wounded. Anders obtained a certificate of disability on the grounds that he had, to date, been wounded eight times. Anders seemed to have a plan worked out because a Soviet official running the hospital where Anders lay had taken money to bribe others and to get Anders' name on the list to be transferred to German occupied Poland.

While he was waiting for wheels to be set in motion Anders continued to serve his country and got a report on the situation in East Galicia (by now occupied by the Red Army) to General Sikorski in Paris. Anders also advised the youth of Lwów, who were beginning to show signs of rebellion, to keep their mood in check. In Lwów all of the leading Polish personalities including judges, lawyers, doctors and Catholic priests had been arrested by the Soviets.

Anders was quite blunt in his allegation that some Polish Jews had cooperated with the NKVD while a militia of 'riff-raff' from the town had been founded. Anders was to learn of further Soviet chicanery when he was visited by Colonel Rakowski, former CO of 12th Lancers. Rakowski reported that the Soviets did not keep their word about how Polish military personnel captured by the Red Army were to be treated. Thousands of Polish troops had been captured and taken east. Rakowski was furious as he had accompanied General Langer to Moscow. In Moscow the Soviet government made many promises and broke every one of them concerning the welfare of captured Polish military personnel and others, especially Polish elites. It was as Anders had suspected: the Soviets could not be trusted.

Eventually the good news came that transport to take the Polish wounded to the German zone of occupation had been organised. Anders was given the necessary documentation and authority to leave the Soviet zone. At the beginning of December 1939 the convoy left for Przemysl under a small Soviet guard. Once the train arrived at Przemysl however, it was held up for a week and rumours began to spread about what was happening or might be happening. Daily conditions on the convoy deteriorated and soon food and water ran short, while dirt and squalor increased. However the Poles were afraid to leave the train in case they got left behind if it should suddenly leave. Eventually Anders was persuaded to leave and was allowed to go to a flat belonging to friends so he could wash and rest.

A rumour spread that the train was to leave at dawn the next day and that everybody was to return that evening. When Anders returned he noticed an increase in the numbers of NKVD men and that the guard had been reinforced. He began to feel uneasy and this sense of uneasiness only increased when even more NKVD officers arrived. Furthermore it was announced that all Polish officers had to leave the train and complete new application forms in order to leave the Soviet zone of occupation. The Soviets gave their 'word of honour' that all Polish officers would be allowed to return to the train in an hour's time. This turned out to be untrue.

In a supposed concern for Anders' welfare the Soviet authorities suggested that he should stay in hospital over-night because they were concerned that the train would be too uncomfortable for him owing to his condition. Anders protested but was ignored and was taken not to a hospital, but to an NKVD post where he suffered a 'most stupid and futile interrogation'. Anders and his entourage were finally taken to a hospital with a guard posted outside each room occupied by the Poles. Visits to the lavatory were accompanied by an escort of two Red Army soldiers with bayonets fixed. Anders did not like how the situation was beginning to unfold.

The next morning NKVD officials came and announced that the train would be leaving soon but Anders did not believe this. He was right not to believe because once he joined the bus which was to take him from the hospital to the train, he met with Polish officers who had been 'filling in forms'. Every one of them had been beaten up and was bleeding. The officers had been confined throughout the night in cellars without food or water. They were now being pushed onto the bus by a strong escort who mocked them and catcalled crying that the 'bourgeoisie' were returning to Poland. As the bus moved out to Lwów, Anders sensed that a new and unpleasant episode was about to begin as he realised he was in the hands of the dreaded NKVD.

For the first three days of his NKVD imprisonment Anders and his compatriots were kept in the cellar of a villa. The cellar was basically a dungeon which lacked everything, even bedding, and had straw on the floor. Daily, and singly, each man was taken for interrogation by NKVD officers described by Anders as 'young louts of about 20' (years of age). What Anders noticed was that the NKVD interrogations were based on bluff and ignorance. The interrogators knew nothing but the Soviet Union and were ignorant of the outside world but insisted that 'they knew everything'. Anders was to confess his crimes, which seemed to have been quite extensive to them but nonsense to any reasonable person. The Soviets were accusing Anders of no more than doing his duty: that of defending his country against external violence, i.e. defending Poland against the Soviet invasion. He was also accused of 'betraying the international proletariat' in fighting against the Bolsheviks between 1918 and 1920. In Soviet eyes, as Anders had fought against the Soviet invasion of Poland in 1939, he was also responsible for Soviet casualties in Poland. As Anders refused to join the Red Army, he was considered to be a spy and had already organised an underground movement in Lwów. If Anders had been a spy, accepting a senior role in the Red Army might well have benefitted his work but of course it was all nonsense.

Anders' answers to the NKVD seemed to infuriate them. The main source of their anger was his criticism of the Nazi-Soviet pact, which he observed was transitional and that eventually war would break-out between Germany and the Soviet Union. His ideas were mocked by his interrogators but Anders predicted the invasion route which he considered the Germans would use. It turned out that Anders' prediction was more or less correct when the Germans did eventually invade the Soviet Union. In time, Anders was taken into the presence of Colonel Krasnov, head of the local NKVD. Once more Anders was offered a senior post in the Red Army. The Soviets made the claim that this was the only route for Anders as he was 'guilty of many serious offences against the Soviet Union'. Anders declined the offer and repeated that he was badly injured and should also be treated as a prisoner-of-war. He was ignored.

Anders was then sent to the 'Brigidki' Prison. Anders referred to it as a 'common prison', or in other words, not a military prison but one for criminals. He was, however, put into the hospital wing where he met with friends who were senior officers and politicians. From them Anders learned about mass arrests of Polish elites by the Soviets and the methodology employed. As in the 'Great Terror' in the Soviet Union in the 1930s, arrests were made at night and most of those arrested were savagely tortured regardless of age or gender. Anders came to realise that so far he had been fortunate and that he was better off in the prison hospital. At the end of 1939, however, he was snatched out of bed by about a dozen NKVD officers and propelled out of his ward. Even though Anders was on crutches he was pushed down every flight of stairs by NKVD thugs until he finally arrived in the basement – with all his limbs somehow still unbroken. He was then thrown into a dungeon.

It was in this cell that Anders almost died, but as we know he was sent to the relatively luxurious conditions of the Lubianka on 29 February 1940. Even if the Lubianka in the eyes of many during the Cold War was symbolic of Soviet oppression, to Anders in 1940 it represented another chance and as we know, his physical conditions were vastly improved compared with those he had endured at the Brigidki. The overall impression that Anders gained from the Lubianka was its silence and secrecy. Routines for moving prisoners between cells ensured that prisoners knew only as much as the prison authorities were prepared to allow. It was possible for prisoners to be unaware of the identities of other prisoners being held in the same building. Finally Anders was taken to his cell which was a clean, four man cell. There was even a small table with a tea kettle on it. Even though Anders considered the Lubianka to be a 'luxury prison' compared with other prisons in the Soviet Union, he learned from his cellmates that it was a place reserved for those of special interest to the Central Office of the NKVD.

Once more Anders was interrogated by NKVD officers, whose methods ranged from kindness to almost insane cruelty. He also learned that the Soviet security forces had amassed quite a dossier on him – including his private life. Anders was genuinely shocked when he was confronted with the contents of the file. There was nothing which incriminated him but it was very intrusive; Anders had had no idea he was being spied on. Once more he was returned to the Butyrki Prison where he remained until September 1940. He was held continuously in solitary confinement but never called for interrogation. For the entire time he was in the Butyrki Prison a powerful light was directed, night and day, into his eyes which became filled with pus. Anders feared that he might go blind. Then suddenly he was back at the Lubianka to share a cell with seven other prisoners.

It was at this time that Anders learned something of the progress of the war. He discovered that Germany had overrun much of continental Europe and that the UK was only just about holding them at bay after the Battle of Britain where British and Commonwealth air forces along with their allies had been victorious and prevented a German invasion of the UK for perhaps a season at least. At first this disturbed him, but after considering the situation as he understood it, Anders came to several conclusions. The main one being that it should not be taken for granted that Germany would defeat the British. The British had an empire to fall back on as well as a very large and powerful navy. Furthermore it was unlikely that the USA would allow the UK to fall. Anders also learnt of the Soviet annexation of part of Romania known as Bessarabia and now modern Moldova, as well as the annexation of the three Baltic republics, Lithuania, Latvia and Estonia. Anders found out about the war between Finland and the Soviet Union which had been fought between November 1939 and March 1940 and ended in a pro-Soviet armistice.

Anders still did not discount war between Germany and the Soviet Union as it seemed logical to him that once Germany had helped itself to Western Europe it would turn on its uncertain ally. Furthermore, during his interrogations Anders had learnt that the Soviet Union was biding its time for when the Western powers exhausted themselves; the Soviet Union would then intervene and expand the world revolution. Then finally, as Anders predicted, Germany did indeed invade the Soviet Union.[33] It should also be noted that the Polish General Staff's Intelligence Section also provided evidence during May 1940 that part of the Soviet plan was of a continuous world or international revolution until the entire world fell under communist rule.[34]

The plight of Anders in his imprisonment in the Soviet Union is not clear as one feels that he is not being honest in his account and is withholding certain information, writing in such a manner that reflects well on him; in many ways Anders was spared the worst compared with many of his compatriots imprisoned or enslaved in the Soviet Union. However, the fact that Anders did endure savage treatment at the hands of the NKVD ensured that once it was possible for talks concerning the establishment on Soviet soil of a Polish Army, Anders would make an ideal commander as he understood so much of Russia and had suffered, unlike the Poles in London who knew nothing and had not passed through Soviet captivity; Anders was the natural leader of these men. Anders was not only the most senior Polish officer in the Soviet Union, but was also the only leader who understood what he and his men had endured between 1939 and 1941. This corporative spirit caused a split in Polish exiled forces because Sikorski and his successors could not understand Anders and other Poles who had suffered at the hands of the Soviets and now refused to enter into a spirit of cooperation with the Soviet Union. In time this translated into distrust as first the Soviet government refused to trust the exiled Poles, and later the British and American governments found it difficult to work with the Poles in the west.

Chapter 3

Amnesty and Evacuation

The German invasion of the Soviet Union on 22 June 1941 was the saving of Anders. Once Germany attacked the Soviet Union, Anders' position radically altered, he was needed by the British government, the Polish Government-in-Exile and, up to a point, the Soviet government. As ever the Soviets were ambivalent in their attitude towards Poles on Soviet territory. Even so Anders was released – but only when it suited the Soviet government to release him – while wheels were put into motion to find common ground between the three governments of which two, the Polish and the Soviet government, were still technically at war with each other. Therefore a priority for the British government was to find a way to remove the state of war between Poland and the Soviet Union. This proved to be one of the most difficult diplomatic endeavours carried out by Winston Churchill, Anthony Eden, the British Foreign Secretary, and the British Foreign Office (FO) during the Second World War.

It is interesting to note that Anders was not released until 4 August 1941, nearly six weeks after the German invasion began and during that period the Soviet authorities tried to maintain the fiction, to their prisoners at least, that there was not a state of war between Germany and the Soviet Union, and that the Germans had not attacked. The Soviets tried to claim that the sound of air raid sirens and anti-aircraft artillery (AAA) was part of on-going exercises. Anders bluntly told his informants not to lie to him as he was an experienced soldier and knew what he was hearing – the Soviets could not fool him. Anders prediction and sketch of the German invasion route, which he had made while being interrogated in Lwów back in 1939, served to cause him problems with the NKVD in 1941 because he was more or less correct and the Soviets wondered if he had had some inside information about the invasion and German intent. However, as German armed forces headed rapidly towards Moscow and Leningrad, the NKVD seemed reluctant to badger Anders too much, and certainly not to the brutal extent of their earlier treatment of him. Interrogators who had previously had no regard for Anders, politely enquired after his health and asked whether, perhaps he would like a cigarette?

Once Anders challenged the lie concerning military exercises being carried out in Moscow rather than the air raids he could clearly hear, Colonel Kondratik of the NKVD started being honest with Anders. Kondratik admitted that the Soviet Union was now in an alliance with the UK and in conversations with the Polish Government-in-Exile. The next few days must have been quite bewildering for Anders as he was taken to a hairdresser and, for the first time in twenty months, shaved and sprinkled 'with a very cheap and pungent eau-de-Cologne' which seemed very popular with his guards who, according to Anders, doused themselves with it. Anders recorded that every second day he was taken to the barber's shop to be shaved and that at 4 pm, 4 August 1941, he was taken from his cell and led along familiar corridors. Anders' little group was joined by the prison commander and for once, nobody pinioned Anders' arms or tripped him or threw him down steps. The prison commander walked alongside Anders, who was aided as he negotiated steps and stairs. Everybody was a model of courtesy. As the walk continued, the surroundings became more luxurious until eventually Anders found himself in a large study which was fully carpeted and furnished with 'soft armchairs'. Behind their desks sat two men dressed in civilian clothes who rose when Anders entered. They addressed him with civility and Anders asked to whom he was speaking They introduced themselves as Beria and Merkulov and confirmed that Anders was a free-man.[1]

The two civilians in front of Anders were two of the most powerful men in the Soviet Union. Beria was the head of the NKVD and Merkulov was his deputy. Like Stalin, they were both Georgians and part of the so-called 'Georgian Mafia'. If Stalin was number one in this mafia, these two were numbers two and three. Anders was briefed by the two NKVD chiefs and told that the Soviet people and Poles had to learn to live together 'in harmony and bury the hatchet', as their sole aim was to defeat Germany. It was explained to Anders that a treaty between the Soviet government and British governments had recently been signed to that effect. Furthermore, an agreement had been reached between the Soviet government and the Polish Government-in-Exile. The terms of this agreement allowed for an amnesty for all Poles in Soviet captivity and for a Polish Army to be raised from Poles on Soviet territory.

Anders was told that he had been appointed by the Polish authorities in London as commander of the force to be raised, and that the Soviet government had granted its consent for this appointment. The Soviets claimed that Anders had been voted the most popular man among Poles in the Soviet Union. It seemed that ninety-six per cent of them had declared themselves for Anders. This bemused Anders because as far as he was aware, such a plebiscite was never held. He also learned that Stalin 'took a great interest' in him.[2] Of course Stalin's 'interest' could prove to be a double-edged sword, or even fatal. Even so, Anders was free.

There are few observations to be made at this juncture regarding the amnesty and the plight of the Poles in the Soviet Union in 1941. The question of an amnesty was unfair as was the use of the word 'amnesty', which suggested that the Poles had been guilty of crimes and were therefore criminals. Indeed, Sikorski tried to get the wording changed but was ignored. Since 1941 Poles have regarded the use of the term 'amnesty' as a slur on their national honour but this continues to be ignored and is now more or less the shorthand in referring to the release of Poles from Soviet captivity between 1941 and 1942. Some burdens have to be borne. However, it should also be noted that the mass release of Poles from captivity was not unique and indeed there were several such releases or 'amnesties' made between 1941 and 1945 as the Soviet state sought to fill the ranks of the Red Army. These amnesties continued right up to the final assault on Berlin in April 1945. In the period of 1941–44, some 975,000 men were released from Soviet camps, commonly known as 'Gulags', with the bulk being sent to serve in the Red Army.[3]

Anders made the observation that most people, not only Poles who found themselves in Soviet custody, were often unlikely to have committed any crimes. It was the nature of Stalinist rule which made them criminals; also, the Poles were not the only people to have been massacred by the Soviets before or after 1939. Furthermore, the Soviet-Polish Agreement was not as amicable as Beria and Merkulov had led Anders to believe, but without doubt Anders would have realised that. Sikorski and his government domiciled in London, however, were not really aware of the horrors endured by the Poles held in Soviet captivity since 1939. They were to discover this later, but never really learned the lessons that Anders was to set them.

The problem was that Sikorski, in 1941, saw an opportunity for himself when the suggestion was made that Poles in the Soviet Union should be released and a Polish Army formed from their numbers. Sikorski had tried to recruit Poles from the Americas and was disappointed with the results.[4] Therefore a large number of Poles suddenly being made available to Sikorski was a god-send – but it was not to be, and anything that came from the Soviet Union seemed to come with a hefty price tag. Sikorski had signed the Polish-Soviet Treaty on 30 July 1941, but it had been the result of incessant arm-twisting by Churchill and Eden and had caused four resignations from the Polish Cabinet.[5] The main bugbear with the treaty was that it was pro-Soviet and so it looked as if Sikorski was pursuing a pro-Soviet policy. A major bone of contention was that the treaty accepted the loss of Polish territories in the east to the Soviet Union, with the hope of receiving German territories in the west at war's end when Germany was defeated. This was to accept the annexation of Polish territories by the Soviet Union even if after June 1941 they were occupied by Germany and remained so until summer 1944. The loss of these territories angered those Poles coming out of Soviet captivity as they had not only been ill-treated, humiliated and seen their countrymen murdered or worked to death, but so many actually came from the areas which were to be handed over to the Soviet Union. Sikorski was never going to truly win these men over to his side and their loyalty to Anders was fierce even after the war because he understood them, and in time delivered them from Soviet captivity.

Sikorski should have known that his Soviet policy was not going to be popular even among his own government as opponents to it included the President-in-Exile, Władysław Raczkiewicz, the Foreign Minister, August Zalewski and General Kazimierz Sosnkowski, the head of the military wing of the Polish underground. From this group came a basic requirement for cooperation with the Soviet government that was a return of pre-war Polish frontiers, which was simply a call for a Soviet withdrawal from eastern Poland. If there was to be any talk of a Polish Army being raised in the Soviet Union it was to be understood that it should be under Polish command.[6] Sikorski had known about this position for almost twelve months but at the time of these decisions being made, August 1940, it all seemed academic; in July 1941 however the situation had dramatically changed and Polish politicians needed to make some realistic decisions rather than those based on wishful thinking.

A further problem for Sikorski was that the Polish military underground and the Polish underground political parties did not support his Soviet policy. This meant that Sosnkowski was able to brief against Sikorski. Meanwhile Sikorski had to be tactful when negotiating with the Soviets as he did not want to antagonise them and cause a very public split within the Polish camp. Therefore Sikorski had to ensure he was perceived as being tough in dealing with Soviet demands so he could not be accused by his compatriots of not having Polish interests at heart in his negotiations with the Soviet government. Sikorski had known this since at least December 1940.[7] Once he had to negotiate for real with the Soviet government or, more often than not, with Stalin, he found it a very difficult tightrope to walk. The problematic relationship between the Polish Government-in-Exile and the British government became a headache as the British government tried to prevent the Poles from insulting the Soviet government in speeches made by prominent Poles, both military and civilian figures.[8]

Initially, Anders was very cooperative in the early days of the Polish-Soviet Agreement; this is not to say he was happy with the settlement, but he did see it as an opportunity to free his compatriots and establish a Polish Army from within the Soviet Union. Indeed he denounced those who opposed the Agreement as he observed that 'everybody without exception', in reference to the Poles who had been in Soviet captivity, had, in his opinion, put their misfortune behind them and supported the Agreement.[9] On 22 August 1941, in his first order to his new army (proposed but not yet formed), Anders declared that the formation of a Polish Army on Soviet soil would be part of the effort to defeat Poland's only enemy – Germany – and that this army would fight alongside all of the Allies, including the Soviet Union, until Germany was defeated.[10] A few days later Anders made a speech in which he recited the litany of Polish military endeavour since the outbreak of war, which included Poles seeing action in Norway, Africa and on the Atlantic Ocean. He did not deny that the way back to Poland would be difficult and bloody. He placed the entire blame for the war onto Germany.[11] Initially, Anders was tactful in his references to the Soviet Union, but this was not to last. Even at the end of 1941 he still supported Sikorski's Soviet policy as, once again, he put it in the context of addressing and correcting the wrongs of the Polish who had suffered while in Soviet captivity, ensuring Poles were freed.[12] As ever, Anders could be identified with the collective Polish suffering endured by himself and his countrymen and women while imprisoned or enslaved in the Soviet Union. Sikorski could never claim that badge of honour.

Anders was to soon learn that he had not been the first choice of the post of commander of Polish Forces in the Soviet Union. In a meeting with General MacFarlane, the Head of the British Mission to the Soviet Union, Anders was given a letter, via MacFarlane, from Sikorski. The letter contained instructions for Anders as well as the information that in principle, General Stanisław Hallers was to be Commander-in-chief of the Polish Army in Russia but, at that time, he was missing.[13] No doubt this was a blow to Anders' prestige, but not a public blow. Anders may not have believed the Soviet story of his overwhelming popularity but to be second choice is always galling. Having to accept second and third rate choices was something that the exiled Poles learned to live with. Hallers was already dead as he had been murdered in April 1940 by the NKVD along with thousands of other Polish officers at Katyń. Even so, Anders set-to with a will and began the task of establishing his army. His main problem was trying to locate Polish troops and other possible recruits, as well as making the Soviets admit to just how many Polish troops and others they were actually holding in captivity. Lieutenant-Colonel Tadeusz Felsztyn, in his 1947 history of 2nd Polish Corps, noted that from the opening days of September 1941, volunteers for the Polish Army being raised in the Soviet Union began to head towards the three main recruitment centres of Buzuluk, Czkalow and Tock in the Saratov-Kujbyszew-Czkalow region. The volunteers came from prisoner-of-war camps, prison and slave labour camps which were spread across the far north of Stalin's prison empire, from the Chinese frontier, from Kalma and Vladivostok. They came in rags, bare-foot, sick and starving. They were in the most wretched of conditions.[14]

Zurowski adds more detail to the plight of Poles heading towards the Polish Army recruitment centres in the Soviet Union. He noted that Polish prisoners of war often simply left their camps, as not all of the camps were fenced in and closely guarded. Once it was announced that they were free to go, they simply left and travelled south. It was the deportees who struggled most because individual camp commanders could decide whether they wished to set their captives free or not – it was dependent on whether a camp commander considered his prisoners valuable as slaves. The camps to which they were heading were largely run by Polish personnel, with Soviet and NKVD oversight. Buzuluk was the main centre for Polish recruitment in the first phase of the establishing a Polish Army in the Soviet Union. A large centre was later set up in central Asia with its headquarters at Yangi-Yul near Samarkand.[15]

Anders knew that on 2 November 1939, after the Soviet invasion of Poland, Molotov, the Soviet Foreign Minister, had announced that 300,000 Polish troops had been captured by the Red Army. A year after the invasion, 17 September 1940, the Red Army newspaper *Krasnaja Zviezda* (Red Star) announced that twelve Polish generals, over 18,000 officers, and more than 200,000 ordinary Polish troops had been captured by the Red Army during the period September–October 1939. Of this number, Anders was already aware that 11,000 officers appeared to be missing and wondered just how many other ranks (ORs) were also missing.[16] There were other problems for Anders to confront: the Poles coming from London and the British representatives sent out to Moscow.

The first Polish diplomat to arrive from London was Dr Józef Retinger who was the Polish Chargé d'Affaires until an ambassador was appointed. Retinger was a personal friend of Sikorski; widely travelled, highly intelligent (rather than merely academically qualified), and popular. Retinger introduced Anders to the British Ambassador to the Soviet Union, Sir Stafford Cripps, Retinger and Cripps already knew each other. Anders did not think much of Cripps and considered him to be naive in his approach towards the Soviet government as well as considering that Cripps failed to understand the problems between the Soviet government and Poland.[17] It was a view that many people held, and still hold, of Cripps, perhaps unfairly so.

Quite simply, Cripps was out of his depth in the Soviet Union and in dealing with the likes of Stalin. Cripps may have been a Socialist, which Stalin was in principle but not in practice, while Cripps was a 'champagne socialist' even if he did seem to endure some puritan ideals in his diet. The problem lay with the fact that Cripps came from a 'gentleman's' background, was privileged and well brought up. Stalin and his cronies were basically gangsters and Cripps was ill-prepared to deal with those of that ilk. Furthermore the Foreign Office had little faith in Cripps and so he became isolated, diplomatically, socially and personally. Even so, the naive Cripps soon learned that it was almost impossible to get anything done with the Soviets, far less get anything done quickly.[18]

Anders also knew this but unlike Cripps he knew that the Soviet government were not to be trusted at all and giving their word, or signing treaties, meant nothing to them. The Soviet leaders could break a pledged bond at will with no compunction.

Retinger was a perfect choice to send to the Soviet Union, but Sikorski made a terrible mistake as he then sent his close aide, Professor Stanisław Kot, as his emissary. Kot acted as Sikorski's political conduit and enraged Anders. Indeed Anders loathed him and his politics which were completely anti-Sanacja, as the inter-war Polish regime was often referred to. Despite Zurowski's contemporary assertion, in 1941 it was considered that Anders was not particularly anti- or pro-Sanacja but this did not deter him from ignoring Kot's advice to remove Sanacja supporters from the Polish Army.[19] Later even the Foreign Office commented on Kot's political activities in the Middle East and beyond. This is borne out in a Foreign Office report of 1942 which asserted that 'M. Kot … a man of very great energy, has got his men into every corner of the Middle East. He is certainly preparing a big future for the Peasant Party [Kot's political party] after the war.'[20] This was a process begun in the Soviet Union during 1941.

Kot also got the Poles embroiled in an unnecessary argument with the Soviet government in which the Polish Embassy in Moscow was accused of being involved in espionage against the Soviet Union. Kot was held to have been partially responsible for this alleged spying but the allegation was to have severe repercussions for all Poles,[21] because after this alleged incident the Soviets could at least go through the pretence of the Poles being poor allies and not to be trusted; quite an ironic stance taken by the Soviet government. Anders certainly thought little of Kot or his abilities, noting that he did not speak Russian or understand Russia at all. In contrast Anders did both as a consequence of having served in the Imperial Russian Army and his recent imprisonment. By September 1941 Anders had told Kot to stop interfering in military matters and by October the relationship between the two had gone from bad to worse.[22] It should be noted, however, that according to Kot, he was appointed as Polish ambassador to the Soviet Union almost against his will as he pointed out to Sikorski that he did not speak Russian and had never been to the country. Sikorski told him that he had to accept the post as nobody else wanted it.[23]

Indeed the archival record for the Polish General Staff in the Soviet Union during November 1941 describes the relationship between Kot and Anders as being fatal. What should be noted is that Kot was considered to have too much political ambition, but it also goes on to say that Klimkowski, an extremely ambitious junior officer who punched well above his weight, and furthermore was Anders' adjutant, had similar ambitions to Kot. Even so, the Foreign Office noted an incident where it seemed that Klimkowski was on his way to Tehran but this was called off and he met with Kot instead, with whom he did not have a good relationship at all.[24] It is without doubt that Kot was planning a political future for post-war Poland; a future that made him a great man. But he was not wrong about the political aspirations of some Polish military officers including junior officers under Anders' command. Kot had written to Sikorski to complain that Anders had ignored his concerns, especially 'Pilsudski-ites' within Anders' entourage. Kot was particularly incensed by the appointment of Captain (*Rotmistrz*) Jerzy Klimkowski as Anders' adjutant.[25] No doubt Kot, who took himself very seriously, was not impressed to be received by Klimkowski rather than Anders on 22 November 1941 because the day before, Kot had been in talks with Stalin.[26]

Klimkowski was to prove to be a controversial and sinister figure at the heart of Anders' team and it is left to history to judge just how much Anders knew about him and his activities. Even Anders, writing letters to Sikorski petitioning for promotion for Klimkowski during September 1941, admitted that Klimkowski did come over as a bit of a fanatic but, overall, was a good man. Klimkowski had been part of Anders' entourage since 1939 and by 1941 Anders had known him for over ten years. Klimkowski was promoted to the rank of captain on 15 October 1941.[27] It should also be noted that Stalin knew Klimkowski because, in a meeting with Sikorski and Anders on 4 December 1942, Stalin asked of *Rotmistrz* Klimkowski, noting that in his estimation, Klimkowski represented young Poles.[28] What Stalin meant by 'young Poles' is uncertain but it could have meant that he already had recruited Klimkowski and that 'young Poles' meant Communist or Stalinist Poles. It is all very intriguing.

Despite Anders' soft-soaping of Sikorski, the Foreign Office later considered that Klimkowski was Anders' 'evil genius' and had to be warned by the British authorities that his 'disturbances' would not be tolerated by them.[29] Klimkowski's activities within Second Polish Corps will be considered later in this work, as will the possibility of Anders' collusion in them and the possibility of their involvement in the death of Sikorski and his entourage in an air crash off Gibraltar on 4 July 1943. What remains unclear is just why Anders supported Klimkowski as much as he did. Was it comradeship from the 1930s or a common love of horses? It is just not clear.[30]

By the end of 1942 the Foreign Office was also aware of some of the shady goings on within Anders' force. One British diplomat, Robert Hankey, drank with Polish officers to get the truth out from them. Hankey got them drunk and reported thus: '...then the truth would come out, not as a result of one's asking.' Hankey learned about the politics of Anders' Army and the personal rivalries as they all tried to establish a hold over the Poles in the Middle East with an eye to political power in post-war Poland. Hankey claimed that Anders had banned politics from his force but still intended to return to Poland as the head of the Polish Army.[31] This certainly smacked of politics and symbolism as even Piłsudski had been sneaked into Warsaw over 10–11 November 1918 by the German government; power was found lying in the gutters of Warsaw and Piłsudski merely picked it up and assumed leadership in Poland. To return to Poland at the head of an army does not sound like a renouncement of politics at all.

However, to return to the summer and early autumn 1941, the greatest concern of the Poles in the Soviet Union and to Sikorski was the relentless German advance into the Soviet Union. As the Germans moved through the western parts of the Soviet Union and headed towards Moscow and Leningrad, Sikorski and Anders agreed a plan to evacuate the Polish Army from the Soviet Union in the case of a collapse of the Russian Front.[32] A letter from Anthony Eden to Sir Stafford Cripps with a message from Sikorski to General Szyszko-Bohusz, Head of the Polish Military Mission (like Anders he had served in the former Imperial Russian Army and so spoke Russian and understood Russia), was enclosed and underlined the situation on the Russian Front regarding the Poles, but also suggested that Sikorski was willing to deploy Polish troops on Soviet soil if the situation demanded it. Sikorski requested that the following message be put before the influential British general, General Sir Hastings Ismay, who had the ear of Churchill. The message ran:

In virtue of the latest developments on the Eastern Front and the particularly rapid German drive in the Southern sector towards the

Donetz [sic] Basin and the Caucasus, the latter had become eminently important to the final issue. The protection of the Caucasian oilfields is now a vitally urgent question. I desire the Polish divisions to take part in their defence. We are not responsible for the delay in organisation and equipment. I do not wish to put forward to the Soviet government the suggestion of moving the Polish forces to the Caucasus, being most anxious to avoid any suspicion. I would be grateful if you will: – Give your kind assistance to the speeding up the equipment-transport [sic] from Archangel to Polish Forces. Induce the British representatives to put forward a proposal to move Polish troops without delay or regard for their state of organisation, to the Caucasus and to equip and arm these troops to the extent which will make it possible for them under the prevailing geographic conditions to render vital services to Soviet Russia and the Allies.'[33]

Sikorski had to be cautious in his request to move the Polish Army as Stalin might well have become suspicious and halt recruitment for it in the Soviet Union. However, after the Japanese attack on the American naval base at Pearl Harbor, Hawaii and the consequent state of war between the USA and Japan; Germany unnecessarily declared war on the USA. This meant that the USA was not only in a position to help the UK, but also to provide aid for the Soviet Union. The USA was to become the great provider of war material and finance to the Allies for the remainder of the war. From this position of largesse, the American President Franklin D. Roosevelt held great sway among the Allied leaders, including Stalin. Therefore it was decided that if Roosevelt approached Stalin regarding the possible evacuation of the Poles from the Soviet Union, Stalin might take it better when Sikorski spoke later to him on the same subject.[34] The passage of time between the original idea of moving Polish troops in September 1941, to that of a possible American intervention on their behalf in December 1941, is interesting as it reveals just how negotiations with the Soviet government, or with Stalin, were slow and ponderous, especially for the Poles.

It did not take long before the Polish and Soviet governments began to disagree about how the Polish Army in the Soviet Union was to be established and organised. The biggest disagreements were about its equipping and deployment. During October 1941 Anders refused to allow the partially equipped (Polish) 5th Infantry Division be sent to the Front. This immediately led to accusations by the Soviet government of ill will on the part of the Polish Government-in-Exile.[35] It did not help that the Soviet government had previously provided the Polish Army with a substantial loan of five million roubles.[36] No doubt the Soviet government, fighting for the survival of its state, did not, and could not, care to understand the Polish motivation for caution. However Sikorski's biggest blow for his Soviet policy was when Anders decided to move Polish military units from the Soviet Union and place them under the command of the British in the Middle East.

The possibility of removing large numbers of Polish troops from the Soviet Union suited both the British and the Soviet governments. The Soviet government was not overly happy to host such a large and possibly hostile build up of Polish forces, while the British Middle East Command was very happy for the transfer of Polish troops to Iraq as the British Army had an acute manpower shortage in that region. Sikorski was outfoxed as he had already lost his leverage, such as it was, in his relationship with Stalin and the Soviet government. He was also aware that if large numbers of Polish troops left the Soviet Union, the Red Army, once it finally arrived in Poland, as was expected no matter how the war looked in 1941, would be able to do as it pleased there and the Soviet Union would be able to dictate policy in post-war Poland.[37] The war was moving faster than Sikorski would have liked and he was being outmanoeuvred on the military-political front.

In 1941 any talk of evacuating the Polish Army from the Soviet Union was hypothetical as much of the effort being then taken was trying to locate Polish troops and possible recruits. The provision of equipment for the Polish Army was also on a long and precarious supply line originating from the UK and then sent by sea to the northern Soviet port of Archangel. From there, the equipment had to be sent to Soviet Asia where most of the Poles found were actually located. The entire enterprise seemed to be one sided, with the Poles supplying the men and the British supplying the equipment, while the Soviets were getting the best of the bargain.[38]

By October 1941 Anders had some idea of what lay before him as he began to assemble his army. He had located 20,000 soldiers in Uzbekistan, which was enough for two divisions, and between 15,000 and 20,000 men were found in

Kazakhstan ready to join the Polish Army. The question of equipment supply remained difficult.[39] During November 1941 Szyszko-Bohusz told Anders that there should be around 30,000 Polish soldiers available from the Soviet Union to serve in the Polish Army being raised at the time.[40] Anders was convinced that there should have been more however, and had been pursuing the true numbers of Polish troops in captivity in the Soviet Union since he had been released in August 1941, and had a short and terse interview with the Soviet General, Brigadier-General Panfilov in Moscow.[41] The Soviet authorities were dissembling and Anders knew it. As a result, suspicion began to grow among senior Poles, both in London and in Moscow, about the fate of those Polish officers captured by the Red Army during September and October 1939. Polish suspicions did not diminish with the passing months.

In early December 1941, during a conversation between Sikorski, Stalin, Kot, Molotov and Anders, who was also interpreting from Russian to Polish for his compatriots, Sikorski asked Stalin about the missing Polish officers. He inquired if perhaps they were still in camps somewhere. Stalin responded with a display of outrage, perhaps false outrage or perhaps genuine, as Sikorski and Anders refused to drop the matter. Stalin claimed that all of the Polish claims were impossible as all Poles had been released under the terms of the recent amnesty setting them free. Perhaps as a sop to Sikorski he indicated that Molotov should look into the matter and check that indeed all Poles had been released. Sikorski persisted in asking about the missing 4,000 Polish officers (it turned out that this was a low estimate, as now the figures seem to be between 16,000 and 22,000 victims of the NKVD, murdered in April 1940). Sikorski told Stalin that he knew from Red Cross returns they were not in German prisoner of war camps but instead seem have to disappeared into Soviet captivity. Stalin maintained the line that the Polish officers had probably escaped while Anders refused to believe him. Furthermore, there were other suspicious circumstances, such as the simultaneous ending of all communication with the officers' families.

Stalin still persisted in trying to convince Anders that the Polish officers had indeed all escaped. Sikorski, sensing an impasse, glossed over the question by noting that Russia was a big country and it was impossible to be sure what was going on at any one time.[42] From this incident we learn three things: Stalin was not only a liar, but a fool as well; Anders was not afraid of him, and

Sikorski was yet to learn any lessons about the Soviet Union, assuming that he ever understood the country and how it was ruled by Stalin. Sikorski was quite second rate when compared with Anders, who easily outfoxed him at every turn. Anders was better connected than Sikorski and simply had better allies, such as his president who declared his complete support for Anders in a message to him as early as September 1941.[43] The President-in-Exile should be seen as an opponent of Sikorski, if not an enemy, owing to Sikorski's Soviet policy and the fact that Sikorski followers ousted Raczkiewicz's choice as prime minister, August Zalewski, in an armed coup in central London during July 1940. The Foreign Office thoroughly approved the removal of Zalewski, who was only in office for a day, even though the British authorities considered the Polish measures were a bit rough.[44]

On 28 September 1941 Anders outlined his plans for the Polish Army on Soviet territory. He estimated that he could build an army of eight divisions from around an estimated 100,000 Poles which should have been available in the Soviet Union. This meant there was a possibility of establishing four infantry divisions, two divisions of motorised infantry, two armoured divisions as well as supply and logistic units. At this time Anders already had enough men for two infantry divisions with 12,000 men in each division. The establishment of a third division was underway but progress was extremely slow as it lacked equipment and supplies. It basically had enough to keep alive but not to progress as a military formation under training. Two questions were considered at the time: the problem of supply given the length of the supply line to Polish troops in the Soviet Union – beginning in the UK and then shipped to Archangel before the long journey to Soviet Asia; and where the Polish Army was to be concentrated. As we have already seen, the possibility of the Polish Army leaving the Soviet Union for Iraq suited both the British and Soviet government.

A conference held in Moscow from 29 September to 1 October 1941 between the USA, the UK and the Soviet Union revealed just how unimportant the Poles actually were in the war. The short conference, which was fairly low key with the UK being represented by the media baron, Lord Beaverbrook and the US by W. Averill Harriman with Stalin hosting the talks, was held to discuss aid to the Soviet Union as long as she remained in the war against Germany. It should be noted that at this point the USA was not at war with either Japan or Germany. The problem for the Poles at the Moscow meeting was that it was not about them and had nothing to do with them. They were yesterday's men and had been for a long time. The Soviet Union stole any thunder that the Poles may have had and were doing most of the fighting as much of the German land forces were drawn to the Eastern Front and away from the West. Anders considered that the conference, and the subsequent agreement, sent the wrong signal to Stalin as to how he should treat the Poles in the Soviet Union in as much as he could disregard them and their ambitions, while noting that Beaverbrook was only concerned with arming the Soviet Union and Soviet matters.[45] It was probably not thought about in depth because Poland was a minor ally and the Soviet Union had just become a major one with the potential of ensuring the defeat of Germany and her allies, even if this was not so obvious in 1941. It was imperative, therefore, that the Soviet Union was not defeated because if they were, Britain and her empire would become endangered once more and perhaps, in time, so would the USA.

There was another problem: Lord Beaverbrook, a Canadian media tycoon did not much like the Poles or the Czechs and did not care who knew this. In his own newspaper he once wrote that Britain was not interested in raising Poland and Czechoslovakia 'out of the gutter, dusting them down and putting them on pedestals with arms in their hands, only for them to be overthrown again'.[46] This was the problem for east-central European countries during the inter-war period: collective security. If there were no aggressive nations on their borders, east-central European states could survive, and even more so if they cooperated in collective security matters. When Hitler came to power in Germany, however, these nations became imperilled, especially as they seemed to squabble among themselves and act, as both Poland and Hungary did, as the aggressors. The Soviet Union stood on the Eastern Front, vulture-like, ready to pick over Germany's leavings. Therefore we can only conclude that when Beaverbrook arrived in Moscow he did Poland no favours. By this time it was quite clear that Poland was seen as a minor ally, as it did not even have a seat at the conference table even though a Polish Army, supplied by the British, was being raised on Soviet territory. Even so, it would seem from the diary of the Soviet Ambassador to the UK, Ivan Maisky, that Beaverbrook's conduct and behaviour at Moscow led some members of the British War Cabinet (not Churchill) to conclude that Beaverbrook had mishandled the negotiations in the

Soviet capital and as a result, consider the possibility of Beaverbrook having to resign his Cabinet post or leave as a result of a reshuffle.[47] Neither happened at the time as Churchill always defended his men. It should also be remembered that Beaverbrook, when sent to Moscow, bore a letter of introduction from Churchill to Stalin in which Churchill had written, 'this letter will be presented to you by Lord Beaverbrook. Lord Beaverbrook has the fullest confidence of the Cabinet, and is one of my oldest and most intimate friends.'[48] With such support it was not really surprising that Beaverbrook behaved in the way he did and took full advantage of the situation allowing his and Stalin's prejudices against the Poles to set the agenda.

Perhaps the Poles were already alive to Beaverbrook's attitude however, as Edward Raczyński, the then Polish Ambassador to the UK, remarked during the summer of 1939 that he had met Beaverbrook at Brendan Bracken's house (Bracken was to become Churchill's Minister of Information). Raczyński noted that Beaverbrook was attacking Poland daily in the *Daily Express* and in the *Evening Standard*. Raczyński also met Churchill and David Lloyd George (a long term opponent of Poland) at the same gathering at Bracken's home. Both Churchill and Lloyd George considered that Poland was 'in league with Chamberlain to prevent the success of the Anglo-Soviet negotiations'.[49] During the summer of 1939 there were some half-hearted attempts by the Foreign Office to encourage the Soviet Union to enter into some form of collective security in east-central Europe with the Soviet Union taking the leading role in any such arrangement. Not surprisingly the Polish government opposed any such move, especially when a key component of such an agreement was that Poland would give free passage to the Red Army across Polish territory towards Germany; of course this was anathema to any Pole. It should also be noted that Lloyd George once said that he would no more give Upper Silesia to Poland 'than he would give a clock to a monkey'. Following Davies' work it should be understood that Lloyd George was not alone in his views; there were some very dubious figures that more or less drew the same conclusion, with varying degrees of venom injected.[50]

Despite the shortcomings of the 1941 Moscow agreement the British government did its best to supply the Polish Army being raised in the Soviet Union with the necessary kit. Kot does suggest that there was a degree of support from the British overall, and even from Harriman for the Polish cause in the Soviet Union, but it seemed that Beaverbrook had been allowed to take the lead at the Moscow talks and prevent any meaningful arming of the Polish Army.[51] During September 1941 it seemed that personalities still mattered more than logic.

During September 1941 the War Office sent 50,000 uniforms; Anders requested a further 50,000 as the Soviets, despite legal obligations to supply such material, actually could not as they had lost vast supplies of war materials in the wake of the German advance into the Soviet Union. The Soviets were beginning to struggle to feed and clothe the Poles, and during September told the Polish authorities that they could only feed and clothe a single Polish division of about 10,000, which was somewhat inadequate. By this time there were already 20,000 Poles at the Buzuluk reception centre while a further 10,000 were waiting to be processed. Anders foresaw that he might end up with a force of about 100,000 men.

Of course the Soviet authorities, with an eye to the future according to Zurowski, were opposed to a large non-Communist (in reality anti-Communist) formation which was subservient to the Polish Government-in-Exile and headed by Anders, who was considered to be a known 'reactionary'. The Soviets preferred that the force should be split up across the Eastern Front under Soviet commanders. It was also not desirable for the Soviet government that Sikorski should be handed such a political and militarily valuable asset; meanwhile, the Soviets were trying to optimise all manpower available to them in order to stave off the German advance into the Soviet Union. Of course Sikorski did not want to see the Polish force being squandered; even though he saw a possibility of it being used to defend oil fields at Baku if the Germans were to advance so far, but overall Sikorski wanted to keep it intact for the day when a Polish Army could once more return to Poland.[52] It was no doubt owing to that ambition that Sikorski, with a sense of futility, asked Anders during November 1941 whether he (Anders) was his man, having been warned that Anders was his rival and that whether Anders' men were his (Sikorski's) men. Anders, somewhat slyly, did not answer directly but instead stated that he and his men were 'all Poland's men', and that in this respect Sikorski could entirely rely on them.[53] This was not the answer Sikorski was looking for as Anders had not pledged himself and his men to Sikorski but instead to Poland. Sikorski could not protest without revealing his hand which was obvious to quite a few figures in British and Polish circles, while Anders had revealed nothing and had pledged nothing. He was for Poland, and for that he could not be faulted.

Sikorski's suspicion was that the Soviets merely saw the Poles as cannon fodder but there were alternative ideas of how to deploy the Polish force once it reached combat readiness. Both Churchill and General Sir Archibald Wavell, the British commander in Libya, agreed with Sikorski's Baku plan but they also considered that the Soviet Union might soon collapse in the face of the German advance and agreed that eventually the Poles might be used to help protect the Middle East.[54] Sikorski was correct to be suspicious of how the Soviets might deploy the Polish force as throughout Russian/Soviet history, the individual has never really mattered to the authorities, both Tsarist and Soviet, and so the Russian populace has always been seen as cannon fodder; foreign troops, especially those with no reason to be loyal to the Soviet state, were always going to be expendable. It was just ironic that this force, once in the Middle East as desired by the British authorities, caused so much pain for Sikorski, as Anders was to make it his own army and defy Sikorski; neither man was ever to see Poland again.

The consequence of the Polish failure to obtain a presence at the 1941 Moscow Conference was that they remained wholly dependent on the Soviet government for receipt of equipment sent by the British and for their goodwill in general – both were in short supply. The meetings in Moscow were swift and business like. The problem was that the Soviet Union was genuinely in dire straits and the Germans were hell bent on defeating the Soviets before the harsh Russian winter set in. Therefore it is not surprising that Harriman pledged that 'we shall work fast'. 'Time' as the London *Times* suggested was 'vital'.[55] In the first meeting in Moscow, Harriman with the full support of Roosevelt, asserted that American support for the Soviet Union was there 'till victory'.[56] It was a very similar vow to that which Churchill had made to Sikorski in 1940.

Churchill remarked to Roosevelt that 'Max (Beaverbrook) and Averill seem to have had great success at Moscow.'[57] Indeed they had; the talks had ended 'speedily' as the Americans and British agreed to supply almost everything which the Soviets had asked for, or more than likely demanded.[58] If anything, the British and the Americans might have over-extended themselves because a new headache arose: where to find the ships to transport arms and supplies diverted from the UK to the Soviet Union. Even if the Soviets were 'satisfied' with the outcome of the Moscow Talks, the British were expected to do without some of the equipment from the USA originally earmarked for the UK.[59] Indeed, Beaverbrook in his report on the Moscow Talks stated that we had to give 'all that we can give'.[60] The problem for the British and American delegates in Moscow and their respective governments was that the Soviet Union was fighting almost the entire German Army, and was struggling. Even though the British held out for over a year against Germany and her allies and had seen her cities and people suffer from heavy aerial bombardments while the USA was yet to enter the war, at least formally, the Soviet Union was actually locked in a life and death struggle with Germany.

The British and American governments had to help the Soviet Union or see Germany overrun Soviet territory, at least up to the Ural Mountains to the east of Moscow. Therefore the talks between the British and American governments with the Soviet government were rushed through swiftly with Stalin and Molotov present, which was probably intimidating. There was also an element of naivety in dealing with Stalin. In an undated note but perhaps towards the end of December 1941, Churchill sent a message to Roosevelt containing the views of Brigadier Hollis of the Chiefs of Staff (COS [UK]) Committee. In Hollis' view the UK and US had to supply the Soviet Union with war material and other materials to fight off the German invasion as 'in this way alone we shall hold out influence over Stalin and be able to weave the mighty Russian effort into the general texture of the war'.[61] This was as naive as the German conservative politicians thinking in 1933 that they had hired Hitler and could control him.[62] And so by the end of 1941, the Polish Army in the Soviet Union was left naked. The Poles were expendable and did not even cross the Anglo-American collective mind as everything possible was done to shore up the Soviet Union. The defence of the Soviet Union was paramount; Polish concerns were already forgotten. Stalin clearly saw this and in the face of the Polish refusal to send a partially equipped division to fight on the Russian Front, Stalin declined to allow a second Polish division to be fitted out.

After the Moscow Conference it would seem that Anders decided to press harder for the evacuation of Poles from the Soviet Union. It was quite clear to him that Stalin and his government only saw the Poles as cannon fodder for the front. The Soviets resorted to chicanery and tried to include exceptions in an attempt to retain Poles as well as to cover up the fact that thousands of

Poles had died in Soviet captivity as a result of ill-treatment, illness or straight forward murder by the NKVD. Anders was well aware of the situation in the Soviet Union and had come to realise that Polish survival was dependent on the capricious nature of Stalin, or evacuation.

The Soviet government continued in its duplicitous attitude as in October 1941 Polish ex-PoWs were being re-routed to Uzbekistan where conditions were extremely hard. In many areas there was a danger of malaria and people died while travelling. There was also great concern for children travelling owing to a scarcity of clothing and footwear for them. During the same month, the Polish Army in the Soviet Union numbered 40,000 men and the Soviet authorities wanted to hold to this number, partially because they lacked the ability to provide for these men, let alone more. It was also at this time that the Soviets began to become quite reluctant to release more prisoners, or even to reveal where they were held. Other reasons including communication breakdowns, bureaucratic chaos and inertia have been cited for the Soviet intransigence regarding the release of Poles to the Polish army.[63] However, of course, the main reason for being careful about the release of Polish prisoners was that thousands of Polish officers had been murdered by the Soviet security forces and eventually, as Poles were released from Soviet captivity, the numbers would not tally.

The question of the evacuation of Polish service personnel remained a live one as it had been agreed that Polish naval and air force members could be sent to the Middle East or to the UK. On 3 October 1941 Sikorski asked Kot to raise the issue with the Soviets. Sikorski had a plan that these people could be sent out of the Soviet Union via Archangel in the very north of the Soviet Union via camps in Vologda and its neighbouring districts. Taking his time, Molotov agreed to the plan on 12 November and that between 15,000 to 20,000 men should be dispatched from Murmansk.[64] This was probably the last positive action between the Poles and the Soviets until Sikorski's arrival in Moscow on 3 December 1941.

Once Sikorski arrived in Moscow the Poles and the Soviets continued to dispute the numbers of Polish troops that should be available for service and who was responsible for what and for whom. By then 44,000 Poles were in uniform, but the Poles were told that 30,000 had been the agreed number, something which Anders totally rejected. According to General Zygmunt Bohusz-Szyszko, Head of the Polish Military Mission in Kuibyshev, the temporary Soviet administrative capital, the total number of released prisoners stood at 100,000 and would soon rise to 150,000. The Soviets continued in their lack of cooperation and obstructed further releases of Polish prisoners citing transport problems. Polish diplomatic staff found it difficult to work for and aid their nationals owing to Soviet blocking and delays. Kot especially was kept in the dark by Soviet officials. Even so, despite the difficulties met from the Soviets; ex-PoWs continued to make their way southwards to Buzuluk even though they ran a very real risk of starvation and death en route.

Polish diplomatic staff for Kazakhstan, Novosibirsk and Archangel was kept down to three while supplies, all valuable in the circumstances, for the Poles were lost or unaccounted for while being transported. Vague promises were made by the Soviets regarding feeding the Poles with an even vaguer plan for their resettlement. No agreement was reached over the extra funds or loans from the Soviet government in order to provide aid for wounded PoWs, women with small children and others who could not fend for themselves. There were a large number of orphans among the Polish exodus. Things did begin to improve as a result of the Kot–Stalin conversation of 14 November 1941. However, a British aide-memoire submitted on 3 November to the Soviet Foreign Ministry might have had some influence. The British recommended that Polish Forces might move south from Buzuluk in order that the British might supply them from Persia (Iran) and India. The British criticised the Soviet government for not fulfilling its promises to supply the Poles with ammunition as well as calling for the release of all Polish PoWs and providing them with the necessities of life as well as providing adequate wages for those released and working in the Soviet Union.

Within two days Andrei Vyshinsky told Cripps that the Soviet government was offering a 65 million rouble loan to the Poles in order to help them with their needs. By the middle of November, Stalin gave in to British and American pressure and agreed that the Poles could expand their force as much as they wanted, but provision for them was no longer a Soviet responsibility. It would seem that the British and Americans already had made plans of how to dispose of those Poles which were to come under their care. The prevailing conditions in the Soviet Union had convinced both the British and American governments that most Poles in the Soviet Union would not be fed, clothed, armed or trained by the Soviet Union and that they should be sent to a designated area in Iran.

From there they would be rearmed and equipped and eventually returned to fight on the Eastern Front. This, according to Zurowski, was the official view taken by the British military, Churchill and Roosevelt. Unofficially at this time the British preferred to see the Poles fighting in the Middle East. This view was not expressed to the Soviet government in case further release of Poles and a move to the south was prevented. There was also a view that the Soviets were not happy with the prospect of large numbers of Poles fighting alongside the Red Army in the Caucasus and that once the Poles left Soviet territory, the Soviets would lose interest in them.[65]

It was believed that it would take six months to return Polish ex-PoWS to a state of fitness ready for battle. There were also complications as the COS, Lieutenant-General Sir John Dill, opposed the Polish evacuation claiming that the shipping of 20,000 to 30,000 tons of stores monthly was impractical owing to the poor infrastructure found in Iran as well as the congestion of shipping in the Persian Gulf. Dill considered that such an undertaking would be at the expense of supplying British forces. As a consequence it was suggested that alternative places of recruitment such as India, East Africa and the Middle East should be considered. Dill thought that the Soviets should be primed for such action as they would eventually have to be involved and there was little sense in keeping things from them, but confidential advance notice should be given to the Soviet government. Dill's final recommendation was that a regular supply of food should be made to Buzuluk and Uzbekistan, but at the expense of supplies to the Soviets. It was recommended that the Americans should be approached regarding medical supplies.

Dill's recommendations were accepted and Sikorski, who was in Cairo at the time, was to be informed. Stalin was also kept in the loop as frankness had been adopted rather than the usual secrecy which was often motivated by a lack of trust on all sides, and possibly a fear of how Stalin and the Soviet government might react to an evacuation of the Poles from Soviet territory. The Foreign Office told Cripps on 25 November 1941 to formally tell Sikorski of the idea to remove over 100,000 Poles from the Soviet Union; Sikorski already seemed to know from his talks with the British Minister of State in Cairo. The preferred evacuation route was via the Caspian Sea, which Sikorski approved of and suggested that military cooperation between the British and Poles should start immediately.

As plans advanced and the necessity to move the Poles towards Iran for supply purposes was established, more official notices of what was afoot were posted. The Polish embassies in the USA and the Soviet Union were told that both Churchill and Eden had approved of the scheme. Meanwhile Kot, who knew of the plan, was yet to be authorised to inform Stalin but did convince him that all released Poles should be placed under the supervision of the Polish Army. Kot also managed to get Stalin to admit that the Soviet authorities were unable to feed and clothe all of the Poles on Soviet territory. It was in this way that Kot prepared for Sikorski's visit to the Soviet Union. Sikorski arrived in Kuibyshev on 3 December 1941 to negotiate with Stalin over the evacuation of Poles from Soviet territory.

Even so, Stalin had already expressed some confusion because the Americans had made a premature foray into the matter when, on 12 November 1941, Harriman sent a telegram to Stalin suggesting the evacuation of the Poles and the equipping and training by the British of Polish troops coming from the evacuation. To no great surprise, in his reply on 29 November, Stalin said that Kot had not mentioned this to him. The following day the Polish Ambassador advised Harriman not to pursue the matter as the intention was that Sikorski was to make all the running with Stalin on this matter. Once conversations between Stalin, Sikorski and Anders began it became clear that Stalin was opposed to the use of Anders' troops in North Africa. Sikorski realised that the continued release of Poles from Soviet captivity still largely depended on the presence of a Polish Army remaining on Soviet soil. Sikorski was also alert enough to understand that this army was the main source of material and moral support for the Polish civilian population still in the Soviet Union. He was also aware that the army, and especially Anders, were beacons of hope for all Poles yet to be released from Soviet captivity. It was at this point that Sikorski relented and only maintained his demand for the 25,000 naval and air personnel to be sent to the UK or the Middle East. Furthermore, Stalin also agreed that the Polish Army coming out of the Soviet Union could expand as far as possible with talk of seven divisions being made, as well as agreeing to Sikorski's request that the entire force should be dealt with as a single unit rather than the separate forces which Stalin had tried to demand earlier. Further developments on the Soviet side of things included increasing the number of Polish diplomats to work in the Soviet Union, more Polish deportees to be released from the far north, while adequate food and transport was provided for their transfer to the reception areas in Central Asia. The original centre was closed down due to severe winter conditions.

In addition to the above it was finally agreed that Anders' force would be deployed on the Eastern Front. Meanwhile, Stalin agreed to equip the Polish 5th Division under the command of General Mieczysław Boruta-Spiechowicz. For once Stalin kept his word about this. Further divisions were to be equipped by the British and Americans. Even Polish civilians stranded in Central Asia saw amelioration in their living conditions as new centres in Uzbekistan, Southern Kazakhstan, Kirghizstan and Turkmenistan were promised; these changes were made over the following six weeks. The financial situation was also improved for the Poles in the Soviet Union as the Soviet government made two loans in total of 400 million roubles available. This allowed for the purchase of arms, equipment and subsidised food.

The transfer of the Polish Army began to take place in the period after Sikorski's visit to Moscow. This made it easier for the British to supply Polish troops while all ideas of Anders' men being sent off to North Africa to fight Rommel's Afrika Korps were temporarily forgotten by the Foreign Office. The War Office also quietly dropped plans to use Polish troops in various British outposts. Sikorski's insistence that Polish troops were to be kept in the Soviet Union made Dill's plan of supplying them with equipment originally earmarked for the Red Army possible. The trick was not to tell the Soviets, and Churchill was emphatic on this particular point. It was estimated by the War Office that the Polish relief programme would need 300 tons of equipment per month using the route via Iran to Soviet central Asia. The British had already sent warm clothing for 105,000 men during December 1941.

There were other complications, namely with the Polish air and naval personnel. The British Military Attaché in Moscow, General Mason Macfarlane, estimated that the evacuation of these men at the rate of 2,000 men per month via Iran to India would never take place. It was realised that not all of these men were actually trained properly and indeed some were raw recruits with nothing to really offer. Anders placed General Józef Zając, who had been the deputy commander of Polish troops in Scotland, in charge of these men. It was also a good way to get rid of him. As the Soviet government was only willing to equip the 5th Division, Sikorski asked the War Office to provide for the remaining

Polish troops. To complicate things, the Soviet government made it quite clear that they would only allow Zając's charges to leave the Soviet Union once all seven Polish divisions had been created, adding that these divisions were sorely needed on the Eastern Front. Obviously this became a stumbling block and a quite unnecessary one as relations between the Allies soured over the next few months.

Despite Mason Macfarlane's pessimism and the awkwardness of the Soviet government, it was reported on 23 December 1941 that Polish airmen and sailors earmarked to leave the Soviet Union were already in India for recuperation and training and would be sent on to the UK in the near future. One assumes trained personnel were evacuated rather than raw recruits who could be used in the infantry. On the same day the War Office agreed to Sikorski's request for supplies but said that this might take time owing to the limitations of transport. Even so, the Poles had already been supplied with 10,000 rifles, 500 Bren guns, 100 3in mortars and 500 Thompson sub-machineguns, as well as the necessary ammunition.

There was a clear improvement to the conditions that Polish captives had had to endure in the Soviet Union prior to Sikorski's visit to Moscow in December 1941. Much of the agreements made between Stalin and Sikorski were honoured by the Soviet government. Some consider that Stalin was impressed by Sikorski's unilateral decision to keep Polish troops in the Soviet Union, while Raczyński claims that Stalin realised that Sikorski was not a tool of the British government but his own man. It is unlikely that either assumption is correct as Stalin was capricious, criminal, and did not have to answer to anybody. He did as he liked and could afford to act with whimsy – he never had any respect for the Poles but even so it does not matter because life for Poles in the Soviet Union improved and that was all that mattered.

An interesting element of Stalin's decision on how to deal with Polish forces being established in the Soviet Union is just why he was determined that they should remain on Soviet soil. Zurowski admits it is all a bit of a mystery given that Stalin promised a Polish force would remain unified and under Polish command as well as being answerable to the Polish Government-in-Exile. It is suggested that given the physical and mental state of these men who had endured the harshness of Soviet captivity and terror at the hands of the NKVD, perhaps the Soviet authorities considered that Poles released from the camps and Gulags would be easy to manipulate and bully. Furthermore, it was obvious that the Soviets were masters of their own front and that at the end of the day, they could place troops wherever they wanted on this front, as well as punish and reward with supplies and money according to their whim rather than what was suitable for Polish needs. Without a shadow of doubt, Stalin would have never accepted a large independent non-Communist army marching alongside the Red Army to eventually establish a non-Communist government in Poland. What was quite obvious, according to Zurowski, was that Stalin had misread Anders and how he affected Poles coming out of the Soviet Union and the psychology of the men who eventually became Polish Second Corps or 'Anders' Army'. Anders was like a messiah, or at least a Moses, leading his people away from Pharaoh – Stalin – and that was the magic or charisma of Anders. No matter where Anders led his people – for right or wrong, for good or bad – he was still the figure responsible for their liberation and lives as he led them from captivity in the Soviet Union. To them, Anders was not a mere man but a symbol of hope and liberation of the individual and of Poland. He was a legend while Stalin was a demon and Sikorski was merely a man of limited influence.

When Stalin realised he had misread Anders, the Soviet dictator began to press for the Polish force to leave the Soviet Union as, curiously, Stalin seemed to accept that he could not master them, perhaps without revealing his hand too openly to the Western Allies. Indeed, Anders considered that the only reason the Soviet government allowed the Poles to leave the Soviet Union for the West was because they were far too difficult to handle. Once the majority of the Poles had left Soviet territory, the Soviet government began to organise a new Polish Army from those Poles remaining on Soviet soil, with the new force being under Soviet control.[66] It should be remembered that by 8 December 1941 the USA had finally become an open ally to the UK and the Soviet Union following the Japanese attack on the US naval base at Pearl Harbor in Hawaii and the unnecessary German declaration of war against the USA. Previously, Roosevelt had been stealthily assisting the UK in the war against Germany. Perhaps Stalin had realised that one way or the other the Allies would win the war with American aid but with or without the Soviet Union and, of course, the Soviet Union was hugely reliant on Western aid, especially American material aid. Stalin wanted to be at the top table at war's end so it was perhaps a small price to pay in letting thousands of very awkward Poles go because he had millions of men who would do his bidding one way or the other; Poland could be picked up on the way to Germany and its millions of people subdued. The Bolshevik world revolution was a long-term project and after larger gains, the occasional sacrifice was therefore worthwhile as Stalin was courted by the British and the American leaderships, so long as the Soviet Union remained committed to fighting and defeating Germany.

It should be noted that following an almost honeymoon period during the winter of 1941–42, the relationship between the Allies and the Soviet Union suddenly began to experience a downturn. It began more or less when the British realised that any hope of deploying a force under Anders in the Caucasus was lost once the Soviets re-conquered Rostov-on-Don. This was fully realised by 15 February 1942. Sikorski also had to relent on his intention to keep a sizeable Polish force in the Soviet Union as he recognised that his people were not being treated fairly by the Soviet authorities and that they would have to be evacuated in order to save them while the British, who were fighting in great difficulties in North Africa, were desperate that Polish troops should be made available in order to increase manpower. Stalin, as we have seen, was just happy to see Anders' force leave the Soviet Union.

By 1942 the problem was that Sikorski was beginning to look weaker than ever once Anders' star began to rise. The treaty he had agreed with Stalin may have improved the lot of Polish prisoners in the Soviet Union, but it was far from ideal; for example the supply of clothing and food was never satisfactory. Under such poor conditions there were periodic outbreaks of disease in Buzuluk and Central Asia while the lack of decent roads and communications in the Soviet Union and in Iran, as well as poor communications in the sea-lanes to the south, combined with the incessant flow of refugees into Polish Army centres, reduced any chance of improving the situation. It was noted that any change in Soviet policies towards the former Polish prisoners caused adversity to the Poles and any delay in British supplies, which did occur in mid-February 1942, was just as bad and caused great harm, especially to the fragile health of thousands of Poles coming out of Soviet captivity. Eden reflected on 22 February 1942 that the effect of the delay of supplies to Poles still stuck in the Soviet Union was that Sikorski's position was made even more difficult than it had been previously. Sikorski was very much in the minority among his fellow Poles when dealing with the Soviets and, without the support of the American or British governments, especially that of Churchill, he would have been long gone. By 1942 the Sikorski brand was becoming toxic and, to escape into hyperbole, it could be argued that Sikorski and his followers were thrown out on their ear from Europe in 1940; in 1942 Anders was leading his people from captivity, slavery and death. Image is all.

Stalin and the Soviet government continued in their policy of denying adequate rations to Poles with only 5th Division getting correct rations and supplies from the Soviet authorities. Stalin neither cared nor concerned himself about the fate of the other Poles while the chaos of war was blamed for the non-arrival of supplies for other Polish units. Stalin also complained bitterly about the British not supplying equipment for the other Polish divisions being established in the Soviet Union. Meanwhile, the British were struggling in their war in the deserts of North Africa, while a second front had opened up as the Japanese had followed their sneak attack on Pearl Harbor with full-blown invasions of Southeast Asia, particularly the British possessions of Malaya, Hong Kong and Singapore. It was a grim time for the UK as the Japanese advance towards India seemed relentless.

Equally, the Poles complained that the Soviets were unwilling to release 30,000 Poles in Soviet labour battalions. They also complained that there was a shortage of winter tents and equipment in Uzbekistan, while typhus was rampant with little in the way of vaccines. Luckily the British were able to supply 100,000 doses of vaccine to combat typhus at least, while against all odds the British continued to supply the Poles. On 20 March 1942, 27,000 daily rations were supplied to Krasnovodsk on the Caspian Sea as well as the necessary tents and medical supplies. The rations however were only for a seven-day period. By mid-March it had become apparent that a permanent solution had to be found.

It was to this end that Anders, accompanied by General Okulicki, went to Moscow to see Stalin. The Soviets had already told the Poles on 10 March 1942 that the supply of rations to the Poles would be reduced to that of 26,000 men from 20 March onwards. The Soviet argument was that wheat supplies from the USA via the Pacific had been interrupted by the Japanese. On 18 March Anders was able to broker an agreement with Stalin, which is said to have gone over the head of Sikorski; the agreement was to allow for the evacuation of all ex-Polish PoWs except for 44,000 soldiers from the Soviet Union. Stalin also agreed to feed the entire force from the end of March, and feed and maintain – but not equip – two divisions. Of course he later broke this promise. There was also a promise to evacuate Polish women and children as well as Polish airmen and the starving (probably all were starving at this point). Stalin also agreed to release the 30,000 Poles from the labour battalions, and that recruitment for the Polish Army in the Soviet Union would not cease after evacuation. But of course recruitment did stop while there were further reductions in arms and rations. Furthermore, the Soviets also threatened to halt British supplies arriving at Krasnovodsk. It was quite odd really.

The evacuation was initially to entail 8th, 9th and 10th Divisions. Their transport was to begin on 23 March 1942 from Krasnovodsk, arriving at Pahlevi in Iran on 26 March. The British informed the Soviets that they could only supply the Poles with 4,000 rations for a single week. The Soviets were still maintaining the line that they wanted the Poles to return to the Soviet Union to fight on the Eastern Front and even said so in their agreement with Anders on 18 March. Sikorski also saw the need for evacuation as it became clearer that nothing the Soviets signed up to was binding; Stalin and his government did as they pleased. Sikorski was also aware of the poor communications from Iran to Soviet Central Asia, the dire straits that Polish ex-PoWs were left in, and the limited ability of the British to supply the Poles. Even so, Sikorski still tried to demand that 30,000 Polish troops should be left in the Soviet Union as a nucleus of a larger Polish Army which was to serve alongside the Red Army and liberate Poland at some time in the future. Anders merely saw it as the second phase of the evacuation. Sikorski also hoped that the presence of 30,000 Polish troops in the Soviet Union would ensure the continued release of Poles from Soviet prisons and labour camps, as well as the continued recruitment for the Polish Army. He was also aware of the deteriorating relationship between the Poles and the Soviets.

The question of the deployment of 5th Division rumbled on. Stalin still wanted it deployed on the Eastern Front even though it lacked arms, armour, and ammunition, including artillery shells, and had nowhere to practise war games. Indeed most of its members were raw recruits; in short they were cannon fodder. Incredibly, fourteen per cent of 5th Division suffered from nyctalopia, a form of night blindness. Sikorski's main objection to 5th Division's deployment on the Russian Front was that it would simply disappear into the maw of the Red Army with no eventual military or political benefit for Poland. It would require at least three to four divisions as a minimal force working together to produce any worthwhile result for Poland and its future.

As far as Anders was concerned, there was no future in keeping Poles in the Soviet Union. The only thing that would satisfy him was a complete withdrawal from the Soviet Union; furthermore, this force was to remain united under his command and he even objected to the idea of sending any of his men to First Polish Corps because they were in Scotland which was too far way and would be lost. It could not be said that Anders lacked ambition and was simply single-minded in his approach. Anders also considered that Sikorski's idea of leaving two divisions in Central Asia was playing into Stalin's hands. Anders' concern was that the Soviets had every intention of turning such a force into a communist puppet army similar to the Berling Army formed later. Even so, it is a matter of conjecture as to whether the Berling Army was ever really communist. As the Soviets continued to renege on their promises and reduce rations to such an extent that Anders considered everybody was at risk of disease and starvation, he considered that Sikorski was divorced from reality as Anders and other Poles were facing it in the Soviet Union. For Anders it was obvious that what Stalin was saying was 'hurry up and go away'. Quite simply, Stalin had no use for a non-Communist army operating alongside the Red Army.

From 23 March to April 1942 a total of 10,789 civilians and 33,069 military arrived in Iran. 704 people died en route while possibly thousands more died waiting at transport points on their journey south towards the Caspian Sea. Such was the mass movement of humanity into Iran that both Sikorski and the British government tried to have the frontier closed as it was feared that the reception centres in Iran would not be able to handle the large numbers of people. It was also feared that disease might break out and that food might run out. Kot was extremely unhappy with the mass migration of Poles into Iran and criticised Anders for allowing such an exodus. Kot considered that Anders should not have permitted civilians to leave as it may have compromised the Polish military's ability to be evacuated from the Soviet Union. Kot was so malicious that he came to believe the Soviets had not wished for the total evacuation of Poles from Soviet territory, but it was actually Anders who had convinced the NKVD that it was in their interests to permit all Poles to leave.

On 31 March, when about 15,000 Poles arrived in Iran, the British tried to stop the transports out of the Soviet Union. In the eyes of the British it seemed that Anders preferred civilians over the military, judging by the type of people arriving. A protest was lodged to the effect that Anders should not despatch civilians who were in no way connected with the Polish military. Once Churchill learned that Anders was sending civilians first, the British Premier wailed: 'Are we going to get nothing but women and children? We must have the men.' Anders certainly showed his humanity as he knew that the women and children would die quickly if he did not act and that his troops could look after themselves for a while at least.

This became obvious as events unfolded. On 29 March General Leopold Okulicki, Anders' Chief of Staff, had also recommended the suspension of further transports owing to the high percentage of sick people and the fact that disinfection had not been carried out in Krasnovodsk. However some influential British officials were also aware of what Anders had already realised. Sir Alexander Cadogan in conversation with Władysław Kulski, the Polish Chargé d'Affairs, observed that Soviet pressure to make the Poles leave was without pity and that the flood of Polish refugees could not be stopped. As Cadogan observed, the local people were hostile to the Poles owing to a general shortage of food in the Soviet Union and if the Poles were prevented by the British from leaving the Soviet Union it was obvious that they would die from starvation.

The overall British plan was to transport the Poles out from Northern Iran and onto Palestine. The Soviet government was told that the presence of refugees in Iran would hamper supplies destined for the Red Army. In mid-March 1942 the official line coming from the Soviet Union was that Polish troops were being evacuated only in order to receive training and for equipping purposes and would eventually return to the Soviet Union to serve on the Russian Front. Stalin still spoke about raising rations to feed 44,000 men, that is three divisions, as well as arming two of these divisions. Concerning the 26,000 Polish troops already evacuated, Stalin promised that once they returned to the Soviet Union and were fighting on the Eastern Front, he would feed and maintain them but still refused to equip them as he considered this to be a Western obligation. Stalin was more honest when he instructed Maisky to say at the beginning of April 1942 that the ultimate destination of the Polish troops was purely a British matter and of no concern to him. The bottom line was that the Poles had left the Soviet Union and were not coming back.[67]

An evacuation of Poles proved to be extremely difficult as the Soviets, even if they did not want a Polish Army on their territory, were determined to hold onto every Pole possible. During March 1942, 33,000 men had been evacuated to Palestine and another 44,000 were on course for evacuation; thus giving a total of 77,000 Polish troops being made available for service in the Middle East. The Soviets continued in their awkwardness and declared that only Poles of 'pure Polish blood', and those who had entered annexed Polish territory after 29 November 1939 would be permitted to leave the Soviet Union.[68]

The idea of 'pure Polish blood' would appear to come from the Nazi and former Soviet ally lexicon of murderous claptrap. While the concept of only Poles who had entered Soviet annexed areas of Poland after 29 November 1939 meant that the original inhabitants of these areas annexed during September and October 1939 were already lost. Indeed the Soviet government had already declared them to be Soviet citizens whether they liked it or not. These conditions were totally unacceptable to the Polish Government-in-Exile and, of course, to Anders.

The terms were not accepted by the Polish authorities, but there was very little that they could do about them. Even so a further 60,000 Poles should have been made available for service in the Polish Army as they were 'of pure Polish blood' and physically fit for military service. However, most of these had already been conscripted into the Red Army and that was even before the German invasion. Furthermore there was a significant number of Poles who had been placed in what were termed 'Stroj-Battalions' which were auxiliary labour units serving with the Red Army. A number of the Stroj-Battalions by 1942 had been dissolved by the Soviet authorities but many Poles remained in non-fighting labour units from which they wished to escape. In addition, many Soviet labour camps ignored the order to release their Polish captives. Therefore, as late as April and May 1942 many men who should have joined the Polish Army remained in Soviet captivity and ignorant of the establishment of a Polish Army on Soviet territory, let alone an amnesty which should have released them. In addition there was still no news of the missing Polish officers because Stalin continued to evade answering the question concerning their fates, while it was discovered that over 7,000 NCOs were also missing. Even so, at the time of this Polish report being released (22 August 1942), even according to the quirky Soviet interpretation of demands there should have been 60,000 Poles permitted by the Soviet authorities to go to the Middle East.[69]

The British authorities were aware of the difficulties that Anders and his compatriots had in dealing with the Soviet government. During a visit to London during April 1942 Anders discussed the problem with General Sir Alan Brooke. Anders underlined his problem to Brooke about just how difficult it was to try to trace every Pole. The Poles had to look through all of the Soviet camps ranging from prisoner-of-war camps to the slave-labour camps. Obviously this was extremely difficult but the 'morass of Soviet officialdom and chicanery' made the problem worse.[70] Sarner also points to a less than clear policy from the Polish side concerning the evacuation of their own people. On 1 April 1942 Sikorski had telegraphed Churchill and told him that 35,000 Polish troops were en route from the Soviet Union to Persia and that a further 10–15,000 could be expected shortly. Sikorski estimated that eventually 77,000 Polish troops as well as an unspecified number of civilians would be evacuated. Sikorski also told Churchill that he agreed with the Soviet decision that the main concentration of the Polish Army, basically two to three divisions in strength, should be deployed in the Middle East. This contradicted Kot's assertion that Sikorski opposed evacuation. Sikorski still wanted a significant force kept in the Soviet Union for the time when the Red Army reached Poland and therefore needed to be alongside it to ensure a Polish recovery of Poland.[71] However Anders decided to ignore Sikorski's wishes and evacuated as many Polish personnel as he could manage. This was controversial because Anders did not fall into line with orders but instead saved 125,000 Poles from death by starvation. Even if large numbers of Poles had remained on Soviet soil and had found themselves in some form of Polish Army fighting alongside the Red Army, there was nothing they could have realistically done to have prevented the Soviet annexation of Poland after 1944, especially as Stalin saw Poland as a buffer state protecting the Soviet Union from further invasions from the West. Anders understood this and so in his mind he had little choice but to rescue as many Poles as possible from Soviet captivity.[72]

Clearly the Soviet government did not want to lose its Polish slave labour force or see a genuine Polish Army established on Soviet territory. However, Anders was happy to report to Brooke that since the founding of the Polish

Army in the Soviet Union, Polish patriotic spirit and morale had soared. It was also considered that the influence of the British government was making itself felt as the Soviets, even though they were not as cooperative as they might have been, were more willing to help the Poles than usual. Anders told Brooke that he was determined to concentrate his force in the Middle East as it would be beneficial to both the British and the Poles. He also informed Brooke that Stalin was not necessarily hostile to the Poles going to the Middle East as it was still possible to support the Soviet left flank from there. During this meeting Anders also briefed Brooke on the Red Army and it was not good news. It seemed that the Red Army lacked everything ranging from war materials, transport and morale. Everything pointed to a German victory. This information was of great interest to Brooke.[73]

A month later, 20 May 1942, there was another conversation between Anders and the British, this time with the British High Command in the Middle East. The independent role that Anders was beginning to assume was encouraged by the British as they showed great willingness to deal with Anders rather than Sikorski, who was in London anyway and ignorant of events in the Middle East. In this meeting Anders told General Claude Auchinleck that a third Polish division was ready and that a cadre force was being formed in anticipation of the establishment of a fourth Polish division and would be ready for the next Polish evacuation out from the Soviet Union. The addition of a fourth division would result on the necessity of the creation of a Polish Corps.[74]

Three months later Anders upped the ante when he met Churchill, General Maitland Wilson (GOC Persia and Iraq Command: significant as this was where the Poles were to be evacuated to) and Colonel Jacob at the British embassy in Cairo. Churchill told Anders that he had studied documents supplied to him concerning the organisation of the Polish armed forces under Anders' command. After examining the evidence before him he had sent it to CIGS and General Wilson. Churchill was cautious though in his policy regarding Polish troops in the Middle East as he understood that Anders did not have the final word in the matter; that was Sikorski's prerogative. Furthermore Anders was not authorised to discuss details of Polish military matters with those outside of Polish circles – which included Churchill. Anders confirmed that that was the situation but Churchill continued being briefed by Anders nevertheless.

Churchill told Anders that the British authorities agreed with him (Anders) on the general shape of his proposed organisation of Polish forces leaving the Soviet Union, but would still have to confer with Sikorski on the entire matter. Churchill revealed that the intention was to locate Polish forces in Northern Persia (Iran) where the Tenth Army was being developed under the command of the newly appointed General Wilson. Anders gave Churchill his opinion of events on the Russian Front and what he expected might happen there. Anders considered that there was every chance of the Germans breaking through the Caucasus. Churchill was not as pessimistic and said that he hoped that the Caucasus Mountains and the river Volga would present the Germans with two extensive physical, yet natural barriers and hold them there until winter fell. Churchill however was willing to defer to Anders' extensive knowledge of the Soviet Union and decided to work on the principle that Anders was correct in his assertions.[75]

Anders told Churchill that if Polish children were not evacuated from the Soviet Union soon they would all die because they could not last another winter there. Churchill informed Anders that he had given orders that Polish women and children should also be evacuated. He thought too that the Soviet authorities were worried that once Polish officers were released they would reveal their ill-treatment at the hands of the Soviets. Anders observed that Poles, once they left the Soviet Union, received good treatment from the British and were restored to full health and it was therefore imperative that the remaining Poles should also be evacuated. He told Churchill that Stalin was refusing to honour agreements made between the Soviet government and the Polish Government-in-Exile, especially concerning military matters. Stalin had halted the recruitment of Poles in the Soviet Union as well as the refusal to arm those already in the Polish Army. This was in response to Anders' refusal to send an under-armed Polish division to the Russian Front. Anders considered that there was no honour in Russia but Churchill told him to keep this to himself as it would not be helpful for this opinion to become public.[76] Churchill was determined not to unnecessarily rock the boat when dealing with the Soviet government. No doubt he was aware that the Soviet government, and especially Stalin, could not be trusted but it remained necessary to keep the Soviet Union engaged in the war against Germany.

Unlike most of the senior Polish commanders, Anders was more realistic about the war and observed that much of the future of the Polish Army depended on events on the Russian Front. During April, he had told a meeting of Polish commanders, including Sikorski, that if the Germans did break through the Russian Front they would probably turn towards the Middle East. Anders outlined his ideas of how he saw the war progressing. He said that if the Germans were to be defeated, either from the east or the west, Polish armies must return to Poland via an eastern route, or from the south, in order to head off the Red Army. A Polish force coming from the west would not have enough time to arrive in Poland before the Red Army got there. Anders predicted that the RAF and the USAAF would bomb Germany into submission, but that the Red Army would physically advance into Germany and capture it – including Berlin. Anders knew that evacuation to the UK was extremely problematic – with shipping being a major concern – and he pointed out that there was a need for a Polish Army in Iraq because the Soviets would use the country for its own offensives. Iraq had been occupied by the British and the Soviets since 1941 after thwarting a pro-Nazi takeover there by local Iraqis. Anders also claimed that troops stuck in the UK would become idle and lose their morale.[77]

For their part the Soviets could not understand why the Poles wished to leave the Soviet Union and fight alongside the British. A letter from Lieutenant-Colonel Ludwik Domon to General Michał Karszewicz-Tokarzewski reported a conversation, which got heated at times, when two NKVD officers visited Domon and other Poles. The NKVD officers said that they did not understand the Polish attitude because the British garrison at Tobruk in North Africa had recently fallen and the Germans had taken prisoner 30,000 British troops. According to the NKVD officers a quick way back to Poland was fighting alongside the Red Army via the Black Sea and Lwów. The Poles retorted that the Soviets seemed to be having their own problems with the enemy invasion along the river Volga. Furthermore, the Poles noted that the enemy had also bombed Kuibyshev, which was now serving as a temporary Soviet capital where much of the Soviet administration, as well as most of the foreign diplomatic missions, had been evacuated to from Moscow.[78] Sarner makes the claim that Domon, whom he cites as holding the rank of Major, was part of a conspiracy which included Karszewicz-Tokarzewski and sought to remove Sikorski as Polish Prime Minister and C-in-C. This was part of a wider conspiracy within 6th Division commanded by Karszewicz-Tokarzewski. It should also be noted that Colonel Grobicki formed an illegal organisation consisting of Nationalist and anti–Soviet elements in 5th Division. Some Polish officers allegedly argued that Poland could only be restored with German assistance.[79] However, how much of this intrigue had its origins in Soviet mischief makes it a moot point. During April 1942 General Boruta-Spiechowicz warned Sikorski that a group of Polish officers headed by Klimkowski was agitating to remove him as C-in-C and replace him with Anders. Interestingly Klimkowski had reportedly told Beria that he was willing to arrest Anders and hand him over to the Soviets which left a question: to whom did Klimkowski's ultimate loyalty remain? The plot to get rid of Sikorski was considered to have been idle talk by bored soldiers but the British Intelligence Service did not think so.[80] These problems were only to intensify once it became obvious that Poland was to be made part of the Soviet area of influence and was not to receive genuine independence at war's end.

During March 1942 however, the decision had already been taken to evacuate Poles from the Soviet Union. There seemed to be no alternative, especially once Stalin began to deny suitable rations for Polish military units being formed in the Soviet Union. Kot realised that Stalin, in using 'the food weapon, has unilaterally changed what was agreed with the Premier (Sikorski) on military issues during the Moscow talks'.[81] And so a log-jam had possibly been broken, but other obstacles were being prepared or had already been put in place by both the Soviet and the British governments. Equally, both Anders and Sikorski were quite capable of shooting themselves in the foot, but a decision had been made: the Poles were to be evacuated to Persia. From there a Polish Army would be formed to fight alongside the British Army with the purpose of eventually returning to Poland. The way ahead was to be fraught with difficulties and disappointments but during 1942 the Poles began to leave Soviet territory for Persia.

Chapter 4

The Formation of Second Polish Corps

O nce the Poles were officially allowed to leave the Soviet Union and start to establish a military formation, Anders did not look back. Anders had achieved what he wanted: virtual independence. It was known that he nursed an ambition to return to Poland at the head of a Polish Army, *his* Polish Army. In the Spring of 1942 Anders was able to begin building such a force. As Piłsudski had done a generation earlier, Anders was also able to establish an armed body loyal to him rather than to the Polish state and its civilian politicians. Anders's force was one that was loyal to his person through the crucible of Soviet captivity. Furthermore, he was in a good geographic position. The Middle East was not an unreasonable place to start a return to Poland, while at the same time sufficiently far enough from Sikorski and the Polish Government-in-Exile to be able to defy them. Ironically, even if Sikorski and the Polish government were in London, they were effectively marooned from power because Anders was able to influence the local British commanders who passed on information to the War Office, while Anders received replies to his concerns and ideas via the same conduit. Simply, Anders was closer to where it mattered despite Sikorski being located in the seat of British political power – London. By 1942 it was the military theatres that mattered.

Anders furthered endeared himself with his compatriots because, without Polish or British permission, he issued orders for the evacuation for Polish civilians from the Soviet Union. As we have seen in the previous chapter the British authorities were furious as thousands of starving Polish refugees arrived in Persia and Churchill had demanded 'are we going to get nothing but women and children? We must have men.'[1] Despite Churchill's frustration at the large numbers of Polish civilians being evacuated from the Soviet Union it was decided by the British government that they were to fall under the care of General Claude Auchinleck, the British Commander in the Middle East.[2]

Sikorski continued with his agenda. He wanted the majority of evacuated Polish troops transported to a place which suited him. Uppermost in Sikorski's mind was the possibility of 15,000 troops being sent to Scotland to become part of a proposed armoured division. He also wanted 10,000 Polish troops to be sent to Egypt in order to beef up the Independent Carpathian Brigade. General Auchinleck opposed these measures and wanted all of the Polish troops coming out of the Soviet Union to be retained in the Middle Eastern theatre of war. The most obvious problem cited was shipping. How could 15,000 men be shipped safely to the UK? There was a lack of ships for this task and it was fraught with risk owing to German U-boats. Auchinleck proposed concentrating all Polish forces in southern Palestine or in Syria.[3]

The British Chiefs of Staff supported Auchinleck's plan and so Churchill wrote to Sikorski who was in Washington DC at the time. Churchill recommended that the majority of Polish troops evacuated should be retained in the Middle East and re-equipped for service there. Churchill said that Polish naval and air force personnel would be sent, as promised, to the UK as well as a small number of troops. These troops were to be sent to Scotland in anticipation of the formation of a Polish armoured division.[4] Sikorski was not easily dissuaded from his course. On 1 April 1942 he agreed to the concentration of two to three divisions of Polish troops to be retained in the Middle East but insisted that 17,000 Polish troops should be sent to the UK in order to establish a parachute brigade as well as an armoured division. Europe was to be most important both politically and strategically once a 'Second Front' was opened in the West in the near future. Sikorski was not totally at odds with Churchill as the British ideas did have some merit in the eyes of Sikorski.

Sikorski feared a collapse of the Russian Front and a German threat against the Middle East. To counter this threat it became necessary to maintain a reserve corps (of Polish troops) in Syria. Sikorski had already spoken on 24 March 1942 to Roosevelt on the subject and so reiterated his concerns and ideas to Churchill. According to Mitkiewicz, Sikorski accepted Churchill's plan for the retention of Polish troops in the Middle East, notably Syria as Sikorski saw the possibility of this force eventually moving from the south, northwards through the Balkans and back to Poland: 'the shortest route to Poland.'[5]

However, as we shall see, the greatest threat to Sikorski was not British plans for the deployment of Polish troops, but from Anders. Tendyra is very

clear that Anders wanted to concentrate Polish forces in the Middle East
to further his own ambitions. Sikorski had to begin to seek allies to try to
contain Anders and his political ambitions.[6] Sikorski made a huge mistake
when he allowed Anders to visit the UK during April 1942. Anders proved to
be very popular and as charismatic as ever. Sikorski was neither. Furthermore,
according to Klimkowski, Anders reached an understanding with pre-war
Sanacja officers as well as other Nationalists. As a result of talks with Anders,
opponents of Sikorski concluded that they had finally found a leader who
understood them.[7] Therefore, by the end of April 1942, Anders had ensured
that he had supporters not only in the Middle East but also among Polish
forces in the UK.

Anders had his own reasons to justify the retention of Polish troops in the
Middle East. He genuinely believed that Germany would defeat the Soviet
Union and then try to link up with the Japanese via Persia and India. Equally
he was also prepared to consider that the German Army could suffer defeat in
the Soviet Union and then be pursued westward by the Red Army. In this case
he argued that there was a need for a Polish Army to be kept in the Middle East
which could then advance from the south towards Poland ready to defend it
from the Soviet Union and the Red Army. Sikorski continued to believe in the
Second Front and the liberation of Poland coming from that route. As a result
he continued to press for reinforcements for Polish 1st Corps which remained
in Scotland.[8]

Zurowski, however, argues that Anders' private views of how the war was
to proceed are irrelevant as they were all tied up with his desire to return to
Poland in the manner of Piłsudski in 1918, if not even more so; entering Poland
in triumph at the head of a Polish Army accompanied by British and American
troops. That was a major reason why he had hoped and predicted the collapse
of the Soviet Union and that was why at one point Anders wanted to retain
his troops in Syria so that they could sit out the Russo-German War and see
how it went before committing Polish troops. Zurowski argues that Sikorski
had a better grip on how the war would be carried out and, referring to his
own treatise on the future of modern warfare and the use of mechanisation,
predicted that eventually the Soviet Union would defeat Germany and that was
the very reason Sikorski wanted to maintain Polish troops on the eastern front
serving alongside the Red Army.[9]

Tendyra observes that Sikorski had some valid points as he noted that Stalin had halted all recruitment of Polish troops from Soviet territory while plans for, and the future of, the evacuation of Poles remained unclear. He also rejected Anders' audacious demand that the entire Polish armed forces, including the air force, should be transferred to the Middle East. Sikorski believed in his army in the UK and Anders believed in his force in the Middle East.[10] Something or somebody had to give way and fairly quickly. Amazingly, it was Sikorski, the Polish Prime Minister and C-in-C who was pressurised by the British to give in to Anders and his plans.

Between 22 and 23 April 1942 the British Middle East Defence Committee and Chiefs of Staff opted to retain Polish troops in the Middle East; Churchill pressed Sikorski to agree with Anders.[11] Sikorski gave in and accepted a mere 8,200 troops for the UK. He also agreed to limit his force in Scotland to that of a single armoured division. Sikorski however warned Churchill that these decisions made him seem weaker in the eyes of his fellow Poles.[12] According to the official history of the Polish Army in the Second World War, what eventually happened regarding the distribution of Polish troops coming from the Soviet Union was that,

> of the 11,339 Polish military personnel sent by rail from Pahlevi (Iran) to the Persian Gulf in April and May 1942 only 1,439 subsequently travelled by sea to Britain while almost 10,000 sailed via Suez to Palestine. The remainder, as well as a small group of army families, travelled by road from Iraq to Palestine, where troops linked up with Polish Middle East Command.[13]

Clearly Sikorski got next to nothing from the troops being evacuated from the Soviet Union while Anders, who remained in London throughout April garnering support, achieved his aims and left Sikorski marginalised by the British government. Anders had unofficially become the most important Polish leader in the war against Germany.

The war had moved on since Sikorski first arrived in the UK in 1940. The arrival of large numbers of American troops in the UK after 1941 reduced further any influence of his, by now miniscule, number of troops had on the defence of Britain. Overall Sikorski seemed to be losing control of events and the future was not going to get any better for him. The British government decided to arm those Poles in the Middle East rather than those still in the Soviet Union.[14] However, those troops were already lost to the UK and it should be noted that, according to Klimkowski, Colonel L.R. Hulls, the British Liaison Officer to Polish Forces in the Soviet Union, put pressure on British officials to back Anders' proposals.[15] The War Office did indeed request that the London Poles instruct Anders to intervene with the Soviets and get a second evacuation of Poles from the Soviet Union accelerated. This was something that the British and the Poles had been waiting several weeks for.[16]

During June 1942 Molotov arrived in the UK for talks with Churchill and other senior British figures. At this time the question of a further Polish evacuation was discussed and it seemed that Churchill requested all Polish troops over the number required by the Soviet Union to be evacuated to the Middle East.[17] Eventually Stalin allowed for the evacuation of three Polish divisions with civilians. Sarah Meiklejohn Terry argues that more than likely Stalin, once he had taken his pick, had always wanted to remove the Polish Army and its dependants from the Soviet Union. Both Tendyra and Terry agree that Stalin, in removing the Poles from the Soviet Union, weakened Sikorski's position vis-à-vis Anders as a central plank of Sikorski's Soviet policy, the presence of a Polish Army in the Soviet Union, had been removed.[18] Furthermore, Anders now controlled the single largest Polish military force and this naturally gave him great influence especially with the British. Meanwhile, Polish soldiers and civilians considered him to be a saviour who had led them from purgatory if not the very depths of hell itself. As a result they all felt that they owed their primary allegiance to him, not to Sikorski. This situation was storing trouble for the future.

After the final evacuation Anders was able to assert ever-increasing pressure on the Polish Government-in-Exile and continue to get it to alter its Soviet policy, especially as relations with Moscow got worse. It was even suggested that Sikorski should step down from office. Sikorski had never really been popular with most of the Polish Army and with the rise of Anders, he became increasingly isolated. Indeed his government came to symbolise everything which divided the exiled Poles.[19] Anders took full advantage of Sikorski's discomfort as he established his military presence in the Middle East as well as setting himself up as the local Polish potentate and ignoring Sikorski's wishes and orders.

At the beginning of August 1942 Anders made an unauthorised appeal to Stalin for the continued recruitment of Poles. Sikorski had already ordered Anders not to discuss detailed organisational matters concerning the Polish armed forces in the Middle East with the British government or its representatives. This role was reserved for Sikorski as Polish Commander in Chief and his Chief of Staff, General Klimecki. Nevertheless Anders, between 14 and 16 August 1942, went to Moscow, apparently in response to a summons from Churchill, to hold talks with him and other senior British officials.[20] Anders was more than happy be seen seated in Moscow alongside Churchill and so Sikorski's position weakened further while Anders' insubordination seemed to know no bounds.

Anders even made life difficult for the British because on one hand he appeared to blame Polish politicians in London for British and American failure to broach vital questions with Stalin related to the Poles and the future of Poland, and on the other he claimed that Churchill and Harriman, now the American Secretary of State, had arrived in Moscow totally unprepared to deliver a démarche to the Soviet government in support of the Poles. Indeed Anders claimed that he was forced to submit a note to the Western delegation outlining the Polish position regarding Polish citizens still in the Soviet Union.[21] Anders' actions in Moscow during August 1942 could only enhance his reputation among Poles but at the expense of Sikorski. Anders only had to be concerned with the fates of those Poles remaining on Soviet territory; Sikorski had to consider the overall Polish strategy and where he wanted it to go in the war and where he wanted it to end at. Anders however, had the effect of providing the British with an alternative Polish leader. The British could pick and choose which leader they wanted; as and when it suited them.[22] This was the very situation that Sikorski feared and so he sent Klimecki out to the Middle East to deal directly with Anders and local British and Polish Commands. Sikorski was worried that Anders was making too many concessions to the British.[23]

Once Klimecki arrived in Egypt he swiftly discovered that Anders was still ignoring Sikorski's orders. Anders was not even supposed to be in Cairo, far less be involved in deep and detailed discussions with the British concerning operational matters. It should be remembered that since the beginning of the war the Poles had been virtually ignored by their allies and suddenly, when it suited the British, they were in cahoots with a Polish commander who was theoretically subordinate to Sikorski. The difference between Anders and Sikorski was that by 1942, Anders actually had something while Sikorski had nothing. He was irrelevant and had been for a long time. Anders had already submitted his plans for the future deployment of Polish Forces in the Middle East and the Soviet Union to General Brooke and General Wilson.[24]

Both Sikorski and Klimecki became quite alarmed at Anders as he seemed to be setting the agenda for Anglo–Polish military cooperation. Klimecki's purpose in Cairo became one of retaining unity in the Polish forces in the Middle East, to ensure their rapid arming as well as their best possible deployment. He also tried to snaffle the largest amount of troops possible to be transferred for the Polish Army in Scotland. Naturally Anders opposed the removal of Polish troops to the UK.[25]

Anders had a better proposal as well as a head start on Sikorski owing to the previous week's Moscow meeting. While he was there Anders had already spoken to General Brooke about his idea, which was quite simple. Anders proposed that the Polish Army should be evacuated from the Soviet Union to Persia from where fighting units could be established and then deployed in the Middle East as well as reinforcing units already fighting in that theatre of operations.[26] Klimecki feared that Brooke would press Sikorski to accept Anders' proposals and so reported that a combat ready Polish force would only be in British interests and not those of Poland. Sikorski was not prepared to fight for British imperial interests.[27]

Sikorski's refusal to fight for British imperial interests as he perceived it was a gross mistake on his part. The war was no longer about Poland and had not been since Poland's defeat in October 1939. Whether Sikorski liked it or not, by 1942 the USA, the UK and the Soviet Union were completely dedicated to the defeat of Germany and would not brook any argument from those who refused to cooperate. Sikorski seemed not to understand this and wrote to Klimecki on 29 August 1942, 'by no means will I agree or allow us to be reduced to the same status as the other allies in the Middle East.'[28] Sikorski was too late: Poland had already reached that state and had been there for some time. By 1942 Poland was definitely a minor ally within the alliance against Germany.

Sikorski not only failed to see that Poland was a minor ally but he still considered that his ultimate war aim was the liberation of Poland. He had not understood that this was already out of his hands and would be a consequence of a final victory over Germany, as had been the case in 1918. The obsession that Poles would be responsible for the liberation of their country was the reason why Sikorski wanted to keep a Polish force under his direct command. Frank Roberts at the Foreign Office noted the distinct possibility of the Polish armed forces taking power in post-war Poland; when he heard of Sikorski's plan for a Polish force to be built up in the Middle East which was designed to form a nucleus of a future army in the region which would then be reinforced by Polish troops coming out of the Soviet, Roberts minuted that such a formation 'will presumably make the Poles the potential masters of whichever country they were placed'.[29]

Sikorski's plan for a Polish Army in the Middle East was to consist of two Army Corps which were to consist of four divisions (two divisions per corps). Each division was to consist of two brigades. Each corps of this proposed army was to have all the necessary armoured and artillery units for both defensive and offensive operations. To this end Second (Polish) Corps in Palestine and Syria were to have been combined with the three Polish divisions arriving in Persia and then combined into a single large operational unit. After a meeting at the War Office on 5 August 1942, the British rejected the Polish plan citing that they were unable to guarantee logistical support for so many divisions. Furthermore, with justification, the British pointed to the serious mismatch between the available manpower compared to the strengths of the proposed units, as well as the shortage of artillery with which to equip the projected formations.

The problem was that Sikorski had based his plans on the increasingly doubtful prospect of Polish reinforcements arriving from the Soviet Union. In a letter to General Brooke, Sikorski accepted a modified version of the scheme which had originally been proposed by Auchinleck. The new plan was the creation of a reinforced corps consisting of two small divisions, which in turn consisted of two brigades each. These were to be tank brigades with a full complement of supporting troops as well as rear base services for the maintenance of tanks etc.[30] A compromise was swiftly reached between the Poles and the British government and a Polish formation was established in the Middle East. Even though the new Polish formation was actually a Corps; it was termed an 'army' in order to enhance its prestige. Tendyra asserts that it was a grand compromise between Sikorski's Second Corps plan and Anders' more muted approach. Its main strength lay with its artillery and anti-tank capacity which leant towards a defensive rather than an offensive role. The armoured units that Sikorski had hoped for were much reduced in number – more so than he might have liked. Overall, Anders' force was to consist of 3rd Carpathian Rifle Division, made up of two infantry brigades; three regiments of light artillery, of which one was anti-tank and another anti-aircraft; a reconnaissance regiment; a machinegun battalion and a communications regiment as well as all of the necessary service personnel. In addition 5th Kresy Infantry Division was to work in parallel with 3rd Carpathian Rifle Division with both infantry divisions being supported by 2nd Polish Armoured Brigade, made up with three armoured regiments and supporting arms and services necessary to complement this brigade. This sounds a fine formation until one looks further; as Felsztyn noted, even though Anders Army had 48,000 members on 1 September 1942, many were quite elderly in terms of serving infantrymen with some being up to 42 years of age. Interestingly Felsztyn, while getting ahead of himself in his narrative as he seems to confuse 1942 with 1943, does make a very good point: what about Polish casualties once they take the field against the Germans on the Mediterranean Front, which quickly became the Italian Front? It was presumed by Polish commanders that Polish casualties were going to be large and then the question would arise of how to replace the dead and wounded. Felsztyn was of the opinion that Anders considered that Poles fighting in the German Army, once captured, would provide the necessary replacements for Polish casualties.[31] It should be remembered that Anders did not necessarily trust Poles who had served in the German Army so it is unlikely that this would have been his first idea. Later it was to prove that Poles who had served in the German Army were, on the whole, politically unreliable even if they were well trained. Nevertheless, despite all of the trouble he might, and would, face regarding Anders' force, Sikorski gave the new formation his unreserved approval on 1 September 1942, the third anniversary of the German invasion of Poland.[32] What else could he have done? If he had opposed it, it would have been political suicide.

Anders had outfoxed his Commander-in-chief. He knew that he had Sikorski in his pocket because now Sikorski would have to agree with Anders' policies in the Middle East or be seen as trying to defy British policies. In other words, Sikorski's already diminished influence in the alliance against Germany had taken another beating while Anders' reputation had grown considerably during the summer of 1942. The fact that the new Polish Corps was referred to as an 'army' rather suited Anders as his influence increased further. Anders wished to refer to the new body as the 'Polish Army in the East' (*Armia Polska na Wschódzie* – APW). Sikorski was very conscious of the positive effect in occupied Poland of the establishment of a new Polish army and so agreed to Anders' wish.[33]

Of course nobody seriously thought that the APW would become 'Anders' Army' as it is nearly always referred to even today when the subject of Second Polish Corps comes up in conversation. Even so, there was another army in the offing; the so-called 'Berling Army' named after its supposed commander, General Zygmunt Berling, yet another Polish officer who had endured Soviet captivity but had chosen quite another route: acquiescence with the Soviet authorities and earning the contempt of Anders.[34] There was never a 'Sikorski Army' or even a 'Sikorski Brigade' as there was a 'Kopański Brigade', those hardy veterans of North Africa and Tobruk. There was an unfair German taunt of 'Sikorski's tourists' as Polish troops were pushed by German aggression from Poland across Europe to France and then to the UK. But there was never any Sikorski military organisation. It is an interesting omission given the history of modern Polish warlords.

Chapter 5

Anders and Sikorski, 1942–1943

A nders' appointment as Supreme Commander of APW in 1942 was fortuitous in its timing as the war had moved on and Anders was able to take advantage of his good fortune for the remainder of the conflict. Even if in his autobiography Anders claims that the only real differences he had with Sikorski related to Sikorski's Soviet policy this cannot be taken at face value. Anders also wrote that Sikorski was the only Polish figure to have any real influence with the Allies and that if he had not died, Polish interests might have been better defended by the Allies.[1] This is highly doubtful, while Anders shedding crocodile tears over Sikorski's death is equally unlikely as the allies often ignored Sikorski while he was alive but, according to Anders, the British and American governments made concessions to the Soviet Union in 1944 which was an easier task because Sikorski was dead.[2] Anders and Sikorski were political rivals in a way that the West did not understand and Anders' was extremely lucky in his promotions and appointments especially his appointment as Supreme Commander of APW.

This appointment had everything to do with politics both external and internal. Anders was appointed over the head of General Józef Zając, Commander of Polish troops in the Middle East. Both Anders and Zając had had divisions merged into single units and both were lieutenant generals. Owing to an earlier promotion Anders did have a technical superiority, but Zając already had command in the area. Neither man wanted to relinquish control over his troops, both had loyal support from his own men and both were ambitious. Anders was appointed because Sikorski was too weak politically to prevent it while Anders also enjoyed good and solid relations with the British government as well as support from some of Sikorski's more outspoken opponents. Therefore any demotion of Anders, perceived or otherwise, would have created further internal strife for Sikorski which he could ill-afford. There were definite tensions within the Polish Army owing to its unprofessional and warlord-like nature. In addition to the difficult relationship between Anders and Sikorski, Anders did not trust Zając because he considered that Zając's loyalty lay with Sikorski, not him.[3] This would not have been a problem in a professional army because Zając's loyalty to Sikorski, or rather to Sikorski's offices of Prime Minister of Poland and C-in-C Polish armed forces, would have been seen as correct and Anders should have demonstrated the same loyalty.

The Foreign Office was quick to notice the politics of the Polish armed forces especially that of the Polish Army, noting that while Anders and Sikorski seemed to support each other when they were in the Soviet Union negotiating with the Soviet government, they had quite different political agendas. By 1942 Anders had a reputation as a 'political soldier' in an army which was largely sympathetic to the pre-war regime and quite anti-democratic. Even so, although Sikorski was personally unpopular, his rank and office still commanded loyalty from the majority of Poles both inside and outside Poland.[4] The notion of individual loyalty to individual commanders was a frustrating feature of the vastly politicised inter-war Polish Army. The British authorities were staggered to learn that the Polish Army, even after defeat, disaster, and the obliteration of Poland, had learnt nothing and still played their childish political games. Major Bryson, a British Intelligence Officer, reported that 'every general officer in the Polish Army had his own group who looked to him to lead in any further struggle against rival factions.'[5] Indeed, Anders more or less proved Bryson's report because earlier he had tried to replace Zając with Karasiewicz-Tokarzewski, the former leader of the military underground and in 1942, Commander of 6th Infantry Division. The same report asserted that Anders was very popular and that most Polish troops considered him to be their best general. A report written a fortnight earlier than the above, however, claimed that Anders had no political ambitions.[6] A lot can happen in a fortnight! It should also be noted that Sikorski had removed Karasiewicz-Tokarzewski from the leadership of the Polish military underground in 1939 because he did not trust him.[7]

The strongest feature of Anders' force was the commonality which the APW enjoyed but it had two strands to it which conflicted in Allied strategy. These two strands were of course a desire to fight and defeat Germany, and a collective hostility towards the Soviet Union. Much of the hostility toward the Soviet Union was part of an ancient loathing of all things Russian which was reinforced by the collective experience of recent, brutal, if not murderous, Soviet captivity. This was part of the reason why many Poles did not wish to fight either as a member of the Red Army or alongside it. Bryson reported that Polish officers openly stated that they would rather be executed than 'fight side by side with the Bolsheviks'.[8] This caused British officials to conclude that only Anders had the ability to convince Polish troops to remain and fight on the Russian Front.[9] This of course was before the widespread knowledge that the Soviets had raised a Polish Army under the alleged command of Berling.

Equally, the APW resented interference by its own government, the Polish Government-in-Exile, as the London Poles tried to improve relations with the Soviet government by making concessions to it, often at the expense of Poland. While it is true that Anders and some of his senior officers attempted to curb the anti-Soviet agitation from within the ranks of the APW, Polish unrest came to the attention of British officials.[10] In the past Anders had caused outrage among the Soviets, the British and, to a certain degree, made some Poles at least uncomfortable. Kot claimed to have been shocked when during September 1942 Anders ordered that the graves of Poles from 'hot Africa to frozen Siberia' should be avenged. Clearly Anders was not only thinking of those Poles who had died fighting the Germans but also those who had been victims of Soviet aggression and cruelty. Anders caused further dismay when the same order was made public in a weekly Polish military newspaper, *Zew* (*Appeal*) as well as in other publications. He went further stating that Lwów and Wilno (today, the Lithuanian capital, Vilnius) were waiting for the return of Polish soldiers. Anders claimed that his message had been misinterpreted but the damage was done.[11] Anders in his statement knew exactly what he was about. He was setting out his stall in preparation for eventually replacing Sikorski. Anders was determined to be seen as the pro-Polish but anti-Soviet champion in exile. He knew exactly which buttons to push: Lwów and Wilno were emotive subjects among exiled Poles and their loss was felt keenly by many. The side of caution on which Anders had to err was to not alienate the British authorities, but he could certainly defy Sikorski at will.

The largest group opposed to Sikorski was the *Klimkowszczyna*. This was a group of about 400 young officers led by Anders' aide-de-camp, Captain Jerzy Klimkowski, from whom the group derived its name. The *Klimkowszczyna* had no real political agenda beyond the removal of the Polish government in London and their absolute antipathy towards its supporters who the *Klimkowszczyna* claimed, by their passivity had betrayed Poland to the Soviet Union and were tools of the Western powers. The basic agenda of these rebellious junior officers was for the Polish government to step down and make room for more energetic, younger men. Most of the *Klimkowszczyna*, as with many Polish officers of the Polish wartime army, were politically sympathetic towards the extreme Nationalist Right.[12] Kot, reporting to Sikorski from Jerusalem, noted that this group did indeed consist of about 400 officers. Sikorski wrote to both Anders and Kot saying that he was aware of the *Klimkowszczyna*, or 'mutinous young officers' as he wrote, and that they saw their future being with Germany. Sikorski was adamant that there was not going to be a 'Quisling Poland'. Bader, the Polish diplomatic representative in Teheran however, doubted that the *Klimkowszczyna* had the support of the majority of the Polish Army.[13] Even so, Anders' attitude towards Sikorski was that Sikorski should mind his own business as he reported within two days of Sikorski's missive that the morale and discipline of his army was very high. Earlier, Kot had been of the opinion that Anders was struggling to control the entire Polish Army in the Middle East.[14] Without doubt he was wrong there but his overall concerns were correct: the *Klimkowszczyna* certainly were not going to restore pre-1926 democracy to Poland but favoured a return to the regime of the inept Polish military juntas of 1926–39. A point that should also be mentioned is that the Poles were stuck out in the desert with not a great deal to do and according to the Polish Ambassador in Teheran, most of the Klimkowski group were masquerading as soldiers; they were often reserve officers who wore military uniforms but had not yet seen action while, politically, were anti-Russian yet curiously sought links with Ukrainians.[15]

Sarner questions the source of Klimkowski's motivations and considers that he was likely to have been a victim of the NKVD or somehow comprised by the Soviet security service and made to work for them. Sarner notes that Klimkowski was one of the first Polish officers to return to Poland from the West after the war. The Communist authorities in Poland actively encouraged him to smear Anders' name, while his memoir of his wartime service, *Byłem Adiutantem Generała Andersa*, was published by the Polish Defence Ministry in 1959. This work totally blackened Ander's name and reputation. This should be contrasted with the treatment of Colonel Franciszek Skibiński, who had served very closely with General Maczek as part of the Polish First Armoured Division and after the war, to the shock and contempt of Maczek, decided to throw his hand in with Communist Poland and return to Poland. Even though Skibiński had never criticised the Soviet Union, Communism or Stalin, he was arrested on his return, imprisoned and tortured – including having all of his teeth knocked out.[16] It was only after the collapse of Stalinism in Poland during 1956 that Skibiński could resume his military career, even though he had been quietly released from prison in 1953 after the death of Stalin. He reached the rank of general in the Polish Peoples' Army.[17] Returning to the case of Klimkowski, despite many people 'knowing' that Klimkowski had collaborated with the NKVD, which included a plot to arrest Anders during July 1942 as a measure to prevent him leaving the Soviet Union, there is no clear evidence to prove such allegations. Sarner claims that rumours concerning Klimkowski and his alleged lack of loyalty were enough to deepen political divisions in exiled circles in both the Middle East and the Soviet Union.[18] What is very odd is that Klimkowski wrote to Sosnkowski on 16 September 1943 claiming that Anders was systematically stealing government money and dealing in stolen diamonds. On 22 November 1943 Sosnkowski replied to Klimkowski, whose address was an APW prison, observing that perhaps Klimkowski had an agenda to run in blackguarding Anders' name owing to being imprisoned by the APW authorities as he awaited trial for various crimes. On 17 March 1945 Klimkowski was released from captivity as a result of an amnesty granted by the Polish Government-in-Exile.[19] It is extremely unlikely that Anders was a thief as Klimkowski claims, but the entire episode does reveal the treacherous nature of Klimkowski. Anders no doubt was quite correct to be cautious about Klimkowski, if only for self-preservation; Klimkowski was clearly a very dangerous individual who seems to have been known to Stalin. What is interesting is that the original script of Klimkowski's controversial work was written in Jerusalem and Rome between April 1945 and June 1947 but not published until 1959 when it appeared off the presses of the Polish Ministry of Defence. Perhaps changes had to be made in Stalinist Russia and beyond before Klimkowski's work could be allowed to appear publicly. He remained a man of shadows and twilight and caused Anders' reputation to suffer.

Despite the lack of compelling evidence to prove Klimkowski's treachery or otherwise; political activities centred in and around him, and his group remain interesting. In early 1942 a Polish diplomat, Karol Bader, reported from Beirut that there was a group of malcontent Polish officers in Palestine who were agitating against the Soviet Union which also had the consequence of translating as being anti-government (Polish Government-in-Exile) in sentiment.[20] Agitation in Palestine was bad enough, but even Sikorski got to hear about Klimkowski and his followers. Sikorski was concerned that Klimkowski was indeed controlled by the NKVD and that through him the Soviets were able to spread discontent and cause 'real damage' to the unity of Polish armed forces. The communiqué containing Sikorski's fears was sent via British channels because Sikorski doubted the integrity of the Polish cipher in Persia. It was suggested that Soviet intelligence had already compromised Polish communications there.[21] The British were also aware that the Soviets were gradually eroding unity within Polish armed forces in the Middle East. A report from British 30 Military Mission operating in Moscow reported to the War Office that the NKVD was 'quietly but steadily' following a programme of propaganda against the evacuation of Polish troops from the Soviet Union in addition to sowing discord between Poland and the UK.[22]

A memorandum from the British Minister of State, Cairo, noted that the *Klimkowszczyna* (not named as such) had been established as a political movement to promote Anders as head of state in opposition to Sikorski. The report described the movement as 'run largely on German lines, with a totalitarian youth movement to ensure a strong Poland after the war'. The British information was quite accurate and described the Polish group's leadership as being made up of: Klimkowski, Colonel Okulicki, Deputy Chief of Staff with the active support of General Tokarczewski-Karaszewicz, Commanders of 5th and 7th Divisions respectively. Major Bohin (group omitted) OC Carpathian Lancers, was said to be disgusted with the whole affair but concluded that it was possible that younger cavalry officers were prepared to support Anders. However, the British report concluded that it might well be the case that Anders was not aware of the aims and motivations of the *Klimkowszczyna*.[23] This was not the first time that the British had observed extreme Nationalist political groups in the Polish armed forces serving in the Middle East; it had been first noticed and reported as early as September 1940.[24] However, in 1943 the Foreign Office suggested that perhaps Sikorski should pay a visit to the

Middle East and try to deal with concerns which related to the future of Poland and to ensure that Anders was not involved in any conspiracies.[25]

It is very unlikely, no matter what the British hoped, that Anders knew nothing of the *Klimkowszczyna*. It was just impossible given some of the personalities involved, and he certainly knew Klimkowski well. At the beginning Anders was certainly aware of Klimkowski's activities because Anders received a letter from him. In this missive Klimkowski argued that a new Polish government was needed to rectify all of Sikorski's mistakes as Klimkowski saw them. Even more usefully he listed them in his letter to Anders; that is every mistake, as perceived by Klimkowski, made by Sikorski since 1940, and left it for Anders to study.[26] The question that can now be raised was: did Anders see the letter? The answer is: of course he did and no doubt they discussed the issue for some time – the two men were very close. However, just how seriously Anders took Klimkowski's views is another matter. Anders was probably willing to tolerate Klimkowski's views because even Anders, as we have seen, remarked to Sikorski that Klimkowski gave the impression of being a fanatic. The British authorities considered Klimkowski to be Anders' 'evil genius' and furthermore Klimkowski was 'seen' (by whom is not disclosed but certainly senior British officials, possibly military or from the intelligence services) and warned that the War Office was not going to tolerate any more trouble from him.[27] This may have also been a warning to Anders if Klimkowski was seen by the British as being the darker side of Anders' influence.

Klimkowski and his followers were not the only group in the Polish Officer Corps with a political agenda that was anti-Sikorski and his government's Soviet policy. Within Anders' command there were at least three groups of conspirators. In 6th Division, a group founded by General Tokarzewski-Karaszewicz, discussed the possibility of replacing Sikorski. The pre-war Polish Finance Minister, Colonel Adam Koc, was part of this particular conspiracy. In 5th Division, Colonel Jerzy Grobicki formed an illegal organisation of nationalists and anti-Soviet elements. Another group led by Colonel Krogulski considered that the Sikorski government was not robust enough in its dealings with the Soviet government and so campaigned for the restoration of the pre-war Polish frontiers. What was most alarming was that a significant number of Polish officers considered that Poland could only be restored with assistance from Germany.[28]

The restoration of the pre-war Polish frontiers was a standard demand from Poles and although the consideration that this could only be done with help from Germany after 1944 began to gain momentum, it was not a universally popular cry among Poles. It certainly undermined the purpose of the war against Germany however, and was totally unhelpful in Polish-Soviet relations, causing the British and Americans to take a long and hard look at their Polish allies as they began to view them with suspicion. For the Allies it seemed that parts of the Polish Officer Corps, especially those in the Middle East, were becoming politically unreliable – if they had not been so previously. This was probably unfair as they were reacting to Soviet aggression against Poland and its people rather than being pro-Nazi, or even pro-German. It was a classic case of Allies not understanding each other, with the Poles not understanding that they were unimportant to the overall war aim – Germany was to be defeated at whatever cost – that was the single aim of the Allies. Everything else was to be a consequence of this ambition once it was achieved; even the war against Japan failed to sway the Allies (especially the Americans) resolve, that Germany was to be defeated first – and comprehensively so.

The British government knew that much of the conflict between Anders and Sikorski was about post-war Poland and that Polish commanders in exile were garnering forces in order to restore military rule once back in Poland. Therefore, from the Polish point of view, it made sense to try to gain as many troops as possible under their individual commands. Members of APW considered that Sikorski was trying to take men from them in order to have them trained as paratroopers in the UK. This meant that airborne Polish troops would be the first Polish military unit to arrive in Poland after a German withdrawal from there. The paratroopers loyal to Sikorski could then seize power in his name and prepare for his return. Major Bryson wrote of the APW 'they regard the parachutists especially as Sikorski's praetorian guard, and while admiring the latter as soldiers, would be loath to see them get first footing in Poland if the result was that Sikorski remained in power.' The British government concluded that the various Polish factions in the Polish military would remain united as long as it fought Germany.[29] But even that was a matter of opinion. It would have been more realistic to have said that only Anders could keep the Polish armed forces, especially 2nd Polish Corps, focused on the war against Germany and only once Germany was defeated could Anders and his countrymen be allowed the luxury of beginning to worry about the Soviet Union and its ambitions worldwide.

Sikorski's position within the allies was further weakened after he submitted a memorandum to Churchill and Roosevelt in which he laid out his plan for an offensive in the Balkans. The British government took its time looking at Sikorski's proposal but his plans were completely contrary to American plans for the war. US service chiefs had already presented Roosevelt with a paper which opposed war in the Balkans beyond that of air and sea supply to local resistance units as well as carrying out aerial bombardments. The Americans were opposed to any diversion of forces – even if Churchill could coax Turkey into joining the war against Germany – that would retard the date and scale of Overlord, the invasion of western Europe, commonly known as D-Day. By 1942 the Western Allies had already begun to consider eastern Europe to be a Soviet sphere of influence as well as considering a good working relationship with the Soviet Union to be desirable.[30]

Sikorski suffered a further blow to his position and prestige when, on 16 January 1943, the Soviet government issued a note to the Polish Embassy in Kuibyshev to the effect that all inhabitants of the Soviet occupied areas of Poland (at the time occupied by the Germans), including ethnic Poles, were now Soviet citizens.[31] This was a great shock to all Poles and it was certainly clear just how the Soviet government saw post-war Poland: a state shorn of its eastern territories. The Soviet Union was not going to return the annexed lands after the defeat of Germany. It was also very clear that there was little, if anything, that the Polish Government-in-Exile could do about the situation while the Allies had little interest in the situation. Anders had previously complained to Sikorski that Allied propaganda had created in the collective mind of the American and British peoples the idea that the Soviet Union was a good and just state.[32]

The timing of the Soviet statement was important as it coincided with allied successes in North Africa as well as the probability of a Soviet victory over the German Army at Stalingrad. The prospect of the Red Army advancing across Europe was sufficiently alarming that prior to the issuing of the Soviet diplomatic note, Sikorski had tried to gain support from the American government for his strategic and post-war plans for Poland. Sikorski arrived in Washington DC on 1 December 1942. He was lucky to arrive at all as he narrowly escaped a potentially fatal accident while in Montreal when the engines on his aircraft failed on take-off. Sabotage was swiftly detected, but not the perpetrators.[33] This was not to be the last attempt on Sikorski's life.

Sikorski's trip to the USA was a complete failure. He did not get any American support for the restoration of pre-war Polish frontiers but that did not prevent him, on his return to London, from claiming that his American trip had been successful. The British government swiftly found that he was lying. It is interesting that a Foreign Office informant suggested that the information supplied to them about Sikorski's visit to the USA should be burned.[34] Lord Halifax, the British Ambassador to the USA, sought the truth behind Sikorski's claim that Roosevelt had agreed to the creation of buffer states against the Soviet Union and learnt that it was all 'pure fiction' on Sikorski's part.[35] Such an audacious lie was easily found out but illustrates just how desperate Sikorski was to pull something out of the hat in order to try to deflect Anders' growing popularity and influence. Of course after this foolish episode on Sikorski's part, it became less likely that the British or the American governments could trust him any further.

A major problem with the Polish troops in the Middle East was that they were marooned in the desert and bored. The Polish journey out to the Iraqi desert had been more fortuitous than anything; even if there was a genuine need to keep a force there to prevent a pro-German takeover of the country, the Polish arrival was still by good fortune. The Poles had initially been evacuated from the Soviet Union to Iran, but their habitual public drunkenness had offended local Iranian sensibilities and the British warned the Poles that they needed to leave Iran as quickly as possible. Therefore, between 10 August and 8 September 1942, the Poles were transported to Iraq where they were joined by other units coming out from Palestine. Civilians were mainly sent to India or to Africa. Initially it had been considered that Iraq remained a stepping-stone to Palestine but Iraq proved to be an excellent training ground and so Poles were taken from Palestine for training in Iraq.[36]

However, being stuck out in the desert while training was creating boredom which became 'rampant and political intrigues were the result'.[37] These intrigues were of course plots and plans to remove Sikorski and his government. Eden observed that there was a need to give Polish troops in the Middle East 'employment'.[38] This was perhaps prompted by the steady realisation that, far from being diminished, the *Klimkowszczyna* were getting worse and posed a bigger threat than had previously been thought. This group had the ability to wreck the alliance against Germany as it had come to believe, and to influence others to believe, that the Soviet Union was a greater threat to Poland than Germany was. Furthermore, it proposed that perhaps Poles should begin to cooperate with anti-Soviet Germans.[39] Sikorski was thoroughly alarmed at this report and warned his ministers that unless this movement of 'madmen and traitors' was stamped out 'we shall squander everything that we possess … including our honour.'[40] He was already too late; many Polish troops, especially those in the Middle East, already considered that Sikorski and the Polish Government-in-Exile had squandered their honour. For them there was nothing left but to revolt against Sikorski and his government.

Even if the *Klimkowszczyna* had a limited political agenda, the existence of the group and Anders' toleration of it raises grave concerns about Anders' loyalty to Sikorski, or at least to his office and the Polish Government-in-Exile.[41] On 18 February 1943 Anders wrote to Sikorski and suggested he should resign in protest at Soviet violations of agreements made with the Polish Government-in-Exile and its dealings in general with Poland.[42] This was not only grossly insubordinate of Anders but also quite sly as he could have easily assumed Sikorski's post and moved the Polish seat of power to the Middle East. In a single move he might have, with the corporate support of the Polish Army, gained the post of Polish Prime Minister. He already knew that the Polish President supported him. As a senior Polish officer with great charisma, Anders might well have been able to control the Polish presidency. His power would have been absolute among his own exiled countrymen.

Anders continued in his insubordination when he urged President Raczkiewicz to form a new government which would be anti-Sikorski in its makeup. Anders took this action as he believed he enjoyed unreserved British support. This he based on the fact that local British officials in the Middle East, including Richard Casey, Brigadier Way of 26th Military Mission and his military advisor, Colonel L.R. Hulls, agreed with Anders' politics.[43] Anders had miscalculated however, as the views of local British representatives did not necessarily reflect those of the British government. The British still considered Sikorski to be the only viable Polish option in terms of British policies towards the Soviet Union. Indeed the Foreign Office treated reports from Way and

Hulls with caution as they were both considered to be anti-Soviet. Frank Roberts described Hulls as 'fantastically pro–Anders, anti-Sikorski and anti-Soviet'. Yet attempts by Sikorski to persuade the British to remove Hulls as the British representative to the Polish armed forces met with failure.[44] Previously Sikorski had complained to Eden that Hulls was a bad influence on Anders; the Foreign Office considered that Hulls should be warned against his interaction with Anders. However, Hulls denied Sikorski's allegations, claiming that they were linked to internal Polish politics. Eventually the entire incident lapsed with no further action being taken by the British authorities.[45] It is ironic to note that the Italian historian, Eugenio Corti, writes that Italian troops who had fought alongside the German Army on the Russian Front would have understood Anders' hostile attitude towards the Soviet Union because they had seen the horror of Stalin's Russia. The perennial problem for Anders was that the British and the London Poles had not suffered Soviet captivity and the torment that lay within this.[46]

Anders continued in his duplicity. He was perhaps emboldened, as he could quite clearly see that there was very little Sikorski could do about him while the British, as long as Anders continued to support British policy in the Middle East, did little or nothing about him. In an 'off the record' meeting with Casey in Cairo, Anders ranted against Sikorski. He claimed that Sikorski had a propensity for party politics and was a 'one government man'. Furthermore Anders claimed that Sikorski maintained a dubious claque and was unsuitable for the dual role of Polish Premier and Commander-in-chief.[47] Anders' comments may have been partially true but they were wholly disloyal to Sikorski and to Poland, not to mention hypocritical. It was not for him to comment on the internal Polish political situation, especially to a representative of a foreign power. Anders knew that despite the meeting being off the record it would be reported back to London, but could easily be denied if needs be. Even so it gave the British government, the Foreign Office and the War Office food for thought if it ever became necessary to replace Sikorski – even if it was that he should not be replaced with Anders.

We know that, despite his ire against Sikorski, Anders' political ambitions were actually no different; Anders' problem was that he sought to replace Sikorski. However, Anders was not privy to the reality of the situation which Sikorski was having to deal with by 1943. Anders may have been popular with the majority of exiled Poles as well as standing in good stead with the British authorities in the Middle East, but this combination of perceived good fortune limited Anders in his understanding of inter-allied military politics. The major stumbling block to Anders' ambitions was that the British government was not even contemplating replacing Sikorski: they saw no reason to do so. It was even more unlikely that they would replace Sikorski with somebody who was deeply hostile to the Soviet Union and all that it stood for. Indeed, the British government would not tolerate any situation which threatened the unity, discipline or fighting capacity of the APW and so became quite nervous at what they were hearing from Casey. Sikorski was therefore urged by the British authorities to go to the Middle East and assert his authority over Anders and the APW, or order Anders to report to London and review the situation in the Middle East. Either way, Sikorski was expected to call Anders to heel.[48]

Sikorski tried to defuse the matter by being very clear that 'politics was not the business of military commanders'. In a private letter to Anders he urged him to 'dismiss conspirators from his entourage and from the army'. Sikorski also observed that the call from Anders for a demonstrative resignation, as requested earlier of Sikorski, would only confirm the Allies' prejudice of Polish romanticism and rashness.[49] It is obvious that Sikorski was also being equally hypocritical about the role of Polish military commanders as nearly all were tarnished by party politics at the expense of their professionalism. It would seem that only Generals Maczek and Kopański were not involved in politics. It could be interpreted that by writing to Anders, Sikorski was unsure or even afraid of meeting him. Even so, Sikorski was quite correct about the Allies' attitude towards what they considered to be traditional Polish traits. Churchill's reaction to a report from Casey concerning Polish infighting and anti-Soviet activity was one of fury. Churchill considered that the APW were a bunch of ingrates. He wrote,

> here we have all of the elements of instability which led to the ruin in Poland through many centuries in spite of the individual qualities and virtues of Poles. In my view, no countenance should be given to subversive movements in the Polish Corps … we have armed and are feeding these Polish troops and they begin their usual Polish fissiparous subversive agitation.[50]

Clearly by 1943 Churchill was tired of the Poles and their shenanigans.

Sikorski was not the only Polish leader with the ability to maintain a credible line between his government and the Soviet government, but he was the only Polish leader who knew secrets of Allied policy, as limited as that was, because the British, American and Soviet governments played their cards close to their chests and only let the minor allies know what was necessary for them to know. Even if Sikorski's knowledge of policy was limited, Anders' knowledge of Allied war policy was even more restricted which thus left him with an extremely narrow and parochial understanding of the state of the war and the politics involved. During April 1943 Eden remarked that Anders did not totally appreciate the international background of the difficulties which reduced Sikorski and his government's room for manoeuvre and discretion.[51] This was just before the grim discovery by the Germans of mass graves containing Polish officers and other Polish elites at Katyń as well as at other sites. Most of the victims had been murdered by the NKVD during April 1940.

Sikorski's weakness was his personality as he was unwilling to share responsibility with others. This led to problems and misunderstandings with other commanders such as Anders and Sosnkowski because when they commented on the international situation connected with Polish interests they often spoke from a point of ignorance and, as a consequence, were deemed disloyal as they gave forth on matters more complicated than they actually realised. This of course gave the impression of disunity within the Polish camp. Sikorski tried to combat this perception with the use of stern lectures on the necessity of an apolitical army but this made things worse. It might have been more sensible to have accepted the situation and to have tried to have made alliance with some of the senior commanders involved, especially Anders. Sikorski should have accepted that on the whole the civilian politicians in his Cabinet were next to useless, all second rate in their time in Poland, while soldiers were highly trusted among Poles, inside and outside of Poland. Anders would have made a formidable ally for Sikorski. With his fluent Russian and extensive knowledge of Russia and how the Soviet Union was organised, not to mention his unfettered reading of Marxist-Leninist theory as well as those of Stalin while, ironically, in Soviet captivity, Anders would have been extremely helpful and an asset to Sikorski in negotiations with Stalin. While negotiating with Stalin, Anders would have been able to throw some of Stalin's own words and ideas back at Stalin himself – and in Russian. This would have been possible because Anders understood all too well what Stalin, under the influence of Lenin's writings, had planned to do once the Soviet Union was able to advance once more and head towards Germany and the West. Therefore Anders, with his knowledge of how the Soviet government was more than likely to behave in its military-foreign policy would, if he had been fully briefed of the situation facing Sikorski in 1943, no doubt have behaved differently as the two men tried to save Poland from Soviet annexation and occupation post war.

An Anders-Sikorski alliance might have been accepted by the British government as the Minister of State in Cairo noted when he reported an 'off the record' talk with Anders where he stated that the Polish Government-in-Exile was out of touch with the APW. It was observed that Sikorski needed to get to understand his force in the Middle East or nothing fruitful would come out of any meeting between Anders and Sikorski. However the Minister was very much mistaken in his understanding of Anders whom he reported (with his army) as being apolitical, and that Anders was a 'soldier first and last'.[52] Certainly this was a misreading of Anders and his officers, as well as a lack of understanding of the Polish concept of the role of the soldier and its political undertones. In Poland the Polish soldier was the most trusted figure of authority and the one most trusted with the liberty of the Polish nation, linking it to the restoration of nationhood in post-war Poland. The British have rarely, if ever, trusted their futures to the military.

The argument remains that if Sikorski had tried to cooperate with Anders and presented him with the challenges that lay in front of the Polish Government-in-Exile, Anders may well have acted as a bridge between the APW and the Polish Government-in-Exile and reduced the tensions between the two bodies. Sikorski failed to do this and made his own task even more difficult than it was already. After 1942, once the Soviet Union went over to the offensive, the Polish voice, small as it was within the allies, was further reduced. Sikorski found his duties as Polish Prime Minister and commander-in-chief were to become even more onerous – and it was all about to get worse.

On 13 April 1943 German radio announced the discovery of mass graves in Katyń Forest and claimed that the NKVD was responsible. Everything pointed towards it being a Soviet atrocity because the victims were all Polish, while the evidence in and around the bodies indicated that the massacre was carried out during April 1940. This was a time when the Soviets occupied the area. On 15 April 1943 the Polish Government-in-Exile demanded an International Red Cross (IRC) Commission into the mass graves. This outraged the Soviet government and it broke off diplomatic relations with the London Poles. The German government had been slick in its announcement of the finding of the graves; its timing was impeccable and completed the Polish-Soviet split.

There is evidence that points towards the fact that the German government had known of the mass graves since the summer of 1942.[53] At the time of the discovery of the graves Eden minuted: 'All the same it is puzzling that the Germans should have kept this information bottled up for so long.'[54] German sources reveal that a Polish work party attached to the German Army had dug up corpses at Katyń during 1942 and therefore knew exactly what was there. Janusz Zawody asserts that the Germans had occupied the Katyń area since 1942 and had begun to dig up the graves during February 1943.[55] The most interesting observations, however, come from Sergo Beria, son of the infamous Laverenti Beria. Beria Junior claims that the Germans knew of the shootings at the Katyń site for two reasons. The first being that the Germans used the same area to shoot Poles; this made it slightly easier for the Soviet government to later claim that they were innocent and that the Germans were to blame. The second reason was that following a conference held in Kraków between 'high officials' of the Gestapo and the NKVD at the end of February 1940, the Soviets executed Polish officers at Katyń, while from 31 March 1940 the Germans carried out a parallel action (Operation AB) which was designed to destroy the Polish elite. The victims of the German action numbered some 2,000.[56] There is further evidence of collusion between the Gestapo and the NKVD as Jacek Ślusarczyk asserts that there were at least four meetings between the Gestapo and the NKVD – two in January 1940 in Kraków and two more in March, one in Kraków and the other at the Polish ski resort of Zakopane. Norman Davies also discusses cooperation between the secret security bodies during March 1940 and confirms an SS action 'AB-Aktion' in the German zone.[57] This confirms Sergo Beria's version of events and even General Bór-Komorowski, who later led Polish underground forces in the 1944 Warsaw Uprising, mentioned cooperation between the Gestapo and the NKVD during March 1940.[58]

Thirty years later in 1973 Rohan Butler, in his review of the evidence of Katyń, observed that the German announcement of Katyń turned out well for the Germans as it came out at a time of 'tension between the Soviet government and the Polish Government-in-Exile in London.'[59] It was in the interests of the German government to split the allies as far as possible as by 1943 it was becoming clear that Germany was going to lose the war. The Soviet victory at Stalingrad at the beginning of February 1943 was a shock to Germany and as the Soviets began to gain the upper-hand in the war, relations between the Poles in London and the Soviet government became further strained. Katyń was fortuitous for the German government as it served the purpose of exposing a Soviet crime against another ally: Poland. Katyń was guaranteed to drive a wedge into the alliance as well as destroying any chance that Sikorski had of any success in his policy of reconciliation between Poland and the Soviet Union. Sikorski was dished by the German government to his enemies: the Soviet government and the APW.

The problem for Sikorski was that there was not much that he could do about the Katyń revelations. Even though the British government was well aware that the Soviets were responsible for the mass murder of Poles at Katyń and other sites, they refused to acknowledge this in public and maintained the fiction that Germany was solely responsible for the crime.[60] The British government could hardly afford to offend the Soviets as by 1943 the Red Army was holding down the bulk of the German Army on the Russian Front. The Allies were clearing North Africa and were preparing to invade Sicily to be followed up by an invasion of the Italian mainland.[61]

Furthermore there was the sore point of the opening of the 'Second Front'; a western offensive against Germany designed to draw German divisions away from the Russian Front. Stalin had been demanding the opening of a Second Front since the German invasion of the Soviet Union in June 1941. In a private letter written to Churchill during April 1942, Roosevelt wrote that the Red Army was killing more Germans and destroying more enemy equipment than both the British and Americans in their operations. Roosevelt feared a Soviet withdrawal from the war or even worse, another measure of cooperation between the Soviets and the Germans if Stalin considered that the Western Allies would never land in western Europe. It seems that Roosevelt was more preoccupied than Churchill in keeping the Soviet Union in the war.[62]

The British government put itself in a difficult position by agreeing publicly that the Germans were the culprits for Katyń. However, Cadogan observed that the Soviet Union had been committing atrocities for a long time and questioned how long the Poles could be expected to cooperate with the Soviet government following the Katyń revelations. He also considered the moral problem that, by not condemning the Soviets over Katyń, the British government would be unable to discuss with the Soviet government the matter of executing German war criminals after the war.[63] Without doubt Cadogan was correct but morality had little to do with reality. In 1946 German war criminals were executed, yet Katyń remained a German crime until 1991.

The British government desperately needed to keep the Soviets in the war and so had to overlook the whole ghastly episode of Katyń. Indeed, on 28 April 1943, three days after the Soviet severing of diplomatic links with the Polish Government-in-Exile, Churchill remarked to Eden, 'there is no use in prowling morbidly round the three-year-old graves at Smolensk.' Churchill urged that the Poles should be made to move on from Katyń. He viewed Katyń and the statement from the Soviet government which confirmed its break with the London Poles as 'a declaration of mortal war'.[64] Anders was less than subtle in his approach towards the Soviet government following Katyń. As early as 18 April 1943 Anders, for his Order of the Day, ordered a Requiem Mass to be said for the dead. At the same time he criticised the events of Katyń and the Soviet government. This was all published in the Polish language military daily newspaper, *Dziennik Polski*.[65]

Anders' actions swiftly drew reactions from Ivan Maisky as well as from Anders' commanding officer, General Henry Pownall, Commander-in-chief, Persia and Iraq Command. Pownall issued exacting orders to Anders which demanded that he suppress all criticism of the Soviet Union by members of the APW.[66] Anders' reaction towards the Soviets was priceless to German propaganda as it exposed the differences between the Polish Goverment-in-Exile and that of the Soviet government. The severing of links between the two governments confirmed this state. Indeed later, during May 1944, in fighting in Italy at Monte Cassino, Anders' troops were taunted by German propaganda which referred to 'betrayal' at Katyń followed by another betrayal by the Allies at Teheran between 28 November 1943 and 1 December 1943. This was a reference to a series of meetings held between Stalin, Roosevelt and Churchill which more or less settled the future of post-war Poland without reference to the Poles. To many people, it seemed that the Western Allies had given the Soviet government a free hand in post-war Poland. This 'baiting' however had the effect of making the Poles fight even harder at Monte Cassino.[67] Anders' reaction to the events at Katyń had been predictable as the APW seethed with indignation towards Sikorski and his pro-Soviet agenda. Katyń made the situation worse, while Sikorski's government acted foolishly in demanding an IRC inquiry thus playing into the hands of both the German and Soviet governments.

Sikorski was left politically naked because the Soviet government felt able to remove itself from any agreements made with the Poles and was therefore able to pursue its own agenda: the pursuit of the 'world revolution' in Marxist-Leninist terms or, quite simply, the return of the Russian Empire. The German government was handed a diplomatic coup and later used the anti-Polish attitude of the Soviets in German propaganda in Poland. Sikorski looked weak and foolish while Anders emerged stronger than ever because he understood the Soviet Union and its agenda.

Katyń was proof of the suffering of those Poles who had endured Soviet captivity between 1939 and 1941 – and even 1942 in some cases. Anders was the single Polish leader in the West who had suffered with them and it had nearly killed him. Pownall's rebuke was further evidence of how little the Allies knew of recent Polish history and later the British and Americans were made to suffer for their ignorance when the Soviet Union emerged from the war as a super-power. A super-power that defied the west for decades and in another guise still does. Katyń was a watershed in the lives of Anders and Sikorski: Anders and his reputation grew, Sikorski was never granted the time to recover.

After the severance of diplomatic links between the London Poles and the Soviet government, the Soviet government began to pour scorn on Sikorski and his government, especially his claim that he represented all Poles. The Soviet attitude towards the Poles grew so hostile and uncharitable that Churchill was forced to summon Maisky for an official reprimand. Maisky claimed that the Soviet government had no intention of seeking Sikorski's replacement or the removal of Raczkiewicz, but did insist that the Polish Government-in-Exile should be 'reconstructed' (basically restructured in such a way that would be acceptable to the Soviet government) in order for diplomatic relations between the Polish Government-in-Exile and the Soviet government to be resumed. Churchill continued in his displeasure of one ally savaging another.[68]

Churchill's words made no difference to Stalin who continued to attack Sikorski and his authority and depicted him as being 'helpless and browbeaten by his vast pro-Hitler following.'[69] Both Churchill and Roosevelt did their best to defend Sikorski but Stalin was remorseless in his vilifying of him. The two Allied leaders tried to tell Stalin that Sikorski was the best and most reasonable Polish leader available and was in grave danger of being ousted by his own people for not being sufficiently anti-Soviet.[70] Stalin, using domestic Polish opposition to Sikorski's Soviet policy, continued to undermine the Polish Premier to such an extent that Churchill, who wished to retain Sikorski, expressed privately that perhaps the Polish Government-in-Exile should be reconstructed owing to its 'foolish and improper blunder over Katyn'. Eden was sufficiently alarmed at Churchill's musings that he secured the backing of the British War Cabinet to make Churchill tone down his message to Stalin.[71]

Attempts by the British government to persuade Sikorski to reform his government were almost impossible. Maisky knew this as he commented to Eden that the only important Polish politicians outside of the Polish Government-in-Exile were even more hostile to the Soviet Union than those who were already members of the Polish government.[72] Sikorski attempted to pursue policies between the two governments but despite Polish attempts to censor its own press, not to pursue with the IRC investigation into Katyń and the British endeavours to quell official Soviet anger over the entire episode, the Soviet government continued in its attacks on the Polish government.[73] Eventually reports were received concerning skirmishes between Polish and Soviet units in Persia. The reports were swiftly denied (or covered up) by the authorities but they were also symptomatic of the volatile atmosphere between the Poles and the Soviets.[74] Katyń failed to reconcile Sikorski and Anders, while Sikorski's attempts at rapprochement with the Soviet government were interpreted by many Poles, including Anders, as being misguided. Katyń was the proof of how wrong Sikorski's policies were in the eyes of many of his compatriots. Sikorski's failure to stem the anti-Polish bile from the Soviet government and his inability to gain unconditional support for Poland from the Western Allies caused further problems and not just from the Soviets. On 17 April 1943 General Anders reported that the APW lacked confidence in the

Polish government. Three days later Anders told the chief of Sikorski's General Staff, Brigadier-General Tadeusz Klimecki, that there should be changes in the Polish Government-in-Exile.[75]

On 1 May 1943 Klimecki warned the Polish government that the situation in the APW was worse than he had expected. Most of the Polish Army was opposed to the Polish government in London, while Anders was openly supporting activities which were directed against Sikorski.[76] There was also a fear that Anders might resign his own post as Commander of the APW in order to expose fissures within the Polish camp and all of the consequences which would result from such a high profile resignation. The British government also feared that Anders might relinquish his command and so took the step of instructing British officials in the Middle East to prevent Anders from taking any 'irrevocable step'. Churchill had already stated that if the APW failed to continue to support the war against Germany, the British government would withdraw its support for Poland. Anders had been put on notice by Churchill that the members of APW had to do as they were told or be cast into oblivion with their country. Churchill did not mince his words when, on 3 April 1943, he sent a minute to Cadogan which read: 'General Anders should be given no encouragement and should be warned that he is answerable for the good discipline and loyalty to the Polish government of the troops entrusted to him. The troops should be aware that any failure on their part of discipline, or of the readiness to act against a common foe in a coherent manner, will relieve the Allies, and particularly Great Britain, of the obligations that they have to secure the existence of a strong Poland after the war.'[77]

Katyń had compounded British anxiety over the morale and potential for mutiny by the Polish Army. By 1943 the Allies had reached a crucial point in their pursuit of the war in the Mediterranean theatre of operations. They had already decided to invade Sicily from North Africa and move onto Italy from there. It had long been expected that the APW would be deployed in the Mediterranean but it had to be a force that could be trusted. Anything which threatened the allied military capability in the region would be removed. The British government encouraged Sikorski to go to the Middle East and restore order among his troops there. Klimecki had concluded that such a trip was essential: he had already established that to his mind the rank and file of the APW were politically sound and that it was only the Command of APW which was addicted to politics with a small group of officers taking advantage of the situation.[78] In 1965 Klimkowski, the leader of the dissident officers, denied that Sikorski's visit to the Middle East was necessary and claimed that there was no question of mutiny by Polish forces in the Middle East.[79] This contradicts the words of the most senior Polish diplomat in wartime London, Edward Raczyński, who recorded on 9 May 1943 that in Anders' HQ near Baghdad the atmosphere was one of rebellion owing to the bitterness of the Polish situation. Karol Bader reported from Tehran that the situation at Anders' HQ could be blamed on Klimkowski.[80] It was very clear therefore that there was a major problem in the Anders' camp but little was being done about the situation as Sikorski lacked the authority locally, while it suited the British to allow Anders to continue as he did providing it didn't undermine Allied operations against Germany. The main point was that Anders was seen as militarily useful; Sikorski was not.

A British security report of the time cast doubt on Klimkowski's assertion. The British security services submitted a report on Sikorski and noted that his position was worsening as thirty to forty Polish generals, which amounted to virtually every Polish general in the UK were becoming emphatic in their demand that Sikorski should cease meddling in politics and confine himself to military affairs.[81] However it was only Sikorski's politics which were keeping the case for Polish post-war independence open, and few, if any, Poles had realised that. And of course, Sikorski was the only Polish leader acceptable to the Western Allies and the Soviet government. Therefore it was only Sikorski who could go to the Middle East and visit the APW. He was encouraged by the British government to make Polish troops understand the necessity of working with the Soviet Union in order to defeat Germany.[82]

Tendyra claims that Sikorski's approach towards Anders in his visit to the Middle East was wrong from the outset. In a meeting with senior Polish officers in Iraq on 10 June 1943 Sikorski raised the question of structural changes in order to address a serious manpower shortage as well as how to meet operational and training requirements. In this guise Sikorski attempted to execute a clumsy attempt in reducing Anders' military standing and popular appeal – but failed miserably. In his attempt to restructure the APW, Sikorski offered Anders a choice: he could become commander of the army or commander of Second Polish Corps. It was a poor choice. If Anders chose to become an army commander he would nominally remain the highest-ranking officer in the region but without a field command. If he opted for the post of commander of Second Polish Corps, another Polish officer would be his superior.[83]

The British government and the Foreign Office, long aware of the definite rift between the Polish Government-in-Exile and the APW, were determined that the situation should not be allowed to fester. A majority of those serving in the APW believed that the Polish government was composed of Sikorski 'yes-men' and were subordinate to Sikorski's personal ambitions rather than what they considered to be beneficial to Poland. Furthermore they suspected that Sikorski was determined to remove Anders. Naturally this led to mistrust of Sikorski by the APW while it was reported, somewhat darkly, that in the event of a 'showdown' between Sikorski and Anders, the APW, to a man, would support Anders.[84] However the Foreign Office could not find any evidence that Sikorski had planned to dismiss Anders.[85]

After two years of unrivalled authority over his military force Anders did not welcome any attempt to diminish his power and authority. Sikorski's aim may have been to restructure the APW but this should be treated with caution because he desperately needed to reduce Anders' influence. If he could have done this by what might have been perceived as a restructuring of the APW for the better, it would have been a bonus. However Sikorski was no match for Anders, but all the same tried to press Anders further regarding Polish-Soviet relations and claimed that progress had been made in this matter.[86] The problem was that Sikorski was a proven liar and his word could not be taken as true.

Equally Anders had to be persuaded by British officials to be less confrontational towards Sikorski. Anders had already said that he intended to speak 'very freely' to Sikorski about his various grievances. It would seem that Sikorski was the weaker of the two men as Hopkins advised Casey to 'urge him [Sikorski] to maintain a moderate and calm attitude' during his forthcoming meeting with Anders on 26 May 1943.[87] Anders also had to be rehearsed by the British in how he was to receive and treat Sikorski when the two men met.[88]

Sikorski failed to understand the justified fears that the APW had concerning his Soviet policy and how it would affect Poland and its people after the war. Instead, Sikorski continued to denounce the politicisation of the APW, especially at senior command levels.[89] The problem for Sikorski was that he had to address the issue as the British and American governments found the politicisation of the APW – and indeed the Polish Army – quite unacceptable. Sikorski's difficulties cut no ice with Anders and his officers, and Anders evaded all attempts by Sikorski to reduce his authority and managed to retain command of both the APW and Second Polish Corps. Once Second Polish Corps was combat ready, Anders proposed to relinquish control of the APW.[90]

Sikorski's visit to the Middle East, as we have already seen began on a mistaken premise: the removal of Anders. This was a politically dangerous course to set out on but there were other dangers: there had already been two attempts on Sikorski's life. Both of these had been in 1942 when Sikorski was travelling in and around North America. These attempts should not and cannot be ignored by historians even if there were attempts to cover up the events in 1942 and for reasons unknown Poles still don't want to know about these episodes, especially in view of the fact that Sikorski died in a mysterious plane crash while travelling overseas, but on the whole they are ignored because they do not fit Polish mythology or indeed Polish historiography.

The first attempt to kill Sikorski concerned Wing Commander Kleczynski, PAF, who managed to smuggle an incendiary bomb onto Sikorski's aircraft bound for the USA from the UK. Kleczynski claimed that he had brought the bomb aboard the airplane as he considered that if the plane was forced down over enemy territory, the bomb could be used to destroy the aircraft and the nature of its journey. Later Kleczynski claimed that he had forgotten that he had brought the device onto the airplane and only remembered it when he smelled burning and panicked because he thought that the bomb was about to explode. British security officials claimed to have been convinced by Kleczynski's account and considered in view of his 'distinguished career' he should not be punished as he was consumed with 'mental anguish'.[91] Two days later Kleczynski was recalled from his post as Polish Air Attaché to the USA to go onto a long leave to 'recover his health'.[92]

The idea that Kleczynski suffered some form of mental breakdown was very convenient to both the Polish and British governments – and it is bogus. Kleczynski was part of a conspiracy. He obtained the bomb as early as December 1941 from Second Lieutenant Eugeniusz Jarewicz, who was involved in the development of sabotage equipment and training officers in its use.[93] Under interrogation by the British security services Jarewicz confirmed that Kleczynski wanted the bomb to destroy an aircraft forced down over enemy territory.[94] The fact that a second person was involved is an indication of a wider conspiracy. As the events took place between 21 and 22 March 1942, an obvious question is just how and where did Kleczynski keep the bomb after obtaining it during December 1941? There are other questions too, such as: who was really behind this and, although it was not mentioned, funds must have been raised, so who was financing the entire enterprise? These questions were not asked because the answers might well have been inconvenient and extremely embarrassing for both the Polish and British governments. To return to the not-very-convincing interrogation it is also unrealistic to accept that Kleczynski 'forgot' about the bomb once it was stowed on Sikorski's aircraft.[95] To add further speculation to this incident, British archives refer to the bomb as a time bomb rather than the incendiary device discovered prior to Sikorski's departure to the USA.[96]

The inconsistency of the accounts as reported by the British and the Polish security services is interesting because it allowed Kleczynski to escape public censure or punishment. The actions of Jarewicz seem never to have been subject to any retribution by the Polish authorities. Kleczynski was placed into an Edinburgh mental health unit but subsequently released. Later he was rather conveniently run down and killed by a tram in Edinburgh.[97] It would not have been unreasonable to expect the British authorities to try Kleczynski and convict him for at least conspiracy against the life of Sikorski and others, and for Kleczynski to receive a lengthy jail term. However, any attempt to bring Kleczynski to trial would have been a public admission of discontent with Sikorski and his Soviet policies and so cause embarrassment for the Western Allies. It was more convenient to allow Kleczynski to retreat into obscurity, his actions perceived of those of a lone madman.

No matter how hard the Western Allies and the Polish Government-in-Exile tried to cover up Kleczynski's actions, a further attempt was made on Sikorski's life. Again it involved aircraft and foreign travel; on 1 December 1942 Sikorski narrowly escaped death at Montreal, Canada, when, as he was preparing to fly onto the USA, all the engines of the aircraft failed. To investigators it was clearly sabotage but they were not certain who might have tried to carry out such an act.[98] Again there was a discrepancy of accounts as Major Victor Cazalet, British Liaison Officer to Sikorski, recorded the flight from Montreal to New York as being at the end of November 1942 in a twin-engine Hudson.

Both engines (rather than four as some reports suggested) failed on take-off.[99] Interestingly, Irving asserts that the British government were so anxious to play down the incident, they tried to persuade Sikorski that there had not been any incident at all.[100]

Concerning his relationship with Anders and the APW, Sikorski considered them to be a worthy body and did his best to keep them on board.[101] However, it should be recognised that he was nervous of Anders, no matter what Polish historiography makes of Sikorski's trip to the Middle East. If Sikorski was not afraid of Anders he would not have allowed members of the APW to sing *Pierwszą Brygadę* (*The First Brigade*), an anthem synonymous with Piłsudski and virtually banned from the Polish Army. Sikorski's gesture, if not blatant sucking-up to the APW, may have angered certain Polish politicians in exile, but it was popular among the Piłsudski loyalists.[102] Sikorski needed Anders and the APW far more than they needed him and so he went to meet them.

It could be said that Sikorski, once in the Middle East, was able to dominate Anders. Sikorski even told Eden that once Anders was confronted, he was like 'a small boy who had done wrong but was now contrite and has been forgiven but would have to watch his step in the future'.[103] The problem with this is that Sikorski was a proven liar and would say anything to make himself look masterful, while the reality was that Sikorski had nothing Anders wanted – save his resignation. Anders had everything, including an army which the British wanted and needed. Sikorski had gone to the Middle East not only to try to confront Anders, but also to make another attempt to split the command of the APW.[104] The Foreign Office noted that on the eve of Sikorski's death, most of the difficulties between Sikorski and Anders had been largely overcome.[105]

This may have been the case but it is equally likely that Anders allowed Sikorski and the British to believe that he agreed with Sikorski, but once Sikorski had left for the UK, Anders returned to his previous behaviour and there was little that Sikorski could do about it. In any event, Sikorski and his entourage died on 4 July 1943 when his aircraft crashed into the sea as it took off from Gibraltar. It was all very convenient for Anders – he was left as the most charismatic Polish figure in the West, and he had an army which was about to become very useful to the Allies. First Polish Corps was still marooned in Scotland while civilian politicians were of little account to many Poles. Anders had now swept all before him.

Chapter 6

Italy and Monte Cassino

I t was all very convenient that the day after Sikorski's death, Anders was laid up with malaria until 11 July 1943.[1] Anders received good news on 17 July 1943 when he was informed that Polish 2nd Corps was to be transferred to the Middle East beginning with 3rd Carpathian Division in mid-August 1943. The original intention was to move them to Syria but malaria was rife there until the middle of October, therefore it was decided to send the division to the Gaza area in Palestine until the end of September. After then 3rd Carpathian Division was to go to Syria for intensive training until they were required for operations, or until winter. If the Division was still in Syria when winter fell, they were to return to Gaza. The same approach was to be adopted for the remainder of the Corps. An interesting footnote concerning the deployment to Gaza is that Kenny, the British bearer of this news, knew that Anders wanted to avoid contact between Jews and his troops. As there were few Jews in Gaza, it seemed an ideal place to locate Polish troops.[2] It should be considered that in a meeting of December 1941 between Polish representatives, including Sikorski and representatives of the Soviet government, Stalin and Anders agreed for once over the question of how good Jews were or otherwise, as soldiers. Both men agreed that in their opinion Jews made very poor soldiers, while Anders seemed to imply that Jews were all criminals.[3] It seems that the oft-denied charge of Polish anti-Semitism had raised its ugly head once more. However, by March 1945 there seems to have been a change of heart regarding Jews and their ability to fight because the Jewish Brigade, fighting alongside the 4th Wolyn Brigade on the river Senio in Italy, were praised and the European-wide prejudice of Jews being poor combatants was challenged.[4]

In late 1943 the organisation of 2nd Polish Corps was discussed in a meeting in Cairo. The Supreme Allied Commander, the American General Dwight 'Ike' Eisenhower, suggested that the Corps should consist of a single infantry division comprised of three brigades with a tank brigade supplemented with army corps units. Sosnkowski, who had replaced Sikorski as Polish Commander-in-chief, demurred. Sosnkowski wanted a single infantry of two brigades with an armoured divisions and an army corps. He was concerned that there might well have been a detrimental effect on Polish opinion and morale if 2nd Polish Corps was reduced to more or less a single division. Eisenhower expressed sympathy but could not allow operational decisions to be based on national pride. He emphasised that he also had to take a robust line with other allies when considering future operations. Eisenhower also noted that operations in Italy had little use for armoured divisions of which he already had a surplus.[5] The Poles considered that an armoured division was essential for a cadre force which would eventually return to Poland and liberate the country, but the type of armoured division they wanted to establish had been outmoded since the North Africa campaign because it did not allow for sufficient infantry to hold territory captured by armoured units and so a new type of armoured division with enough infantry was being used by the Allies. The Allies were swift to roundly condemn the Polish idea.[6] Decisions were quickly made about the deployment of 2nd Polish Corps; they were to arrive in the Mediterranean theatre of operations between 20 December 1943 and 1 March 1944.[7]

The Allied return to Europe began on the night of 9–10 July 1943 with the invasion of Sicily (Operation HUSKY), which was launched from North Africa. HUSKY nearly didn't get off the ground as the American High Command deeply distrusted the British and the 'distraction' of a Mediterranean campaign. At times even Churchill, despite the fact that he is often seen as the brainchild behind the entire enterprise, was concerned about the outcome of HUSKY as he worried that the Germans might be able to assemble sufficient forces taken from northern France and drive the allies back into the sea. The British had thrice been ejected from the European mainland since 1940: Norway, France and Greece; the British could not fail in any attempt to return to Europe.[8]

The overall Allied objective was the conquest of Italy. A campaign against Italy had long been in the mind of the Allies as had been laid out to Stalin during August 1942 when Operation TORCH, the landing of allied troops in North Africa, was discussed. At the time, Churchill was trying to defuse Stalin's black mood once he was told that the Allies would not be landing in Europe during 1942, thus relieving some of the German pressure against the Soviet Union. Churchill explained to Stalin that any landing in northern France during 1942 would be rebuffed by the Germans, while in North Africa there was a good chance for victory which could be followed up by moving onto Europe, and thus helping the Soviet Union. Stalin asked if TORCH was aimed at Germany – Churchill replied that it was against Germany's weakest ally.[9] It was clear that Churchill meant Italy.

An invasion of Italy was a risky strategy and it was observed that nobody had successfully captured Rome from the south since AD 536. Napoleon was supposed to have claimed to have said that 'Italy is a boot. You enter it from the top.' Quite simply, geography was against any invader moving northwards towards Rome because the way consisted of high mountains riven with fast flowing rivers. The only direct route from the south was along the Via Casilina (Route 6). Eighty miles south of Rome the route passed through the valley of the Liri river and this was where the German commander-in-chief in Italy, General Albert Kesselring, chose to make his stand. Over the entrance of the Liri Valley stood the colossal monastery of Monte Cassino which was to block the Allied advance to the north.[10] The taking of Monte Cassino is seminal in the tale of 2nd Polish Corps and will be discussed later in this narrative.

Churchill's fears of the Allies being pushed back into the sea were shared by General Brooke when, on 14 September 1943, Allied armies landed at Salerno, heralding the beginning of the Allies' invasion of the Italian mainland. Brooke was not to be reassured until 18 September when he wrote in his diary 'Salerno landing now seems safe.'[11] Italy had already withdrawn from the war on 3 September 1943 following the removal of the Italian dictator, Benito Mussolini and the signing of the Armistice of Cassible. This left the Germans, supported by Italian fascists loyal to Mussolini, in control of much of Italy, which they were determined to defend as long as possible. The result was a long and grinding campaign as the Allies began to advance northwards.

On 27 March 1944 Field Marshal Alan Brooke noted that (General) 'Alexander stuck at Cassino'.[12] The Italian Campaign had come to a shuddering halt, as had the attempted landing at Anzio, north of Rome. Anzio was a particularly disappointing event as Churchill let it be known. Regarding Polish forces, Polish troops had been in Italy as early as December 1943 when men from 3rd Carpathian Brigade were sent to relieve British troops on the Sangro river; 3rd Carpathian Division lost seventeen officers and 182 ORs that winter in raids on German positions or while patrolling. In early 1944 the remainder of 2nd Polish Corps arrived in Italy from Palestine and Egypt. By April there were 50,000 Polish troops in Italy.

The establishment of 2nd Polish Corps was as follows: 3rd Carpathian Division commanded by Major General Duch; 5th Kresy Division commanded by Major General Sulik; the 2nd Armoured Brigade commanded by Major General Bronisław Rakowski and a considerable artillery force commanded by Major General Roman Odzierzyński. Halik Kochanski observes that even though on paper 2nd Polish Corps looked formidable, it was hampered by a manpower shortage. The divisions had two brigades rather than the customary three and there was a severely limited reserve. Anders arrived in Italy on 6 February 1944 and five days later at the Allied HQ at Caserta, he meet his CO, Lieutenant General (yet to be confirmed) Oliver Leese, Commander of the British 8th Army. The two men did not speak each other's languages so they conversed in French, Anders fluently, Leese with some risible schoolboy French which often humoured Anders. Indeed it was said that when Leese left Italy at the end of September 1944 he left Anders as a friend, but one wag claimed that if Leese had not left when he did, Anders' fluent command of the French language would have been 'irretrievably ruined'.[13] Leese took an instant liking to Anders and was sympathetic towards the Polish situation.[14] Indeed Captain Ion Calvocoressi, Leese's ADC, noted in his diary on the evening of 12 May 1944 that the Poles were very gloomy after the failed opening attack (Monte Cassino) and that Leese was trying to cheer Anders up.[15] What is interesting is the question of manpower for 2nd Polish Corps as a long treasured Polish ideal was that those Poles captured fighting for the German Army should be trained to fight for the Polish Army alongside the Allies, however Anders seemed to question the wisdom of this. In April 1943 in a report on Polish PoWs, Anders learnt that thousands of Poles had been conscripted into the German Army and that many could not be identified as they feared for the safety of their families. Anders mused over what a Pole who had served for two and a half years in the German Army really thought and that all Polish PoWs should be screened before they were accepted as recruits to the Polish Army.[16] In Italy it is clear that ex-German Army Polish prisoners were still not trusted as none were allowed to serve on the front-line, but were kept in rear depots or base establishments in the Middle East. They never came to Italy. This contradicts Holland's assertion that Poles slipped over from the German lines and joined

General Anders at the Polish Institute and Sikorski Museum (PISM), Princes Gate, Kensington, London, 17 September 1967, twenty-eighth anniversary of the Soviet invasion of Poland. (*Courtesy of Janusz Jarzembowski*)

Jever, Germany, 1946. Anders is greeted by General Klemens Rudnicki, back to camera, (Divisional Commander, First Polish Armoured Division, 21 May 1945–10 June 1946) accompanied by (right to left): Lieutenant General Guy Simonds, CO Canadian II Corps; General John Tredinnick Crocker, commanding (OC) British I Corps, who commanded First Polish Armoured Division from 28 September 1944 until 8 April 1945 when the Division reverted to Simonds' II Corps. (*Courtesy of Janusz Jarzembowski*)

Valentine tanks possibly from Majewski's Brigade – Infantry Tank Mk III, Valentine II, 16th Tank Brigade, First Polish Armoured Corps. (*Courtesy of Janusz Jarzembowski*)

Anders' visit to First Polish Armoured Division. Left to right: General Klimecki, Chief of Polish General Staff, Anders and Majewski (with beret), Scotland, April 1942. (*Courtesy of Janusz Jarzembowski*)

General Maczek wearing a
Rogatywka (garrison hat),
Klimecki, Anders. (*Courtesy of
Janusz Jarzembowski*)

Visit to First Polish Armoured Division by General Anders, Jever, Germany, late
May 1945. The division withdrew from Wilhelmshaven on 22 May to Jever airfield
(approximately 12 miles north-west) designated Advanced Landing Ground
(AGL) B-117. The airfield had served primarily as a German night-fighter base and
because of its grass runways had never been identified or bombed by the Allies.
Post-war, the base was used as a displaced persons camp until taken over by the
RAF in 1952 and was eventually returned to German control in 1961. Anders is
seen arriving in a British Army Auster AOP V, used by airborne artillery observers
and a liaison aircraft by senior officers. (*Courtesy of Janusz Jarzembowski*)

Anders greets Colonel Tadeusz Majewski CO 16th Armoured Tank Brigade, partially hidden is Maczek and to his right, General Klimecki. The British Liaison Officer appears to be from the Irish Guards (buttons in fours and the Order of Saint Patrick on the cap). (*Courtesy of Janusz Jarzembowski*)

Lieutenant General Anders addresses the First Polish Armoured Division alongside General Rudnicki and invited guests. (*Courtesy of Janusz Jarzembowski*)

Awards presentation: Anders awards Lieutenant General Guy Simonds the Order of the Virtuti Militari (Silver Cross), General Crocker to his right – others unknown. (*Courtesy of Janusz Jarzembowski*)

General Anders, late 1960s, possibly at the Royal Albert Hall or Olympia. (*Courtesy of Janusz Jarzembowski*)

Awards ceremony presentations by Anders – figures in image unknown and from various units. However, note the figure nearest the camera is wearing the badge of 10th Dragoons regiment. Shoulder straps seem to indicate three bars for a Lance Sergeant and three stars for Captain. (*Courtesy of Janusz Jarzembowski*)

A Mass is held. Left to right: Simonds, unknown, Anders, Crocker, second row middle, Maczek, on his left (bald head) Lieutenant Colonel Ludwik Antoni Stankiewicz, Chief of Staff First Polish Armoured Division. (*Courtesy of Janusz Jarzembowski*)

Song sheets of the song 'The Red Poppies on Monte Cassino' in memory of the Polish sacrifice in the final battle for Monte Cassino. (*Courtesy of Janusz Jarzembowski*)

Souvenir complete with Polish symbolism. (*Courtesy of Janusz Jarzembowski*)

Anders in conversation with Field Marshal Alexander – interpreter centre. Taken from a personal album of a Polish soldier. (*Courtesy of Janusz Jarzembowski*)

the Polish Army or Second Polish Corps; it was extremely unlikely as they would have had to be screened by Allied security forces, while Anders' attitude towards ex-Wehrmacht Poles should be noted. The Poles cite security fears for the men's families back in Poland but the fact that once more Poles were being screened in separate camps makes it clear that Anders and his commanders did not trust Poles who surrendered to them and certainly would not let them anywhere near the frontline in Italy.[17] Anders preferred to fight with the men he could trust, even if they were in short supply; put simply, Anders could not risk the possibility of allowing himself and his men to be betrayed by their countrymen who had served in the German army. It is interesting to note that Field Marshal Alexander in his memoirs wrote that Anders once came to him and said that he had a problem as Polish 2nd Corps was only permitted 100,000 men and that he now had 120,000 men. This astounded Alexander as he knew that since the fighting for Cassino the Poles had taken large casualties but Anders told him that the numbers had been made up by Poles who had been serving in the German armed forces captured by Polish troops.[18] This may have been so, but again it is extremely unlikely that these men served on the frontline as Anders seemed unwilling to trust them among his forces in Italy. Davies provides another side to this story as he relates how 176 ex-members of SS 14th Waffen Grenadier Division (1st Galician) captured by the Allies in Italy were screened and judged to be fit to join Polish Second Corps.[19] There are many twists and turns of how Ukrainians from Poland served the Germans quite willingly and by 1945 many things had changed in the collective thinking, especially regarding who were Poland's enemies. To be frank, a review of the archival literature of Polish activities suggests that Polish personnel who had been captured in Italy, and then served in Italy with Polish Second Corps are more myth than fact.

Kochanski gives a comprehensive review of the battle for Monte Cassino as there was more about the fighting than the Polish capture of it because there had been several previous attempts to capture the monastery before the Poles prevailed. The Monte Cassino massif totally dominates the Rapido and Liri valleys and is a natural defensive position. A feature of the massif is Monastery Hill and the great and vast Benedictine monastery which can be seen everywhere in the area. Equally, from this position and the surrounding high ground the German defenders, predominately paratroopers, could see every move of the

Allies in the valleys below. As a result the Germans, almost at will, shelled Allied operations in the area. Two hills, Castle Hill and Hangman's Hill, defended the approaches to the monastery. Behind Monastery Hill ran Snakeshead Ridge and below that a gorge (also known as Cavendish Road) along which it might have been possible to bring armoured formations. The Germans certainly recognised this possibility. The rear of Monastery Hill was in full view of Germans positioned on the dominating heights of Monte Caira.[20] The entire position appeared to be impregnable, at least from the ground, but it still had to be taken as it brought the entire Allied advance through Italy to a halt. Fred Majdalany, who wrote one of the earliest comprehensive studies of the battles for Monte Cassino, noted that the mountains around the area made for a difficult terrain as their slopes were made up of hard volcanic material with boulders strewn about. Furthermore, there were gorse thickets which gave good cover, while the entire region was riven with ravines and gullies. The nature of the slopes precluded any hope of digging in and it was only the defending Germans, who had had three months to blast holes in the rock, enlarge existing caves and create new ones using dynamite, who were able to create excellent defensive positions. On the other hand the attackers had little cover, if at all, and no paths, merely goat tracks, which meant that all supplies had to be brought up by mule.[21]

However G.A. Shepperd asserts that if the Allies had bombed the final slopes before Via Casilina, where German paratroopers were desperately holding out, the monastery at Monte Cassino could have been by-passed because the slopes had a better vantage point and dominated routes northwest of Monte Cassino.[22] If this is true, it would have saved thousands of lives and casualties, as well as preventing the razing of the monastery and the towns and villages in the surrounding area owing to allied bombing and the resultant fighting which lasted for several months.

The first assault against the Cassino position was made by the 135th Infantry Regiment of the US 34th Division on 1 February 1944. The Americans advanced along the line of Snakeshead Ridge towards Monte Calvario, also known as Point 593. This was a steep-sided hill about 2,000yds. from the monastery. Units from 135th Infantry Regiment also advanced along the parallel Phantom ridge towards Colle Sant' Angelo. The Germans strongly counterattacked the Americans. By 11 February it was clear that this operation was a failure; no advance could be made and the first battle for Cassino was abandoned.

The presence of the monastery on its lofty perch played tricks on the minds of Allied troops as it seemed indomitable. The Germans had promised the abbot of the monastery that they would not reinforce the building itself, but the hills around it became a warren of dugouts, mortar pits and artillery emplacements. On 15 February 1944 the monastery was bombed by the US 15th Strategic Air Force and totally destroyed. The abbot left for Rome with his grievances about the bombing and the Germans reinforced the ruins of the monastery.[23] The bombing of the building actually made it easier for the Germans to defend as they created defensive points within the rubble. A major problem for the Allies was the lack of information about the monastery and how it had been constructed. General Tuker, commanding officer of 4th Indian Division, on learning from the Americans that Monastery Hill was the key to the position at Cassino, went to see what was confronting the Allies. Like everybody else who was confronted with this position in 1944 Tuker seemed to have been hypnotised by the brooding dominance of the abbey. Tuker sought information about the monastery but there was little in the way of intelligence concerning Monte Cassino. Tuker was not one to give up and eventually, after scouring bookshops in Naples, finally came up with a book dating back to 1879 which gave some details of the construction of the monastery at Monte Cassino.

The monastery had been converted into a fortress during the nineteenth century and Tuker noted in a memorandum to his corps commander, General Freyberg, that the main gate had massive timber branches in a low archway, which consisted of large stone blocks measuring 9 to 10 metres long. The gate was the only way into the monastery. The walls were about 150ft. high, made of solid masonry, and 10ft. thick at the base. Overall the monastery should be considered a modern fortress; it was thought that even a 1,000lb bomb would be next to useless and anything that military sappers might attempt would be futile. It was not even known at the time if the Germans were actually in possession of the monastery or not.[24] There were further observations about Monte Cassino itself: it was a 1,700ft. high mountain with rocky sides and a zigzag arrangement of twisting roadways for five miles on one face of the mountain. This offered shelter and mobility for tanks and guns with the advantage lying with defending artillery, all of this topped with the monastery. The most important military advantage of Monte Cassino was observation: even though a battalion of soldiers could be housed there, a single soldier with binoculars and a wireless set could be just as effective directing fire of any number of artillery guns from his post. Therefore a trained observer was more effective in this case than a battalion of soldiers.[25] This was the problem that confronted Allied soldiers of all nations as they pressed home attacks against Monte Cassino at great cost in 1944.

The second battle for Cassino was an offensive by the 4th Indian Division and 2nd New Zealand Division against the Monte Cassino massif. 4th Indian Division followed the American route from the previous attack, while the New Zealanders were to cross the river Rapido north of Sant' Angelo, capture the town of Cassino and open up Highway 6 in anticipation of an advance by the US 1st Armoured Division. The attack was timed to take advantage of the bombing of the monastery, but little progress was made. On 18 February the assault was called off. The third battle for Cassino began on 15 March and again the New Zealanders and the Indians were involved. Castle Hill and Hangman's Hill were captured but Monastery Hill was stoutly defended by the German 1st Parachute Division and any advance by the Allies was prevented. Higher on the massif tanks from 20th Armoured Brigade had been carefully moving along the Gorge when they were spotted by the enemy and wiped out. In two battles at Cassino the New Zealanders lost 1,600 men and the 4th Indian Division lost over 3,000 men.[26] On 23 March the offensive was called off.

After the three failed attempts to capture the Monte Cassino massif, General Alexander began to plan Operation DIADEM. This attack was to be more adventurous and was part of an advance on a twenty-mile front by the British 8th Army advancing on the right, while the French Expeditionary Force under General Alphonse Juin was in the centre and the US 5th Army commanded by General Mark Clark advanced on the left. On 24 March Leese met Anders with the outline of the plan; it was projected that 2nd Polish Corps might be involved in the coming offensive. It was proposed that the Poles would attack the Monte Cassino massif and capture the monastery. This was to be followed up with an advance on German reserves in the village of Piedimonte on the Senger Line or 'Hitler Line'.

Anders was given ten minutes to consider this proposal. Kochanski considers that perhaps Leese was offering Anders a chance to refuse the task, one which had defeated the forces of several nations while Anders only had a limited force available to him. The New Zealand commander, Lieutenant General

Sir Bernard Freyberg, had already refused to risk his own force, which, like Anders', was reduced in size. Freyberg was no coward and had been awarded the Victoria Cross, the Distinguished Service Order and three bars to this award in addition to being wounded several times in the First World War, but his men had twice been through the mincer at Cassino and perhaps enough was enough. Anders however, being politically aware of the glory and positive publicity the Poles would gain if they were successful, was more willing to take on the task.

Anders' thinking was that even though Monte Cassino seemed to be an impregnable fortress which had caused the deaths of thousands of Allied soldiers as they attempted to capture it, if he refused to accept the task, 2nd Polish Corps would be wasted in the Lire Valley, where they would still take heavy casualties but over a longer period of fighting because the battle in and around the Cassino area would continue. But if the Poles captured the position, it could only aid their quest to return home because world attention would be focussed on them. Anders agreed to take on the task and was prepared to accept losses of around 3,500 men. Sosnkowski, who was in Italy at the time, was less enthusiastic and told Anders that in his opinion 2nd Polish Corps was too weak to carry out the offensive. Sosnkowski suggested that 2nd Polish Corps should either operate with British 13th Corps in the Liri Valley, or at least request the reinforcement of an infantry brigade as well as more artillery. Leese gave the Poles more artillery but not the infantry.

Anders set about planning how he would conduct the attack on Monte Cassino and visited those generals who had commanded divisions in the previous attacks. Anders found Freyberg and General Charles Keightley, commander of British V Corps, very helpful and cooperative. On 7 April 1944 Anders flew over the massif itself to see what he could learn, as well as studying reconnaissance photographs and topographical maps with his staff. Ground reconnaissance was impossible as the Germans overlooked the entire area and so detailed knowledge of their defences remained unknown. A staff officer, Colonel Piatkowski, noted that there was nothing which could be considered to be orthodox defences in the German positions. On 5 May a German deserter described the German defences to the Poles. From information gleaned from the deserter, Anders concluded that the enemy defences were basically two rings joined to form a figure eight. The first ring ran from Massa Albaneta,

Phantom Ridge, Colle Sant' Angelo to Albaneta Farm, the second from Massa Albaneta to Colle d'Onofrio and included Monastery Hill.

From this information Anders decided that at least half of one of the defensive rings had to be captured in a single attack. He identified two targets: Point 593 and Colle Sant' Angelo. Each of his divisions was to take one each before an attack on the monastery itself could be attempted. 5th Kresy Division was to hold Monte Castellone with a single brigade as well as take Phantom Ridge and advance on to take Colle Sant' Angelo in addition to capturing nearby hills. This would then put the division in position to cover the operations of 3rd Carpathian Division which was to attack Point 593 and the Massa Albaneta before moving onto an attack against the monastery. It would seem that 5th Kresy Division were being required to do a lot.

During the night 23-24 April, 2nd Polish Corps moved into positions. The Poles filled the Rapido valley with smoke to obscure the moonlight and then contrived to camouflage their artillery positions, traffic and storage dumps from the enemy. British soldiers took the Poles around the battle positions at night and put them in the picture. The British noted that the Poles hated the Germans. This attitude dominated the Polish outlook for the coming offensive. Conditions at the Front were appalling as there was a perpetual shortage of water and rations and to add to this discomfort the Poles lay in shallow foxholes surrounded by decomposing corpses from earlier fighting. To intensify this vision of misery, the Germans shelled the area nonstop. However, the Poles were able to take advantage of the previous attacks against Monte Cassino. By May the problem of supply in the mountains had been largely overcome by 4th Indian Division who developed the existing original primitive goat tracks into proper trackways, useful to supply a modern army. Prior to Polish Second Corps' attack, huge ammunition dumps were established near their forward positions. Furthermore, the Polish attack was not a limited assault but one part of a concentrated assault along the entire front. Even so, conditions remained difficult and the Poles endured the worst of them.[27]

Before the Polish infantry attack on Monte Cassino went in, there was an intense artillery barrage to try to soften up the defending Germans. The artillery could not see their targets because the mountains were so steep that German positions could not be identified. Even anti-aircraft guns were pressed into action owing to the acute elevation of their guns. After realising that shells were only bursting if they hit something hard, the artillery adjusted their fuses in the hope that the shells would burst in the air and shower German trenches with shell splinters and shrapnel. After the first day of fighting it was learned from German prisoners that the artillery bombardment had come as a great surprise to the enemy.

At 01:00 hours on 12 May the Polish infantry assault began. The attack was closely supported by tanks operating from the gorge but this was quickly halted by enemy mines and artillery. The infantry failed to occupy the entirety of Phantom Ridge and was prevented from advancing towards Colle Sant' Angelo and Point 575. Briefly, Polish infantry held Point 593 on Monte Calvario and Point 569, but German counterattacks had driven them back. It was quite clear that the Germans were well equipped and well prepared. 5th Kresy Division had received twenty per cent casualties even before they had reached the foot of Phantom Ridge at 02:30 hours, having taken twice as long as expected when the operation had been planned. Quite simply, German artillery blasted the Poles so effectively that all that they could do was lay prone and hug the ground.

Initially 3rd Carpathian Division's offensive had gone well as it took Point 593 within twenty minutes of crossing the starting line. On the right-hand side of the offensive the forward divisional battalion had to clear the gorge but 400yds. short of the farm before reaching Masse Albaneta, the attack ran into difficulties. The gorge was strongly held and covered by fire from Colle Sant' Angelo. Sappers were sent forward to clear minefields in the area but were virtually wiped out by murderous enemy fire. This left armoured support marooned as the tanks were held up by heavy gun and mortar fire. At first light, to the left of the offensive, Germans who had taken shelter came up and counter-attacked the Poles. Seven enemy counter-attacks were beaten off by the Poles at Point 569 but by 11:30 the position was lost. Furthermore, German artillery in the Belmonte-Atina area fired into the rear of the Polish attack with 'devastating effect'.[28] The slow progress of 13th Army Corps in the Liri Valley, news of German reinforcements and the high Polish casualty rate persuaded Anders to issue orders to return to the start line.

The high casualty rate shocked the Poles and the long line of jeeps bringing in the Polish wounded seemed endless. The temporary graveyard appalled those who went to seek the graves of their fallen comrades and were confronted with more burials than they were comfortable with. Anders, when he visited

Leese, was visibly traumatised and Leese responded with great sympathy. He also told Anders that the lack of reinforcements available to the Poles meant that they could only fight one more battle, but at present they were to take a few days out of the line to recover before attacking again.

Leese visited Anders at 2nd Polish Corps HQ at 15:00 hours on 12 May and expressed the view that he was satisfied with the progress of the fighting at Cassino. He made particular tribute to the Poles saying that they had made a valuable contribution by inflicting heavy casualties on German paratroopers and had prevented them from helping elsewhere on the front. Leese told Anders that he did not anticipate the Polish attack being resumed until at least the night of 14-15 May. Anders told Leese that he would like an artillery barrage to precede any such attack possibly beginning at about 04:00 hours, bombarding the enemy for an hour and then the infantry would begin their attack at 05:00. Anders' reasoning was that it would give both the artillery and infantry their chance to see objectives and fire tasks. Leese agreed.

Leese however did urge caution and patience as he told Anders that he intended that 13 Corps should advance before the Poles attacked once more. He requested that the Poles should carry out 'active patrolling'; Anders agreed and outlined his orders for such work. He also requested more 4.2 in mortar ammunition be allotted to 2nd Polish Corps. Mortars were essential in the fighting in the hilly and mountainous terrain. The following day Leese once more visited, discussing and approving Anders' plan for attack. Leese outlined the situation which lay before them. He told Anders that there were indications that the German 90th Parachute Division was moving south towards Monte Cassino and its area. Meanwhile, mopping up in the Liri Valley was taking its time and proceeding slowly but bridge-building in the area was going well. Leese also hoped that 4th (British) Division would soon be able to get into striking distance of Highway 6 (Route 6) so as to attack at the same time as 2nd Polish Corps. Leese was also getting 13 Corps to move 78th Division forward towards the river Liri.

At 11:30 hours on 14 May 1944, Tac (Tactical) Army phoned Brigadier Frith to ascertain the deadline by which 2nd Polish Corps needed to be informed whether the proposed attack was to be carried out or not. Anders and Colonel Wisniowski replied '22:00'. This information was passed onto Eight Army via Major Bruce, Liaison Officer, by phone. Delay seemed to be the order of the day because on 15 May at 18:45 hours, Tac Army once more rang Brigadier Frith and once more postponed the Polish attack. This postponement was due to a very limited advance being achieved by 78th Division.[29]

On 16 May 1944 at about 16:30 hours General Kirkman, CO 13th Corps, arrived with his G.1. (General Staff Officer, Grade 1, usually of lieutenant-colonel rank) to see Anders who was absent at the time as he was with 5th Kresy Division. Owing to Anders not being available Kirkman went with Brigadier Frith to see Colonel Wisniowski, BGS (Brigade General Staff) 2nd Polish Corps. Kirkman informed Wisniowski that it would not be possible for 2nd Polish Corps to join forces with 13th Corps to launch a combined attack on the Cassino area. The intention was to attack the next day, 17 May. Kirkman then outlined his plan to Wisniowski. The start line was to be at PYCHLEY with the infantry scheduled to cross the line at 07:00 hours. The first objective of the offensive was to be some 300yds. north of FERNIE. The second objective was to be BEDALE (all of these are objective codes, not clearly defined in existing archives but the overall mission is quite clear in the narrative) with the final objective being the seizure and holding of Route 6 in the area.

After joining up with 2nd Polish Corps the intention of the objective was a defensive 'cutting off' of Cassino and area. When this was achieved Kirkman wanted the Guards Brigade and 4th Division to move in and 'mop up' Cassino. Anders arrived back at his post just after Kirkman had outlined the above plan of attack. Kirkman put Anders in the picture regarding the proposed offensive and Anders added his view of the plan. Anders had wanted to attack at 05:00 hours following an artillery barrage of an hour's duration against enemy positions. However, Anders agreed with Kirkman's idea and decided to conform to it, which meant an artillery barrage beginning at 06:00 hours and finishing at 07:00 when the infantry attack could begin. Kirkman was grateful for Anders' compliance and then a fuller plan was discussed. After Kirkman left, Anders asked Brigadier Frith to go to Eighth Army, explain to Army Command the change of timings and to obtain agreement to the Kirkman-Anders' plan. Firth visited Tac Army where he discussed the matter with Leese, who was entirely in agreement with the plan; indeed he considered it to be the best plan yet for an assault against Monte Cassino.[30]

On 17 May at 07:00 hours, 2nd Polish Corps renewed their offensive. The plan was more or less the same as the previous operation but its timing was to coincide with an attack by 13th Corps in the hope that the German artillery might be forced to split its defensive firepower. During the night prior to the morning attack the Poles had sent a reconnaissance patrol, about a company in strength, out to the Phantom Ridge position and after some confused fighting the position was taken. Initially progress was slow as the troops were still exhausted from the previous fighting. One of the main things to hamper the Poles was the necessity of carrying large amounts of hand grenades in addition to the usual infantryman's equipment for battle. The grenades proved essential in close quarter fighting. By the end of the first day the Poles had broken the German northern defensive ring and had captured Colle Sant' Angelo and Point 593. However the Polish position remained precarious.

The British took great interest in the Polish progress during 17 May. At 12:15, Army Command phoned Brigadier Firth for an update, Anders was kept informed. At 13:40 Leese arrived to see 2nd Polish Corps and Anders put him in the picture; the fighting was extremely hard but was going better than expected. The Poles were counterattacking from the west on Colle Sant Angelo but this required air support which seemed difficult to get. Colonel Kent G.1. (Ops) Tac Army arranged aerial support. Leese then outlined the situation on the rest of the front: 78th Division had captured their secondary objectives but could not get onto the road until the slopes of Monte Cassino had been cleared. 4th Division had got their carriers onto Highway 6 south and southeast of Monte Cassino. The Canadian Corps had moved towards the enemy while Goums (French North African troops) were reported to have either cut the enemy line or were in a position to deny the enemy the Liri-Pico route. It also transpired that 26th and 29th Panzer Divisions were still in the Rome area and that there was little sign of them moving southwards towards the fighting at Cassino. During the afternoon Anders asked Frith to telephone Army Command with a request that 78th Division should advance to the road and possibly advance to the Villa Santa Lucia Valley to help threaten the rear of the German Paratroop Division which was holding up the advance of 2nd Polish Corps. Army Command stated that at the moment this was not possible, but that 13 Corps would do all in their power to assist the Poles using supporting fire.[31] Colonel Klemens Rudnicki (2ic), 5th Kresy Division, recalled that Polish casualties had been enormous with much of the ammunition used up, leaving more or less nothing to fight with. There was also confusion in the Polish ranks as platoons and battalions had got hopelessly mixed up due to heavy fighting and the ensuing chaos this had brought about. Rudnicki was uncertain what dawn would bring.

However, during the night of 17-18 May, the commander of German Tenth Army, General Heinrich Vietinghoff-Scheel spoke to Kesselring. The two men agreed that the German position at the Monte Cassino monastery was untenable and so throughout the night the Germans began to withdraw from the monastery and area. At 08:00 hours 18 May, a Polish patrol cautiously approached the ruins of the monastery and discovered all was quiet. At 10:20, after a patrol had carefully checked the area, an improvised Polish flag (pennant of 12th [Podolski] Lancers) was raised by the patrol.[32] The vast sentinel had finally fallen and a Polish flag flew over it. The Polish victory coupled with considerable British progress in the Liri valley meant that the daunting Gustav Line was broken and that the way to Rome was open, but the war in Italy was not yet over. There was still plenty of fighting yet to come but Polish symbolism was clear; the Polish casualties were 3,779 dead, wounded and missing.[33] However, Parker observes that once the advance up the Liri Valley began, the monastery could well have been bypassed or contained. There had been no need for the Poles to attack it again; the fresh Polish attack had been for either psychological or political reasons rather than any genuine tactical reason.[34] It was certainly most fortunate for 2nd Polish Corps that the Germans withdrew from the Monte Cassino area because it was unlikely that the Poles would have enjoyed victory and might well have been destroyed as a military formation, given the lamentable report of Lieutenant Colonel Rudnicki.

Anders immediately contacted Sosnkowski giving him the news of the victory at Cassino. He gave a précis of the fighting to his Commander-in-chief mentioning a splendid foe, difficult terrain and hellish fighting but victory had been granted owing to the heroism of the soldiers. Anders also paid tribute to Allied cooperation and the splendid aerial support received during the fighting. Anders was able to report that the spirit and morale of the Polish Army in general – not just his own men – had shot up. Of course the fighting had not been without its casualties, including senior commanders. Anders listed those that had been killed: Colonel Kurek, Lieutenant Colonel Kamiński, Lieutenant Colonel Fanzlau, Major Rojek and Major Stojewski; senior officers wounded: Colonel Peszek, Lieutenant Colonel Domoń and Lieutenant Colonel

Stoczkowski. Anders was certain that most of the wounded would be able to return to their duties in time.[35] Leese was swift to congratulate Anders and sent a personal telegram expressing his extreme pleasure at the Polish victory in which he gave the Poles full credit for the victory at Monte Cassino.[36] A few days later Anders received a message to the effect that King George VI passed on his congratulations for the victory at Cassino and had made Anders a Companion of the Order of the Bath. General Alexander decorated Anders with the award in the name of the king.[37] Anders was to receive many plaudits in May 1944; one can only wonder at the speed he was censored and more or less ignored within twelve months.

Chapter 7

Italy after Monte Cassino

Despite the victory at Cassino and the opening of the way towards Rome, the war in Italy was far from over; at 11:00 on 18 May 1944, or within an hour of the notification that Monte Cassino had fallen, Leese was at 2nd Polish Corps' HQ and briefing Anders. Leese told Anders that 78th Division was pushing on westwards with armoured units in the vanguard in order to reach the Adolf Hitler Line. The Canadian Corps hoped to get to the Hitler Line by dusk the same day. Fifth Army was also doing well and had taken control of the Itri-Pico Road. Leese reported that elements of 26th Panzer Division were in the Pontecorvo area. Leese gave 2nd Polish Corps the task of mopping up the Cassino Massif but also to patrol to Ponto Corno and Villa Santa Lucia with the ultimate aim of capturing Piedimonte. Brigadier Frith raised the question of forward areas for Polish artillery somewhere southwest of Cassino as they would soon be out of range for operations. Leese agreed that this had to be addressed and told Anders to address the problem with Brigade Royal Artillery and Central Command Royal Artillery 13 Corps. Leese hoped that once the Hitler Line was broken; he could rest 2nd Polish Corps for three to four weeks in order to refit. Anders expressed his pleasure at this news and said that it would be adequate for the Corps to prepare for further action.[1] When 2nd Polish Corps did enter Piedimonte three days later, Leese was ecstatic and sent his congratulations to Anders writing: 'This action will materially effect [sic] the enemy resistance for the Hitler Line.'[2] During the first week of June, Leese expressed his thoughts regarding the conduct of the Italian Campaign in a memorandum. Leese considered that the first phase of the campaign was over as Fifth Army, on the left hand side of the operational theatre, had entered Rome. On the right hand side, Eighth Army had made history by breaking the Gustav Line, capturing Cassino and Monastery Hill. This was swiftly followed up by the breaking of the Adolf Hitler Line; the close pursuit shattered several German divisions and had prevented the enemy from reorganising. Fifth and Eighth Armies had jointly won a great victory. According to Leese the enemy was thoroughly disorganised and 'on the run'. The Germans needed to gain time and try to delay the Allied advance using stubborn rear-guard tactics, demolition and minefields. The Allies' task was to prevent this and to harry the enemy at all times, keeping them on the move day and night as 'every hour gained, every German killed or captured brings nearer the annihilation of the German Army in Italy'.[3] The capture of Rome went almost unnoticed because it was overshadowed by the Allied landings in Normandy; Operation OVERLORD, or the 'D-Day landings'.

One gets the impression from the above narrative and observations that after Cassino and up to the capture of Rome, fighting in Italy somehow got easier. This is definitely not true if one examines the operations at a more local level. An example of this more localised fighting concerning individual units is that of 'Children of Lwow' 6th Armoured Regiment, 2nd Polish Corps. On 17 May 1944 at 18:30 hours, 3rd Squadron of 6th Armoured Regiment was ordered to move overnight closer to the Front in the Santo Michael area. Once there half of the squadron moved to the river Rapido to provide covering fire for the right wing of 2nd Polish Corps advance across the river. The next morning the remainder of 6th Armoured Regiment moved to its holding area around Santo Vittore in anticipation of a coming offensive.

During the night of 19-20 May, Lieutenant Colonel Henryk Świetlicki, CO of 6th Armoured Regiment received new orders for forthcoming operations from Brigade. 6th Armoured Regiment under the command of Lieutenant Colonel Bobiński was to attack the town of Piedimonte with infantry support from 18th Infantry Battalion and artillery support from a battery of field artillery from 7th Anti-Tank Regiment as well as units from 9th Anti-Aircraft Regiment. Sappers were also made available for this offensive.

The attack against Piedimonte was in three parts. During the night of 19-20 May 1944 3rd Squadron was reunited with 6th Armoured Regiment and at 05:00 hours on 20 May, the entire regiment left Santo Vittore and moved to the region of Monte Scholastic about two kilometres west of the monastery at Monte Cassino. The three operational directions of 6th Armoured Regiment were: 'A' – one kilometre east of the town of Cassino; 'B' – in the S. Vittore area and 'B2' – in the Venafro area. The tank squadrons received further orders: 2nd Squadron was to support a British infantry battalion from 21st Indian Brigade.

1st Squadron was to give covering and support fire for this joint offensive in addition 1st Squadron also had to capture and occupy the section of Route 6 to Piedimonte. By 15:15 hours both squadrons had reached 3rd Squadron's position and had moved onto their operations.

The operational CO, the artillery observer, platoon commanding team, as well as the communications officer all operated from the tanks of 1st Squadron. Communications between the Polish armour and the Indian infantry was coordinated by Second Lieutenant Franciszek Haluszczak operating from his tank as part of 3rd Squadron. As the operations began the Polish tanks moved swiftly towards their operational objectives. Three tanks from 4th Platoon 3rd Squadron went to the front of the formation in order to protect 3rd Squadron's right flank as it moved towards Piedimonte.

Within fifteen minutes of leaving the Start Line 3rd Squadron had reached its first objective: the route linking Piedimonte to Route 6. Infantry supported by tank fire moved towards the road as they tried to scout ahead to see what opposition, if any, lay ahead of them. They soon found out what lay ahead as enemy artillery shells rained down on them. The German artillery was trying to separate the infantry from the armour. 1st and 3rd Platoons from 3rd Squadron were still about 60yds from Route 6 and found entry onto the highway was almost impossible owing to enemy fire which also hampered the Polish ability to keep in communication with each other.

Meanwhile, 2nd Squadron found they had advanced too far and were enduring heavy artillery fire so had to be ordered to withdraw to safety. Radio communication in 2nd Squadron also broke down while two of the tanks became stranded. One of the tanks was then hit by two anti-tank shells and set alight. Two of the tank's crew, Sergeant Baran and Trooper Jaremkiewicz, were rescued. Near houses along Route 6 the CO of 2nd Squadron's tank was hit by several rounds of anti-tank artillery and caught fire. Cadet Officer Silberberg, carrying his CO's map case managed to leap from the blazing tank along with Lieutenant Masztak.

In the fighting around Route 6, British infantry also suffered heavy casualties as they tried to winkle out enemy machinegun nests which were frequently well dug-in and well positioned. Many of the Germans were veterans of the Russian Front including Stalingrad; the British had fought largely in the deserts of North Africa and had little experience of urban fighting, while many Poles had had little if any experience of combat. Even those Poles with combat experience, of which many were now senior commanders, had never experienced anything like the close-quarter action of Italy. The advantage lay with the Germans. Even so the Poles remained determined to play their part.

Tanks from 6th Armoured Regiment fired on German positions while 2nd Squadron sent out two tanks to reconnoitre the area. One tank moved along Route 6, the other northwards. The reconnaissance patrol came under anti-tank fire as well as discovering the burnt-out remains of a tank. After making contact with the enemy, 1st Squadron brought in thirty enemy prisoners, but 4th Platoon of 1st Squadron failed in trying to find an entry point into Piedimonte which would allow for the entrance of armour. The fact that 4th Platoon had exhausted all of their ammunition and was nearly out of fuel when it returned bore witness that 4th Platoon had made very aggressive attempts in trying to gain entry to Piedimonte.

Polish records show that there was heavy enemy artillery fire later, with loud reports all around reinforced by machinegun fire and mortars, all attacking the Polish move. The Poles requested that the British infantry try to deal with the entrenched German defensive positions; the Polish tanks could continue to fire but always needed infantry support for such a situation. Infantry was nearby but the situation was tense. Lieutenant-Colonel Świetlicki noted that several enemy soldiers were in an area near Piedimonte and so gave orders for the area to be checked. The result was a haul of thirty-two prisoners. Between 22:00 and midnight the Polish tanks withdrew to the rear of the battle lines in order to refuel and rearm their tanks, receive water and no doubt eat something as well as rest. This lasted until 04:00 hours, 21 May. The first day's fighting had cost 6th Armoured Regiment one dead officer, a squadron commander as well as seven dead ORs. One OR was wounded.

At 06:00 hours, 21 May, 6th Armoured Regiment with its own artillery support and with British infantry returned to battle. German defence was strong and Polish casualties were high; this included 6th Armoured Regiment's CO, Lieutenant-Colonel Świetlicki being seriously wounded as well as five other officers and four ORs. Second Lieutenant Stanisław Kałucki died as he was being medic-evacuated; 1st and 2nd Squadrons withdrew to about a kilometre to the rear between Monte Cassino and Route 6 where they were hidden from enemy observation. During this time the CO of 3rd Squadron received orders to capture Piedimonte.

The plan was that 3rd Squadron, in conjunction with infantry units which were holding the countryside to the east of Piedimonte, were to attack and capture Piedimonte. A further eighty men from 18th Rifle Battalion with another eighty from 12th Ulan Regiment (Podolski Lancers) were also assigned to the offensive against Piedimonte. At 11:30 hours half of 3rd Squadron under the command of Captain Alfred Kuczak-Pilecki moved onto the offensive from the southeast of Piedimonte. The remaining half commanded by Captain Mihułk gave supporting fire to Kuczak-Pilecki's group as the moved along Route 6. As Mihułk's group began to cross the route, which linked Route 6 to Piedimonte, they came under heavy enemy anti-tank fire and lost three tanks. Four ORs were killed on the spot while an officer and a single OR were wounded. Mihułk's group withdrew from the area and took up another position. From this post they returned to giving supporting fire for Kuczak-Pilecki's offensive; the fighting continued for another half hour, by this time a further three Polish tanks were destroyed. There appeared to be no way to get into Piedimonte, but the Poles continued to try and lost another two tanks. Kuczak-Pilecki's group, however, found what they thought might be a way into the town.

Night fell; the remaining tanks from 3rd Squadron with their infantry support guarded the area around Piedimonte. Seven tanks from 1st Squadron joined 3rd Squadron at 04:00 hours they sought to hold the land taken. At 10:00 hours, 22 May, 1st and 3rd Squadron returned to the offensive along Route 6; they were joined by Lieutenant Masztak's Squadron, less infantry support. The objectives for the day were to destroy enemy positions on the western flank at Piedimonte and secure the route towards the northwest. There was a report of a 'Tiger' Regiment (Tiger 1 – Heavy German tank) on the Canadian flank which was possibly a threat to the Polish flanks.

At 14:00 hours the Poles prepared for a joint infantry and armoured offensive. The infantry came from 5th Infantry Battalion fresh from the battles for Monte Cassino and Cassino town. 5th Infantry Battalion had stormed Piedimonte, pushing their way through criss-crossed machinegun fire and received heavy casualties. Their Commander, Major Tarkowski was killed. The combined Polish assault headed directly towards the centre of the town but the streets were too small to allow for armoured operations which meant that 1st

Squadron was forced to abandon six tanks which were damaged. The squadron then tried another route but again entry was denied to them by the enemy while another three tanks were left behind, wrecked.

Lieutenant Masztak's Squadron also met with heavy enemy resistance as the Germans bombarded the Polish tanks with artillery fire, anti-tank fire, mortar fire and automatic weapons. This left one tank ablaze and two more damaged. Masztak was forced to press his reserve four tanks into action owing to the destruction of the other vehicles. During the evening 1st Squadron gave supporting fire and laid down a smoke screen so that Masztak's Squadron could withdraw to safety. During the night enemy mortar fire destroyed stocks of ammunition for the tanks' main guns; at this point the Polish and German frontlines were only 200 metres apart. 6th Armoured Regiment's casualties for 22 May 1944 were seven ORs killed, one officer and 15 ORs wounded.

At 09:00 hours 23 May Captain Kuczuk-Pilecki prepared once again to get tanks into Piedimonte and thus make an entry point for the infantry. The Polish attack was broken up as three tanks were damaged by mines. The knocked-out tanks blocked the way for the continuation of the offensive. The remaining tanks received orders to withdraw to safety, however one slid off the track which was to lead them to safety and fell into a ravine. Corporal Adam Antonik was killed and Cadet Officer Średnicki wounded. Captain Kuczuk-Pilecki raced to the scene to try to rescue the crew of the overturned tank. Corporal Dżuman and Cadet Officer Jena went with him.

The Germans watching opened fire with mortars. One of the bombs fell among the Poles and as Second Lieutenant J. Jabezyński related later, their 'beloved' commanding officer fell, mortally wounded. Lance Corporal Juliusz Matzenauer was also killed while Corporal Dżuman was wounded. A burst of machinegun fire, described as 'Spandau fire' hit the chest of the already dead Captain Kuczuk-Pilecki. The death of Kuczuk-Pilecki hit the Poles hard and they mourned him. They considered that he had died a selfless hero's death and reflected that it was only the previous night that Kuczuk-Pilecki and his men had been fighting off very strong and determined German attacks against Polish positions. Kuczuk-Pilecki's men entrusted his remains to the sanctuary of a ruined church, burnt out as a consequence of the heavy fighting that had been and was still going on. Their staunch Catholicism allowed them to believe that Mary, the Mother of Christ, would guard and guide their fallen comrades to the afterlife. It was a very emotional time for these already hardened troops as they had to bid farewell to their dead and move on; there were still battles to be fought and won before the war was over.

During the night of 23-24 May the enemy launched a heavy attack. The enemy, taking full advantage of the ruins nearby, attempted to destroy immobilised tanks. This led to a hard-fought battle and the Germans were eventually forced to withdraw. During the morning of 24 May, Major Feliks Motyka was appointed Commander of 6th Armoured Regiment. At around 11:00 hours there was a move onto the offensive in combination with Lieutenant Jadwisiak's squadron; the group's task was to cut off Piedimonte from the north. Through splendid cooperation with motorised infantry and artillery support, Jadwisiak's squadron was able to destroy many enemy positions, including knocking out two German anti-tank guns. The territory which lay before Piedimonte had not been entirely captured by 6th Armoured Regiment, but progress had been made. At 19:00 hours, Motyka's squadron returned bringing in enemy prisoners while during the night, 13th and 15th Infantry Battalions were withdrawn from the area surrounding Piedimonte. From first light on 25 May there was plenty of activity in 6th Armoured Regiment's Lines. From dawn, Polish patrols had gone out towards Piedimonte where it appeared that the Germans had withdrawn from the town. Under the ruins of the town were many dead. At 09:00 hours, 2nd Squadron was sent to an airfield at Aquino to see what enemy activity there was and to secure the area. When they returned at around midday, Piedimonte had been taken by the Poles.[4]

After the capture of Piedimonte, 2nd Polish Corps were due, as we have seen, a month or so leave away from the front line to recover their strength, re-equip and reorganise. A report from the War Office on 2nd Polish Corps operations in the Adriatic Sector explains why this did not happen. The report opened with a discussion of the general situation on the Italian Front during the latter half of May and the first half of June 1944. Events in Italy began to move rapidly during this period owing to the success of the Eighth Army in the Liri Valley and that of the Fifth Army along the Mediterranean Coast, which made possible for a general move along the Italian Front. The rapid Allied advance made the German position precarious; first the enemy centre was threatened, followed by a threat to its left flank. As a result the Germans began to withdraw.

The first drive forward was made on Eighth Army's right flank by 10 Corps which up to that time had been in a defensive position. 2nd New Zealand Division started the drive on 25 May heading in the direction of Belmonte-Atina, which resulted in the capture of Sora on 1 June 1944. This advance pushed out 2nd Polish Corps, which was in the Cassino-Pass Corno area. As a result, 2nd Polish Corps passed from Eighth Army's command to Army GP Reserve. The last Polish units left the Cassino area on 31 May 1944. They were then concentrated in the Campobasso area for a rest period with the exception of 2nd Armoured Brigade which was in the Prata area. The original intention was to have rested the Poles for a month, as well as a proposed reorganisation and the bringing up of reinforcements. However this period was reduced to a mere two weeks owing to the rapid developments on the Italian Front. After being rested, 2nd Polish Corps was to be sent to the Adriatic Sector where they were to take up positions.

The successes gained in the advance on Rome and its capture meant that there was a need and desire to take full advantage of the situation. This led to the commander of the Italian Front to personally ask Anders if 2nd Polish Corps could relieve at least one Indian Division at the earliest opportunity. The Indian troops were urgently needed in the fighting in mountains to the north of Rome. They were the only troops in Italy except for the Poles trained for this type of warfare because the French Expeditionary Corps, which consisted largely of mountain troops, had been diverted to their homeland to take part in Operation DRAGOON, the Allied drive from the southern French coast as part of the campaign to liberate France.[5] Anders agreed to this request even though it meant that one of his divisions would be deprived of much needed rest. As the Allies advanced ever northwards, the Germans fought a brilliant rear-guard action and destroyed much as they retreated – as well as laying extensive minefields over a large area. Eventually the advance came to a halt and defensive positions were taken up. This was more or less the situation when 2nd Polish Corps took over the entire Adriatic Sector.

The first Polish units to arrive in the Adriatic Sector were those of the 3rd Carpathian Division's artillery units less one field regiment, which relieved 10th Indian Division on 5 June 1944, taking over the artillery tasks of 4th Indian sector. On 12 June 1944 the rest of the Carpathian Division started to move from its rest area and by the next day 1st Carpathian Brigade had already relieved 7th Indian Brigade (4th Indian Division) and began operating towards the Capelle-Atri region. The relief of 4th Indian Division was complete by 14 June 1944. There was a bit of fine tweaking still to be done as 2nd Carpathian Brigade arrived in the Treglio area on 14 June 1944. On 15 June a battalion from 2nd Carpathian Brigade relieved the only battalion in the 11th Indian Brigade's line at Monte Silvano. On 15 June, 3rd Carpathian Division took over 4th Indian Division's sector and so came under the command of 5th Corps. 3rd Carpathian Division was to consolidate the Guillanova-Teramo line and to patrol the immediate foreground.

There were further measures as, on 16 June, 12th Podolski Regiment relieved the Central Indian Horse (CIH) Regiment in the area Castel di Sangro (H 0954) – Sulmona (H 9483) – Opi (C 8553) and passed directly under the command of 5th Corps. More armour between 15 and 16 June, moved to the area between Ripa and Milliano while 2nd Armoured Brigade between 16 and 22 June moved to the area between Lanciano and Santo Vito. 5th Kresy Division made their move to the Castel Bordino area between the rivers Osento and Sinello beginning on 16 June and completing the move by 22 June. The Carpathian Lancers were sent to 2nd Armoured Brigade's area. On 17 June, 2nd Polish Corps assumed the command of the Adriatic sector. Apart from 2nd Polish Corps the following units were also placed under the control of Anders: CIL (*Corpo Italiano di Liberazione*) an Italian Corps of three Brigades, 1st and 2nd Brigades and the so-called Nembo Group, the entire CIL consisted of battalions: 17th and 26th Medium Regiments, Royal Artillery, two battalions of British sappers also numerous supply units. 318 Polish Fighter Reconnaissance Squadron, which had been cooperating with 5th Corps began working with 2nd Polish Corps on 17 June 1944. On 16 June 1944, 2nd Polish Corps was given a new task: the pursuit of the enemy and the capture of Ancona.

At this time, 3rd Carpathian Division had forward elements along the river Vomano with the bulk of its force in the area of Atri and Silvi; it received orders during the night of 15-16 June that it was to pursue the enemy along two axis: along coast road No. 16 and along the so-called 'Blue' Road which took the route of Atri-Notaresco-Bellante-Ancarano-Offida-Ferma-Ancona. 3rd Carpathian Division was reinforced by 11th Medium Regiment from AGRA. CIL was given the task of advancing along Route 81 towards Teramo-Ascoli then along Route 78 towards the Amandola-Macerata area. One battalion was to be detached from the main body of CIL to go to Asquila in order to secure the network of roads in the region.

This advance began on 17 June and brought the leading elements of 3rd Carpathian Division to the river Tordino. 3rd Brigade of the division actually reached Notaresco but the bulk of the brigade, as well as 2nd Carpathian Brigade, remained on the south bank of the Vomano as they could not cross owing to the destruction of bridges by the retreating Germans, as well as the river rising after recent rains. It was more or less impossible to cross until sappers arrived and erected a bridge over the swollen river. This was all part of the problem for the Allies as they advanced through Italy; the retreating Germans knew how to fight a rear guard action well. Not only did the enemy destroy wholesale anything remotely useful to the Allies; they also mined all possible approaches – including fords. The numerous minefields helped to slow down the Allied advance while the frequent rain (for which the enemy could not be blamed) helped to swell rivers and generally make life miserable for the pursuing troops. The lack of reconnaissance regiments was also felt, as such units were able to secure and assess information regarding what lay ahead more swiftly than the more orthodox formations, therefore the dearth of reconnaissance regiments meant that often advances were made into fairly unknown country. Part of the skills of reconnaissance regiments was to probe further inland and find country lanes and tracks which were quite suitable for armour or other vehicles in dry weather. Despite the difficulties which lay ahead of 2nd Polish Corps, their advance was on average fifteen kilometres a day.

On 19 June the leading battalion of 1st Carpathian Brigade captured Cossignano and its patrols reached Ripa Transone; in the same day the vanguard of 2nd Carpathian Brigade captured Colonella and its patrols crossed the river Tronto. The next day 1st Carpathian Brigade captured Fermo and then sent patrols ahead that surprised enemy sappers preparing to blow up a bridge over the river Tenna. One enemy officer and ten ORs were captured and the bridge saved. 2nd Carpathian Brigade captured Pedaso the same day. First contact with the enemy was made by 1st Brigade of 1st Armoured Cavalry Regiment along the river Chienti on 21 June when its vanguard crossed the river. On 22 June part of 3rd Battalion from the same regiment crossed the river on the Morovalle axis and attacked the enemy in the area inflicting heavy losses and then advanced to the Morovalle railway station which was approximately two kilometres north of the Chienti. As Terlicki notes, the river Chienti was a serious natural obstacle which the enemy, pursued by 3rd Carpathian Rifle Division, crossed and then defended from the far banks. The river flowed rapidly off the nearby Apennines Mountain range, was deep and near its estuary; its steep banks made it a natural defensive position but still the Poles assaulted the German positions across the Chienti as Sherman tanks of 1st Krechowcki Uhlans Regiment cautiously entered the waters of the river, becoming stranded mid-stream. [6]

This situation was not to last however, as the lack of tanks, and of Brigade Command to bring sufficient reinforcements to hold the bridgehead, allowed the enemy to counterattack during the night of 22-23 June. Polish units in advanced positions were isolated and surrounded by the enemy; they came under heavy fire and were forced to withdraw south of the river Chienti, suffering huge casualties – dead, wounded or missing – during this move. Other units from 1st Carpathian Brigade which were still north of the river also came under heavy enemy fire and were ordered to withdraw. Reconnaissance patrols along the coastal (Adriatic) sector by 2nd Carpathian Brigade confirmed the presence of the enemy and all Polish patrols were fired upon; it was clear that the Germans were still willing to put up a fight.

In conjunction with the task of capturing the port of Ancona as swiftly as possible, 2nd Polish Corps HQ issued instructions on 22 June dealing with operations by Polish formations towards the Gothic Line. 3rd Carpathian Division was to operate along the present Divisional operational axis with its main efforts being on the left-hand side of this axis. 5th Kresy Division was to be used for bypassing enemy defences from the south at Ancona and cutting off enemy forces in operations against the river Esino through Offanga to the Chiaravelle area. CIL using detached units was to secure 5th Kresy Division's left flank. The bulk of 2nd Armoured Brigade was ordered to operate on 5th Kresy Division's axis, while most of 2nd Polish Corp's artillery was to support 3rd Carpathian Division in its operations.

To ensure that 5th Kresy Division was brought up swiftly into its operational axis, a Battle Group consisting of one battalion of the Lwow Brigade, 15th Poznan Reconnaissance Regiment and an armoured squadron from 4th Armoured Regiment was sent to the left flank of 3rd Carpathian Division to the general area west of Monte Santo Giusto on 23 June. The 12th Podhalian

Reconnaissance Regiment, also operating in the same area, was placed under the command of the 5th Kresy Battle Group. Reconnaissance of the river Chienti in the Battle Group's sector revealed that the enemy was holding the line in strength.

An attack by CIL on enemy positions on 26 June was a failure. Strong enemy defences along the Chienti caused the corps command to consult with 2nd Polish Corps command in order to decide how much further operations should be conducted. 2nd Polish Corps decided that the enemy was to be smashed in a combined infantry and armoured attack. The offensive was to begin on 4 July 1944 using the combined force of 5th Kresy Division and 2nd Armoured Brigade. Prior to the proposed offensive the Poles began to conduct aggressive patrolling but on 30 June the Germans withdrew from the Chienti. On the same day at 10:00 hours, 2nd Polish Corps command issued orders for the pursuit of the enemy.

Using skilled rear-guard actions the retreating enemy slowed the Polish advance. It soon became very clear that in order to drive the Germans from positions guarding the river Potenza, greater force was needed than was at the disposal of the pursuing Polish force. Even so, during the afternoon of 30 June 1944, the Poles inflicted defeats on the enemy. At Monte Lupone for example, 3rd Carpathian Division and 5th Kresy Division captured or killed the entire enemy garrison. Despite this victory, river crossings became the greatest headache for 2nd Polish Corps because they were heavily contested as the Germans made the Poles fight for every crossing in frontal assaults. Rarely could a way be found around these crossings.

The battle for Ancona, beginning at 07:00 hours on 17 July 1944 with an armoured crossing at the river Musone was the scene of heavy fighting. The Poles suffered few casualties and the port was captured on 18 July. The capture of Ancona was extremely important as it gave the allies a large port through which supplies could be sent. During the Adriatic Campaign, the Poles captured twenty-eight enemy officers as well as 3,346 ORs of which 421 were Polish. Polish losses were sixty officers and 617 ORs killed, 221 officers and ORs wounded, while three officers and 137 ORs were missing. The Polish total casualty was 284 officers and 3,385 ORs: a grand total of 3,669. Anders' commanding officer, General Sir Oliver Leese, wrote to Anders and noted that the Poles had provided all of the jumping off points for future operations by capturing positions such as the river Metauro, the river Cesano and of course, Ancona. The capture of Pesaro was the crowning achievement of the campaign.[7] However, the fighting for the Adriatic sector was not totally over as a Polish intelligence summary, dated 28 September 1944, noted. The summary suggested that events just prior to 28 September considered that the enemy continued to regard the Adriatic sector as one of the most threatened, and feared an allied break-through. To try to prevent this, the Germans brought in fresh troops at the expense of other sectors of the Italian Front.[8]

The story of 6th 'Children of Lwow' Armoured Regiment helps to fill out what is, in many ways, a bland military report. After the capture of Piedimonte back in May 1944 the 6th Armoured Regiment was by no means at the end of its war. By 18 June 1944 the regiment was on its way towards the Adriatic Sea ready for coming battles. The regiment's tanks came by rail on freight transporters via Caserta, Benevento, Foggia, Termoli and finally to Santo Vito Marino, the last functioning railway station along the line. Once the armour was unloaded the regiment prepared once more for action. As their tanks came north by rail, the remainder of the regiment also travelled in the same direction by road along Highway 16. Over the course of several days they travelled via Pescara then Santo Benedetto, moving onto Fermo. From there, 6th Armoured Division moved towards Loreto. The Polish troops could not but help notice that even though Italian civilians welcomed them, the Italians' faces were etched with sadness and fatigue. The lot of the Italian civilian during the Italian campaign was one of misery and the end of the war could not come soon enough for them.

However, the war was set to continue and so 6th Armoured Regiment pressed on. After forcing a crossing over the river Musone, which was mined, and putting the regiment in an area about one kilometre from the north of Lorento, 6th Armoured Regiment was given the task of ejecting the Germans from nearby high ground. This offensive called for cooperation between units from 3rd Carpathian Infantry Division and the Carpathian Ulan Regiment which was operating on the right hand flank. 6th Armoured Regiment headed in the direction of Crocette and the Seranello Hills, the terrain was difficult to cover. By evening 6th Armoured Regiment had received casualties: one officer and four ORs had been wounded. During the night of 2-3 July 1944 there were sharp exchanges of artillery fire between the Poles and the Germans.

An armoured platoon from 1st Squadron, 6th Armoured Regiment seized a cemetery and buildings near Highway 16 as well as fighting off a German counterattack.

On 3 July armoured reconnaissance sent to Crocette by 6th Armoured Regiment's commanding officer discovered that the enemy was present in the town. This led to two squadrons of tanks being sent out to conduct aggressive reconnaissance towards Crocette and Seranello. This activity was to take up much of the afternoon. By 14:00 Polish infantry had cleared much of the area while the presence of Polish tanks ensured the capture of large numbers of the enemy. Even more importantly, large quantities of enemy-hand held anti-tank weapons were also captured. The capture of Crocette ensured that a large allied military presence was able to gather in the area while 6th Armoured Regiment was given new orders.

The orders were concerned with how the momentum of the offensive was to be kept up and not to give the enemy a moment's peace, thus preventing him from re-grouping or gaining time to think, plan or rest. 6th Armoured Regiment was ordered to send self-propelled guns supported by tanks in order to attack and capture the hills at Fornaci and at Casa Pigini. They were also ordered to overrun the enemy's route of retreat via Castelfildardo. 1st and 3rd Squadrons were detailed to support the self-propelled artillery and the offensive was to begin at 20:00 hours, 3 July. Tanks from 6th Armoured Regiment's CO's squadron moved out and captured the eastern suburbs of Castelfildardo. The cost to 6th Armoured Regiment for the fighting of 3 July was one officer and thirteen ORs killed as well as thirteen ORs wounded.

Throughout the next day, 4 July, 6th Armoured Regiment protected the flanks of 2nd Polish Corps as well as providing fire support from their tanks to the British armoured regiment, 7th Queen's Own Hussars. During the evening, 6th Armoured Regiment moved to their night positions at Casa Tannoni. During the night operational orders were received for the next day. 6th Armoured Regiment was to continue to work with 7th Queen's Own Hussars towards the direction of Badia in hope of moving towards the town of Osimo.

During the morning of 5 July, 6th Armoured Regiment crossed the river Tannoni using a Scissor Bridge and moved out with 2nd and 3rd Squadrons in the vanguard. Badia was already under heavy German artillery fire as the enemy defended the Ancona region. Two Polish tanks were hit by artillery fire and set ablaze. Three ORs were killed while one officer and six ORs were wounded.

Dusk fell: 1st Squadron arrived at 2nd and 3rd Squadron's positions and set about consolidating the area which had been captured that day. The infantry assisted in that task as well as helped to ensure the safety of the area during the hours of darkness. Many prisoners had been taken during the fighting and they had to be secure and detained. During the afternoon of 6 July, 6th Armoured Regiment moved to Casa Sabatini in order to receive replacements for those who had either been killed or wounded. The Polish troops were also afforded fresh and replacement equipment as well as a chance to take a short break from the fighting.

While this fighting was going on, preparations for an offensive against the port of Ancona were being made by 2nd Polish Corps. The plan was to use an 'armoured fist' (*pięści pancernej*) on the Corps' left flank. On 7 July 1944, a battle group was to be formed consisting of 3rd Armoured Squadron (6th Armoured Regiment), a platoon of Stuart tanks, a platoon of self-propelled artillery, a company of motorised infantry and a squad of sappers. The group was commanded by Major Stryjewski, (2ic) 6th Polish Armoured Regiment and the group's orders were to discover the strengths and positions of enemy fire. The Poles attacked the Germans relentlessly all day, which caused the defending Germans to reveal the locations and strength of their positions as the Poles had wanted. This was at the cost to the Poles of one wounded officer and five ORs being wounded.

During the evening of 14 July 1944, 6th Armoured Regiment moved to their next offensive. The regiment travelled via Recanati, Montefano and Santo Biaggo and finally reached the northern reaches of the Montoro region to the east of Filotrano. In order to disguise 6th Armoured Regiment's move, artillery fire was laid down in an attempt to muffle the sound of the regiment's tank engines and so not betray their movement towards their new front. The intention was to try to convince the Germans that the Polish armour had not moved at all. The tank crews wore green berets rather than their usual black ones and once they entered the new operational area the tanks were carefully dispersed and covered up with sheaves of corn. At the same time further armour was hidden in front of enemy positions in the Montoro area. The idea was to gather in secret a concentrated armoured force in the Adriatic coast area and to try to launch a shock attack against the Germans.

The plan worked well and the Germans were unaware of the Polish armoured regiments in their area. During 15 and 16 July, following careful reconnaissance patrolling and intelligent planning, an entry point for armour was identified on the river Musone and the final plans were put into place. On 17 July, 6th Armoured Regiment was to attack beyond the Monte Torto-Croce di Santo Vincenzo axis; 4th (Polish) Armoured Regiment, positioned on the right but beyond 6th Armoured Regiment's offensive, was to attack in the direction of the Della Crescia Hills. On the left of the offensive was the 7th Queen's Own Hussars Regiment. Before the main offensive began, commandos working in cooperation with a squadron from 1st Krechowicki Ulan Regiment moved at dawn to the town of Casa Nuova to discover the strength of German anti-tank artillery.

6th Armoured Regiment was supported by two companies of infantry from 15th Infantry Battalion. This was supplemented by splendid and close artillery cooperation, all underpinned by collaboration from the skies, which the allies had more-or-less cleared of enemy aircraft by 1944 in Italy. The main enemy defensive points were at: Monte Della Crescia with the centre of anti-tank defences located at Casa Nuova and Croce di Santo Vincenzo. The route towards Monte Torto, along which 6th Armoured Regiment were supposed to make their move towards their objectives, a minefield was located which would block the regiment's way. Even so, at 06:25 hours, 17 July 1944, 6th Armoured Regiment moved out, supported by artillery and aircraft. The regiment's tanks moved in a line, as if they were queuing for something, to the Musone. 2nd Squadron took the lead followed in turn by 3rd Squadron then the CO's Squadron with 1st Squadron bringing up the rear.

Once in place and ready to begin operations, the Polish tanks unleashed murderous fire and were able to advance freely. Within 200 metres of the far side of the Musone, the Poles were bringing in their first prisoners. At 09:15 hours, 3rd Squadron reported that they had reached the area of their first objective, Monte Tort, however they had been held up for some time owing to a lack of infantry support. Infantry was essential to the tanks owing to the need to clear and consolidate captured enemy territory as well as the need to liquidate threats to armour. While 3rd Squadron waited for infantry support, some of their number helped the Stuart tank crews take dozens of prisoners to the rear lines and out of danger.

Once infantry support arrived and took over the territory captured by 3rd Squadron, the tanks moved off once more and headed towards Croce di Santo Vincenzo. The axis of 3rd Squadron's advance was hampered by the terrain and heavy enemy anti-tank artillery fire which slowed and endangered the Polish advance. 3rd Squadron took the decision to go for an all-out attack against the German positions and within minutes the German positions had been knocked out. Three 75mm anti-tank guns and two heavy caterpillar-tracked towing vehicles were captured by 3rd Squadron. A platoon from 3rd Squadron reported the presence of German self-propelled artillery and tanks. After a short battle involving both 3rd and 2nd Squadron from 6th Armoured Regiment, the Poles were able to report the destruction of a 105mm artillery piece mounted on a tank as well as the destruction of two Mark III tanks and the capture Croce di Vincenzo. This operation was observed by both Anders and Sosnkowski.

1st Squadron moved onto its offensive and advanced about three kilometres to the hill at Monte Auguliano. 2nd Platoon from 2nd Squadron moved in the direction of Monte Polvergi from where they led prisoners, complete with horses and carts, away from the front. During the evening 15th Poznań Ulan Regiment arrived at 6th Armoured Regiment's position. The Ulans were en route for Monte Auguliano where they were to link up with infantry who were to help guard the tanks overnight from enemy infiltration. 6th Armoured Regiment's casualties for the day were two ORs killed and three wounded. Enemy casualties were vast and disproportionate compared with those of the Poles. The disorientated Germans surrendered in large groups and were largely overcome by the war in Italy, which is surprising given that many had fought on the Russian Front, but too much war had become just too much. The overwhelming allied firepower no doubt was another factor. However, given that the Germans had claimed racial superiority over the Slav Poles it is not surprising that many Poles jeered at these specimens of the 'Master Race'. At the point of capture they were far from this claim, but were instead shabby and frightened-looking prisoners captured by the Polish Army.

On the morning of 18 July, 1st Squadron with 15th Poznań Ulans continued to chase the enemy. It was during this time that the Squadron's CO's tank caught fire; two ORs were killed while an officer and two ORs were hurt in this incident. Meanwhile, taking advantage of a smoke screen, 1st Squadron pressed onto Monte Camerata Picena. En route, 1st Squadron destroyed a German Mark IV tank and a self-propelled gun. After passing Camerata Picena the squadron reached the river Esino and took post there. From this post they shelled enemy positions. As on previous days many prisoners were taken. The remainder of 6th Armoured Regiment later reached Camerata Picena where orders were received to establish a bridgehead on the Esino. 2nd Squadron, with firing support from 3rd Squadron, moved to find a place to cross the river but found that the enemy had heavily mined the river banks. By dusk no progress had been made in establishing a bridgehead. During the night sappers set about removing the mines so that the advance could continue at daybreak.

By 06:00 hours of 19 July, 2nd Squadron had already crossed the river and was pushing onto Chiaravelle. Despite heavy enemy anti-tank fire and unceasing artillery fire directed against 2nd Squadron, Chiaravelle fell to the Poles at about 10:30 hours. 3rd Squadron seemed very determined to press ahead and, after finding a route, seized an asphalt road and a railway track at midday that could be used to take the suburbs of the town, which were situated on the left-hand side of the offensive. In preparation for that afternoon's offensive, 1st Squadron moved to 3rd Squadron's position and, moving together, reached the fork on the route to Borghetto and Monte Santo Vito by 15:30 hours.

The Germans hiding in the area were very determined to break up the Polish offensive and, using anti-tank artillery hidden in the Chiaravelle area as well as 'tank-hunters' and machinegun nests and mortar positions, all carefully hidden, opened fire on the advancing Poles. The only purpose of the German defenders was to destroy the Polish tank crews and their infantry support. The Polish response was swift and determined however. Using overwhelming fire from their tanks and machineguns the Poles cleared the Germans out from their hidden positions in huts and hayricks. The Poles were able to destroy the German counterattack before it had really got going. The squadrons remained in the area they had captured during 18 July, overnight of 18-19 July. When they were relieved by infantry on 19 July, the armoured units were able to withdraw back to Chiaravelle. The next day, 6th Armoured Regiment left Chiaravelle and moved to the region of Santo Luigi around Offanga for nearly a month's well deserved rest and respite from battle.

During the silence of July and August the Poles prepared for their next operation. It was during this period that news came in the form of a joint statement from Sosnkowski, Anders and the Commander of Polish 2nd Armoured Brigade. The statement, dated 25 July 1944, while praising the entire Polish armoured brigade for its work and success thus far in the Italian Campaign, singled out the 'Children of Lwow' 6th Armoured Regiment for particular accolade, especially in its role in the fighting and eventual capture of the port of Anaconda.

After the capture of Senigallia 2nd Polish Corps moved to a position on the river Cesena. By this time, 16 August 1944, 6th Armoured Regiment was located close to the Front in the Borghetto area. From here the regiment was preparing to return to action between Cesena and the river Metauro as 2nd Polish Armoured Brigade had been detailed to break through a network of German defences in the area. The enemy defences had been organised in two belts in the hills running parallel between rivers there. The Poles had a plan for another armoured attack. The Polish plan was that the two enemy defensive belts were to be taken one after the other. The first objective according to the latest orders from Brigade was an attack on the German position on a hill by the Metauro. In order to execute this plan it was first necessary to capture the suburbs of Santo Constanzo from where heavy anti-tank fire had been encountered previously. This meant that there was a need to branch out in operational plans so that 1st Krechowicki Ulan Regiment had to conclude its offensive at the heights of Monte Fano in the direction of the mouth of the Metauro. While this was being done 4th (Polish) Armoured Regiment and 6th Armoured Regiment operated beyond the Rosaria-Cerasa-Hill 215 Axis.

On 18 August a battle group centred on 6th Armoured Regiment was formed. This battle group consisted of 6th Armoured Regiment, two companies of infantry from 17th Infantry Battalion, self-propelled guns from 7th Anti-Tank Regiment and a squad of sappers. At 19:00 hours, the CO of the group, Lieutenant-Colonel Feliks Motyka received his orders. The group was to capture Cerasa and then to move onto Hill 189 to link up with 4th Polish Armoured Regiment. The linking up of the two armoured regiments was to try to prevent 'friendly fire', or in other words ensure that they did not fire on each other by mistake.

The battle group moved out at 20:00 hours. It was already dark when 6th Armoured Regiment moved in front of 4th Polish Armoured Regiment's position. At 21:00 hours Motyka established a forward position. All that night, 19-20 August, German artillery shelled the Polish tanks at their posts. On 20 August 6th Armoured Regiment in order to aid 4th Polish Armoured Regiment's efforts moved onto the offensive at 07:45 hours. The offensive was preceded by an artillery barrage but even so, the spearhead of the regiment's attack quickly ran into enemy anti-tank and tank fire. Successive waves of enemy artillery struck the Polish tanks but Polish infantry continued to advance and closed in on the enemy, attacking German infantry with hand grenades. By 11:00 hours it had been learnt from enemy prisoners that there was a number of German anti-tank guns in the hills nearby and that there were four assault guns on the Rosario-Santo Angelo route towards the Metauro. Orders had been issued to the German gun crews that they were to maintain their positions as long as possible. Each German infantry company opposing the Polish assault had been issued with nine hand-held anti-tank weapons, similar to the American bazooka, as well as having two tanks in support.

The result of this information was that 6th Armoured Regiment set out to discover the whereabouts of the German defences and how best to deal with them. To this end the regiment headed towards the area of the battle group's spearhead at Hill 164 close to an armoured squadron which had been under fire from 105mm artillery guns. In spite of heavy anti-tank fire from enemy 88mm guns and 'Panther' tank fire along the Cesara-Rosario-Hill 146-Hill 137 Line, 6th Armoured Regiment pressed on. Every tank as it emerged on the horizon was hit by German anti-tank fire which meant that 6th Armoured Regiment endured its highest casualty rate to date and the casualties were very high.

The offensive had to continue and the stubborn German resistance overcome if not utterly destroyed. Seven light and four heavy artillery regiments poured concentrated fire onto German positions at Rosario, Cerasa and Hill 146. 1st Squadron 6th Armoured Regiment headed towards Rosario while 2nd Squadron made for Cerasa. Each squadron was supported by a platoon of infantry which scouted ahead following the artillery fire as it swept the German positions. However the artillery fire had limited effect on the German positions because as the infantry advanced they were met with strong enemy automatic weapon fire and mortar barrages.

1st Squadron's commander ordered 1st and 2nd Platoons to attack Rosario. With 'foot down' crossing the horizon, the tanks hurried to the embattled infantry positions and, taking advantage of smoke cover and an artillery barrage, by 16:20 had forced their way into Rosario. Most of the defending German armour was on fire while the majority of the Germans came forward to surrender to the Poles. The remainder of the German garrison was doing their best torpidly withdraw; 1st Squadron's CO requested that the artillery cease fire so that the Polish infantry could advance into the town. At the same time 2nd Squadron advanced on the right-hand side of the offensive as the infantry took many prisoners. The consolidation of the captured territory and its clearance fell to the infantry. Finally the remainder of 17th Infantry Battalion arrived and a group of armour from 6th Armoured Regiment held the captured territory in Rosaria and the fringes of Cerasa. After seizing the route in the region of Hill 141, 1st Squadron had to remain with infantry units until they were relieved. The day's fighting saw two ORs from 6th Armoured Regiment killed while two officers and two ORs were wounded. Two Sherman tanks were destroyed as were two enemy 'Panther' tanks and two self-propelled guns. Two artillery pieces mounted on tank chassis were captured by the Poles.

On 21 August 6th Armoured Regiment was left as Brigade Reserve. The British regiment, 7th Queen's Own Hussars, on the same day was already leading an offensive in the direction of Hill 215 which began at about 11:00 hours. At about 15:00 hours 6th Polish Armoured Regiment's battle group received orders to move towards 7th Queen's Own Hussars to the west of Cerasa. At around 20:00 hours 1st Platoon from 3rd Squadron was sent instructions to link up with forward elements of 5th Kresy Infantry Division who were on Hill 201, to the north of San Giorgio di Pesara. 1st Platoon's task was to find out the situation in the area where they had been sent and to find a position suitable for the establishment of an operational base for 2nd Armoured Brigade. At the end of their task the platoon had to hide overnight on both sides of no-man's land, an area of about eight kilometres, without betraying signs of a single tank of theirs being in the area, such was the secrecy of their mission and the need for surprise. Information gleaned from 1st Platoon's reconnaissance mission was given at about 14:00 to a Polish patrol at Hill 210 which then withdrew from the area. 5th Kresy Infantry Division took possession of San Giorgio di Persara the same day.

At 06:50 hours, 22 August, 6th Armoured Regiment received orders to seize Hill 215 and reconnoitre towards Montemaggiore. At 07:22 the regiment moved with one squadron, 3rd Squadron, ahead rather than the usual two squadrons moving as a vanguard. By 07:40 3rd Squadron had already passed Hill 215 and was heading towards Montemaggiore which was later captured by the Poles at a little past 09:00. At 11:30 German artillery began to shell the town and several tanks were damaged. 3rd Squadron received fresh orders to leave a single armoured platoon in Montemaggiore while the remainder were to go out and link up with the rest of the regiment who were in the area of Hill 215. The tanks remained in the area until 20:00 hours waiting for the infantry to arrive. During 22 August 1944 3rd Squadron suffered one OR killed and two tanks damaged. Between 20 and 22 August the enemy had suffered twenty-seven dead, five wounded and forty of their number taken prisoner; in terms of equipment they had lost two 105mm howitzers, many hand-held anti-tank weapons (*offenrohr* and *panzerfaust*) as well as two 'Tiger' tanks being destroyed and the destruction of a pair of self-propelled 75mm guns.

After this action several days were spent on reconnaissance missions, clearing mines from river crossings and the establishing of bridgeheads. From the Metauro on the left of 2nd Polish Corps' flank stood 5th Kresy Infantry Division which was supporting the Canadian Armoured Division. 24 August 1944 saw the formation of 5th Wilenski Infantry Brigade in anticipation of an offensive towards Monte Delle Forche in which 6th Armoured Regiment was expected to participate. At around midnight of 25-26 August a Polish artillery barrage opened up in support of the movement of Canadian armour on the left-hand side of the Polish offensive. During the night the Canadians crossed the Metauro. The Canadian crossing was then supported and held by British infantry.

During the morning of 26 August, after crossing a ford on the Metauro, 3rd Squadron moved to a waiting position in the Borgo Lucrezia area. At 14:00 hours the squadron moved onto the offensive on the axis of 14th Infantry Battalion's offensive which was assigned as Hill 124 and Monte Delle Forche. On the right-side close to this operational axis, 15th Infantry Battalion could also be found near Monte Delle Forche. 3rd Squadron operating with two platoons to the fore preceded the infantry as they moved out. In this manner within a couple of hours the formation had reached Hill 167. During this time the remainder of 6th Armoured Regiment moved to Borgo Lucrezia. The infantry with its armoured support had reached its next objective, Hill 171. With supporting tank fire, the infantry attacked the hill; operations did not cease until nightfall.

1st Platoon, 3rd Squadron drove at dusk onto Delle Forche which caused the enemy to panic and led to enemy casualties. That night, 26-27 August, was completely different as the Germans counterattacked. The Luftwaffe strafed and attacked Polish positions with rockets while German artillery and mortars also shelled Polish lines. Overall the Front was very busy. The next morning, 27 August, 2nd Squadron supported an infantry offensive against the Monte Delle Forche – Hill 155 – Carignano axis. Between 08:00 hours and 11:00 hours, all three objectives were captured. On 3 September 6th Armoured Regiment was removed from the line to Casa Beverano and a couple of days later to Calibano Santo Pietro. Here the Polish troops noticed that the local Italians seemed to have almost forgotten that a war was being waged and had returned to tilling their fields and tending their cattle. It all seemed so timeless. During the second half of October 1944, 6th Armoured Regiment moved to Sarsina as reserve for British 10th Corps. On 31 October some of the regiment was moved to Poppi and others to Bibbieny. By then it was already 15 November 1944.

6th Armoured Regiment was in Bibbieny until the end of January 1945. The regiment lived a standard garrison life while there. This included studying a number of courses necessary to fighting as an armoured regiment. The courses were wide ranging from tank commander, driver, radio-operator and gunnery. At the end of January the regiment moved to their new position at Montefano. On 2 February, 2nd Squadron moved to Brisighella in the Apennines with the purpose of relieving 3rd Squadron of 4th Polish Armoured Regiment. Shortly after arriving on 7 February 1st Platoon, 3rd Squadron set up a defensive position and the next day was reinforced with the addition of two self-propelled guns from 7th Anti-Tank Regiment. For the following two days 1st Platoon was subordinated to the CO of 14th Infantry Battalion and then from 9 February fell under the command of 1st Battalion of 87th Italian Infantry Battalion. The remainder of the squadron was at the disposition of 5th Corps and then from 13 February came back under the command of 2nd Polish Corps. The local winter conditions, both regarding the weather and terrain, were terrible. However life was varied – tank crews were rotated weekly and those on duty led in battles both large and less so. It was also during this time in Montefano that new equipment was provided for 6th Armoured Regiment's Shermans. The most obvious change was the fitting of 105mm main guns (M4 105), while twelve of the Shermans were provided with 17 pounder main guns (Fireflies). This meant that tank crews needed training in order to become familiar with their new equipment.

On 12 March 6th Polish Armoured Regiment moved from Montefano to Faenza where 2nd Squadron had been in a defensive position on the river Senio since 6 March when they had relieved New Zealand armour. The squadron came under the command of the CO of 6th Rifle Brigade of the 5th Kresy Infantry Division. At the time of the move 1st Squadron remained at Montefano as its crews needed to attend a course on the mechanics of their new tanks. Finally, on 26 March 1945, 6th Armoured Regiment returned to action. 2nd Platoon from 2nd Squadron in cooperation with their infantry support liquidated an enemy attack by a German infantry company. The Poles suffered no casualties but killed sixteen Germans and captured an officer and eleven ORs. 1st Squadron returned to 6th Armoured Regiment on 29 March and on 4 April the regiment was sent to a reserve area and took up a position in the region between Forli and Faenza.

In the following few days a large and general Allied offensive opened up on the entire Italian Front. The purpose of the offensive was to utterly destroy the German military capacity in Northern Italy. As part of this offensive a formation known as 'RAK' was placed with 6th Armoured Regiment. RAK formation consisted of a company of motorised infantry in carriers from 13th Infantry Battalion; a squad of self-propelled guns form the Royal Horse Artillery (RHA) British Army, a battery of self-propelled guns from 7th Anti-Tank Regiment as well as sappers. On 13 April the RAK formation moved to the area where they were to be concentrated near to the town of Solarolo. While at Solarolo that 6th Armoured Regiment received orders concerning its next objectives which included infantry units from 3rd Carpathian Infantry Division leaving for the direction of Bubano-Sasso Morelli-Casoli Canina via Canale di Medicina in the direction of C. Bassa in order to occupy Poggio Piccolo.

At 07:00 hours on 14 April 1945 6th Armoured Regiment moved onto the offensive, heading towards its new operational area with 1st Squadron in the vanguard. While forcing the Fosso Gambellara the Poles met with heavy enemy opposition; after fierce fighting however, 1st Squadron with the Karpacki Ulan Regiment took Sasso Morelli at 16:00 hours on the same day. At nightfall 1st Squadron returned to 6th Armoured Regiment's lines in the Pera di Sopra region having left seven tanks with infantry support in a defensive group at Sasso Morelli. 6th Armoured Regiment's casualties for the day were quite light given the savage nature of the fighting as only one officer and seven ORs were wounded, but the self-propelled battery supporting the regiment took severe casualties, mainly from enemy artillery fire.

The next day, 15 April at 10:00 hours, 3rd Squadron supported by a platoon of motorised infantry in carriers with a squad of sappers travelling on the outsides of 3rd Squadron's Stuart tanks were set out to establish a bridgehead on the river Silaro in the direction of Giardino-Castel Guelfo. Once 3rd Squadron's group reached Giardino they linked up with a company of infantry from 13th Infantry Battalion. The Silaro was strongly defended and its banks sown deeply with mines. One of the infantry carriers ran over a mine and was wrecked as well as leaving three Polish infantrymen dead and two wounded. Almost immediately one of the tanks was damaged by a mine. Even so 3rd Squadron pushed on; the momentum of the Polish assault was not to be lost. Under the cover of tank fire and with artillery support from self-propelled guns as well as aerial backup, the infantry finally managed to secure a bridgehead by around 16:00 hours and brought in twenty enemy prisoners. Even though the banks of the river were quite soft and muddy, three tanks from 3rd Squadron managed to cross the river by 20:00 hours with the remainder of the squadron's tanks crossing during the night of 16 April between 02:00 and 03:00 hours.

In a series of counterattacks the Germans attempted to destroy the Polish bridgehead but each enemy counteroffensive was broken up by Polish tanks, artillery and infantry. Amazingly, fighting off these attacks only cost 6th Armoured Regiment a single death as one of the ORs was killed in the fighting. The infantry had five men killed and about twenty wounded. Allied aircraft destroyed a German Mark III tank which was about 200 metres from the river bank. The Germans suffered about thirty dead.

The German defence within the attacking 6th Armoured Regiment's operational area was stubborn but the Polish units, who were well equipped and well trained, managed to overcome the enemy. On 16 April at around 07:30 hours, 2nd Squadron advanced via the bridgehead at Sillaro and continued to pursue the withdrawing enemy. At the same time 2nd Squadron acted as a guard for the overall group in the axis along the axis of Castel di Medicina, mainly to the north-west. A kilometre beyond Castel Guelfo the squadron ran into heavy enemy opposition. 2nd Squadron managed to destroy two 150mm guns and a caterpillar-tracked tractor. It was reported that German tanks were present along 2nd Squadron's operational axis. The squadron received aerial support from airbase 'Rover-David'. The bridge at Canal di Medicina had been blown up by the Germans while heavy enemy anti-tank fire prevented any further advance for the present by 2nd Squadron. One of the squadron's number was killed and they lost a tank to enemy action on the canal. At about 20:00 hours the squadron withdrew leaving a single platoon of armour and infantry by the canal. The remainder of 6th Armoured Regiment by then was in a defensive position in the canal area. All that night there were waves of firing and fighting.

At around 06:00 hours on 17 April 1945, a Polish infantry patrol crossed the canal under the cover of tank fire and threw a scissor bridge across the water. Taking full advantage of the bridge, 2nd Squadron crossed it, established a bridgehead and took prisoners. At about 10:00 hours the Regimental Group moved to the reserve and had to move together with echelons of the Commander of 'RAK' Group. Throughout 18 April in the face of strong enemy defence work on the river Gaiana, this Polish formation supported by 13th Infantry Battalion faced the enemy, head on, without flinching. The purpose for this boldness was the establishment of a bridgehead on the river. This attack was further supported by tanks from 4th Polish Armoured Regiment and 6th Armoured Regiment which included ten tanks firing armed with 105mm main guns.

The next day, 19 April, after heavy fighting at 10:00 hours, 4th Squadron 6th Armoured Regiment managed to cross the Gaiana and establish a bridgehead. At midday tanks from 2nd Squadron drew up alongside 4th Squadron. Until the evening, 6th Armoured Regiment with Polish commandos extended and cleared the area before them. Enemy casualties were heavy. On 20 April 6th Armoured Regiment moved to the Quaderno Canal area where it received its next set of orders which to proceed with two squadrons from the Karpacki Ulan Regiment and capture Bologna. However a report from '*Kubusia*' said that the Polish national flag was already flying over the city. Advancing units of 3rd Polish Rifle Brigade had already taken Bologna and were now pushing further along Route 9. The Germans had surrendered in Northern Italy. The war in Italy was over.[9]

Chapter 8

1945–1948: A New Poland and a Divided Europe

The war in Italy may have been over, but the war in Europe continued until the second week of May 1945 when finally, after Hitler committed suicide, as did Goebbels and his wife after murdering their six children, the Nazi spell was finally broken and the German High Command agreed to an unconditional surrender. Poland may have been on the side of the winning Allies, but they had not really won anything. Poland had not retrieved its independence and certainly was not democratic. Indeed, in May 1945 Poland was occupied by its long term enemy, Russia – or the Soviet Union as it was known in 1945. This was a process which had begun in 1939 and had re-started in 1943. Poles throughout the world could not enjoy the wild celebrations which swept Europe as the guns fell silent because, for one thing, a civil war had already begun in Poland and times ahead were far from certain. Anders and his men from 2nd Polish Corps were beside themselves with frustration; peace had been declared but they knew they could not go back to Poland because they faced arrest by the NKVD, and possibly execution. It was a world turned upside down as far as the Poles in the West were concerned. While Polish troops had fought their way up through Italy or had chased the Germans back to Germany, such success was not being mirrored on the diplomatic front as Polish politicians and diplomats suffered defeat after defeat.

The Polish defeat began with politics and failed diplomacy in 1938 and was to dog Poland for the next half century. The most concentrated talks took place during 1945 as Poland was disposed of by the Western Allies. The Poles had always had a weak case, but after 29 November 1944, when Tomasz Arciszewski formed his government after the resignation of Mikołajczyk, the Western Poles had lost much influence. Sikorski had had the personal word of Churchill that he would stand by him; Mikołajczyk got along with Churchill but did not enjoy Sikorski's standing, while Arciszewski had nothing. Indeed during January 1945, Churchill told Eden that he was working with Mikołajczyk (the

Yalta Conference was coming) and was 'anchored' alongside him, but was yet to meet Arciszewski. Even so, when he (Churchill) was to meet Stalin at Yalta he was going to tell him that the British government continued to recognise the Polish Government-in-Exile as the official government of Poland.[1] Churchill had also referred to the Arciszewski government as *faute de mieux*, that is one in power owing to the lack of a better alternative. Churchill would have liked to have seen Mikołajczyk return to power because Arciszewski served no purpose at all.[2]

Cadogan, from his view at the Foreign Office had a different opinion of the Western Poles. On 20 February 1945, Cadogan and Eden had talked with Mikołajczyk and Romer about the Yalta Conference, or Crimean Conference as Cadogan was apt to refer to it. Cadogan was aghast that the Poles displayed no gratitude for what he considered to be British achievements for a post-war Poland. Indeed in his diary, Cadogan wrote: 'They of course exhibited no gratitude, and were merely critical and unconstructive – like all Poles.'[3] This was scarcely productive ground if it was how a senior British diplomat perceived the Poles; his committing of these words to his private diary without doubt displayed his true feelings and of course he was far more diplomatic in public, but his real feelings towards Poles should be noted. Even so, British diplomats and Eden continued to fight Poland's corner against the Soviet government and Stalin's imperialist ambitions regarding Poland. A conference to be held in San Francisco had become a bone of contention; the Soviet government was threatening to boycott it because the Western Allies continued to criticise Soviet actions in east-central Europe as the Red Army advanced towards Berlin, annexing all territories that fell before it. Stalin had even sent a message to Roosevelt that accused the British government of reaching a secret agreement with the Germans. The whole issue became more complicated with the death of Roosevelt on 12 April 1945.[4] It is interesting to note that at the time of the Yalta Conference the British were aware via ULTRA intercepts (signals intelligence obtained by breaking high-level encrypted enemy radio and teleprinter communications) that leading Nazis including Hitler, Goebbels and Ribbentrop were desperately hoping to reach an agreement with Stalin, possibly through the Japanese. Equally, Stalin was vexed by the possibilities of the British and Americans reaching some accommodation with the Germans.[5] It was clear that nobody really trusted each other at Yalta, the Soviets were trusted the least of all and, in turn, they trusted nobody either. It was all part of the paranoia of the Stalinist Soviet Union.

The meetings between the Allies in the USA were to prove just as difficult and ponderous as ever, especially in the matter of Poland and its future. Another problem was the personality of Molotov who believed he had the full support of Stalin, but of course this was on the condition that he did as his master bade. Molotov had some colourful nicknames but only behind his back; his public demeanour was humourless and stubborn to the point of absurdity. However, the new American President, Harry Truman, told Molotov bluntly what he thought of Soviet behaviour in general. Molotov said, 'I have never been talked to like that in my life.' Truman riposted, 'Carry out your agreements and you won't get talked to like that.'[6] This was in response to the Soviet government totally disregarding their commitments, made at the Yalta Conference, regarding the future of Poland. As we have seen, the Soviet Union basically annexed the country while pretending to liberate it, as well as arresting anybody who might oppose Soviet rule in Poland. Cadogan was outraged when it became obvious that fifteen Polish leaders –who were supposed to have been consulting with the Soviets regarding the formation of a new Polish government – had been arrested by the Soviet authorities instead. Even if Cadogan described the Soviets as 'animals' in his diary, he realised that, beyond protests and giving the Soviets 'a bad press', there was little that could be done about Soviet activities on the ground in Poland.[7] The Soviet annexation of Poland was a fait accompli and Stalin, as well as Molotov, knew it. Even worse from the Polish point of view, there was a general election in the offing in the UK. Churchill was about to be swept from power and a Labour government returned at a time when British working class sympathies were with the Soviet Union and not with the Western Poles. It is interesting to note that Stalin was baffled by the result of the 1945 British general election, but the historian S. M. Plokhy remarks that Stalin never understood public opinion (nor did he need to).[8]

Within a matter of a few weeks, the Western Poles were to be shorn of all support they might have still possessed while the Soviet Union, and especially Stalin, remained lionised by an irresponsible British public. Even Churchill had fallen under Stalin's spell, although Eden had cautioned him to be very wary of Stalin and Soviet ambitions. On 17 July 1945 Eden minuted to Churchill his concerns over how the Soviet government was ignoring every treaty it had agreed with the British and American governments. Eden wrote: 'The truth is that on any and every point, Russia tries to seize all that she can and she uses these meetings to grab as much as she can get.'[9] At least Eden was alive to the situation vis-à-vis the Allies and the Soviet Union, but he was powerless to do anything about it other than protest ineffectively; it made negotiations held at Potsdam during July 1945 more-or-less irrelevant as the Stalin and Soviet government did as they pleased in east-central Europe, notably in Poland. Cadogan was quite clear that most of the time it was Stalin personally that was obstructive in discussions about Poland and its frontiers.[10] Even with a change of government in the UK following the July 1945 general election and a new Foreign Secretary, Ernest Bevin, nothing changed regarding negotiations with the Soviet Union, especially in direct negotiations with Stalin. On 31 July Cadogan noted to his wife that negotiations had gone fairly, given that Stalin held all the winning cards, but Cadogan was relieved that Stalin was willing to compromise in the treatment of Germany because to have held Germany in perpetual servitude to the Allies would have cost the Allies a fortune. Cadogan noted that the new British Prime Minister, Clement Attlee, allowed Stalin to do most of the talking while Attlee 'nods his head convulsively and smokes his pipe'.[11] It was game over for the Western Poles; their government was no longer recognised and Stalin and his Polish collaborators were in charge in Poland, while the new Polish frontiers were a reality, whether the Allies or the exiled Poles liked it or not. It was over and a new Soviet friendly Poland was being formed no matter what. Perhaps it might have helped if the British and American leadership had spoken a bit more together in 1945 as Roosevelt had exclaimed on 24 March 1945, a few weeks before his death, that it was as Harriman had warned – Stalin had broken every promise made by the Soviets at Yalta.[12]

The problems for Poland vis-à-vis the Soviet Union began in earnest after the Soviet victory at Stalingrad and the later victory at Kursk, the titanic series of battle between German and Soviet armour which more-or-less saw the end of German ambitions in the Soviet Union; they were on the run for ever after that. The German defeat at El Alamein and overall events in North Africa by May 1943 had confirmed that the all-conquering German Army was fallible after all. The Luftwaffe had already been defeated at the Battle of Britain during the summer of 1940, thus preventing a German invasion of the UK, while a few months earlier, in April 1940, most of the German Navy's large surface fleet vessels had been destroyed by the Royal Navy in operations in northern Norway. Again this had repercussions for a German invasion of the UK as Norway confirmed the supremacy of the Royal Navy around British waters at least. The ability of the Soviets to hold and eventually repel the German invasion of the Soviet Union in June 1941 and then mount a counter-attack, was perhaps not foreseen – even by those who desperately wished for it. Of course much of the Soviet counterattack was going to affect Poland adversely. As we have seen, the Soviet Union in 1939 as an ally of Germany had invaded and annexed eastern Poland; eighteen months later, invading German forces seized the Soviet loot. Once the Soviet counteroffensive began to succeed, it was obvious that Poland would not be left in peace at war's end.

By the end of 1944 only a small fraction of Polish territory west of the Curzon line had been captured by the Red Army and so Polish people had not had the opportunity to consider what the Lublin Committee, in essence the nucleus of the provisional communist Polish government made up of Stalinist Poles, meant to them but that did not prevent the Soviet government announcing on 31 December 1943 that the Lublin Committee had transformed itself into a provisional government of Poland, and that the Soviet government had recognised it as such. The Polish Government-in-Exile from London denounced the situation and denied that the Lublin Committee had any legitimate claim to represent the Polish people.[13] Churchill would not have been surprised by such a turn of events because Stalin had, in July 1944, made it very clear that he did not consider the exiled Polish government in London to be a government unless it became a core of a provisional Polish government 'made up of democratic forces'.[14] Ironically 'democratic forces' meant Stalinist and was far from being democratic. Equally, Churchill warned that in the Stalinist lexicon 'fascist' meant anybody who defied Stalin's will.[15]

From New Year 1945 the Soviet government began to press with more urgency their true agenda for the post-war world – the spread of Soviet power beyond the frontiers of the Soviet Union. At the same time, the Lublin Committee had began to attack Mikołajczyk rather than Arciszewski which confirmed two things – Arciszewski and his government were lame ducks as Churchill had earlier suggested and that in the eyes of the Soviet government (the Lublin Committee would have never done anything with a blessing from

Moscow) Mikołajczyk, despite being out of office, still represented political power within exiled Polish circles. This was an interesting development and British officials considered that the Soviet government was trying to push the agenda further before the Yalta meetings.[16]

Another interesting development was the revelation, oblique of course, that Polish Communists recognised Polish armed forces in the West to be an enemy, but one that needed handling carefully and with a limited amount of respect when it suited the Communists to do so. In other words, they were afraid of them. General Michał Rola-Zymierski, defence spokesman for the Lublin Committee and a future Polish Marshal made a speech which appeared to target the Polish Army in the West. For once, instead of the usual condemnation of the Polish armed forces loyal to the Polish government in London being fascists and reactionaries, Rola-Zymierski saluted them and their achievements to date. He even praised the AK which was a major departure from the normal round of insults and slurs against the underground military wing. What was most interesting however, was that Rola-Zymierski claimed that the Polish Army was a 'child of democracy' and that a new Polish Army would be established for a 'new Poland'.[17] This was all very interesting and cynical as democracy in Soviet terms actually meant dictatorship, one only has to look at countries which claim to be 'Peoples' Democracies' or 'the Democratic Republic of...' to realise the falsehood of such an idea and of course there was to be a new Poland one way or the other. The world had been altered out of recognition as a consequence of the Second World War. Of course, linking the Polish Army to the foundation of any concept of a new Poland was one that was certain to find favour among Poles because the Polish Army enjoyed the trust of the people perhaps second only to the Catholic Church, leaving civilian politicians trailing somewhat as perhaps the least trustworthy in public life.

This sense of bonhomie for the military in the West did not last long because Stalin had made it quite clear how little regard he held for the Polish forces in the West. In a message to Roosevelt, Stalin asserted that the AK were mere bandits and terrorists under the control of the Polish Government-in-Exile. He also informed the American president that civil war beckoned in Poland as a result of the ambitions of 'a handful of emigrants in London'.[18] Stalin was correct that civil war did indeed beckon – it had probably already broken out – but much of this lay at his door as the Soviet forces began to run riot once in Poland.[19] As Stalin once remarked however: 'the Bolshevik slogan is: to turn the imperialistic war into a civil war.'[20] This is what was happening in Poland as the war was finishing in Europe; it was not in the interests of the Soviet government to allow true peace to prevail, but instead to ensure that chaos and violence continued until the Soviet government was able to achieve what it wanted: a Soviet-friendly Poland. By April 1945, as final victory over Germany was no longer in doubt and the Red Army was just about to assault Berlin itself, Rola-Zymierski altered his position and observed that the AK was no longer a military organisation but a political one.[21]

This was partially true as the AK had been formally dissolved on 19 January 1945 by order of the Polish Government-in-Exile. However, AK veterans merely reorganised and so WiN (*Wolność i Niezawisłość* [Freedom and Independence, Polish anti-Soviet underground movement, 1945-1948] was established out of the ashes of the failed uprising in Warsaw during the summer of 1944, which had seen so many AK fighters killed or captured. During January 1945, Arciszewski's Secretary, Jerzy Jan Lerski (*nom-de-guerre* 'Jur'), after parachuting into Poland, investigated what was happening as the Red Army advanced into the country. He sent his results to the former Minister of War, Leslie Hore-Belisha, in a memorandum entitled *The Polish Home Army and Underground Movement in Danger of Extermination*, which basically recorded the activities of the Soviet security forces once they entered Poland during the summer of 1944. The Red Army may have liberated the Majdanek death camp situated on the outskirts of Lublin but this did not prevent the NKVD, on 19 August 1944, from repopulating the camp with Poles as staff officers from the 8th and 9th Polish Infantry Divisions, along with General Halka, who had been captured earlier, as well as 200 officers and NCOs and 2,500 ORs.[22] The problem was that this kind of behaviour (there is no suggestion that the NKVD were using Majdanek as a death camp but the attitude should be noted) was already known to the British government and there was little they could do about it; Hore-Belisha hadn't had any real influence since 1940 when Churchill removed him from his post as Minister of War. Furthermore, Hore-Belisha even denied having received the document.[23] It was becoming a case of the unimportant pursuing the insignificant. Rola-Zymierski, in trying to reach out to the Polish armed forces in the West, was probably trying to gain some legitimacy for the Soviet takeover of Poland, but what he could not get around was the fact that Poles in the West, especially Anders and his men, hated foreign rule in Poland – especially that of Russia and even more so the alien and brutal rule of the Soviet Union. Anders and members of Polish forces in the West, even if they were only symbolic, were to remain a thorn in the side of the Soviet Union and its satrapy in Poland until Communism collapsed in east-central Europe during 1989.

At all times Anders did his best to thwart any chance of the Allies and the Soviets being too close when they discussed Poland and its future, unless of course plans were to be favourable towards Poland – but this never happened. During January 1945, a few days prior to the Yalta Meetings, Anders arrived in the UK. His only intention for being present in the UK was mischief as he tried to launch, albeit subtly, what might almost have amounted to a coup within the Polish armed forces. Anders' arrival in the UK caused dismay and made the British government extremely uncomfortable and anxious when they realised that his arrival in the UK was connected with a scheme to grant him, by Polish Presidential decree, total command of all Polish forces in the UK, France and in Italy. From President Raczkiewicz's diaries it can be clearly seen that Anders arrived in the UK on 21 January 1945 and left on 4 February; during this period there were a series a high level meetings between Raczkiewicz and his senior officers as well as Polish civilian officials.[24]

Owing to his extreme anti-Soviet views, Anders was anathema to the Soviet government and the fear that he was about to take total command of Polish forces in the West was one that the Soviets would not stomach – it would only be a short step to Anders having command of the military underground in Warsaw – or what was left of it after the Warsaw Uprising – and before long, Poles who were supposedly loyal to the Red Army would no doubt be clamouring for Anders to be their commander. How this might have worked out would have been interesting, and possibly bloody, given the Soviet zero tolerance of support for Anders. The Allies considered the presence of Anders in London only a few days before the Yalta Conference awkward and the proposed post inappropriate; Mikołajczyk agreed.[25] As ever with Polish military leaders Anders was seeking a political role as leader or dictator; the Poles fudge this with the term *Wódz*, which is more-or-less leader, but can be also interpreted as 'warlord' or even '*Fuehrer*' – it amounts to the same: an unelected leader seeking illegitimate power with an armed force behind him.

At the time of Yalta the situation for the Polish military underground was dire. A Polish report passed onto the British and American governments during February 1945 asserted that 5,000 Poles had been taken by the NKVD from Hrodua; 10,000 from Białystok and 75,000 from Poznań and deported to the Soviet interior. It was also estimated that about twenty per cent of the AK and its successors had been arrested by the NKVD and subjected to 'harsh and brutal examination' – no doubt weasel words for torture. Furthermore the AK leadership, consisting of Okulicki and fifteen others, were arrested and put on trial during June 1945.[26] It was as though the Soviet occupation of Poland between 1939 and 1941 had happened all over again, but this time the entirety of Poland rather than just the eastern provinces.

The British government was fully aware of the plan to make Anders Commander of Polish armed forces because a week earlier there had been a meeting between General Brooke (CIGS), General Stefan Kopański (COS Polish armed forces) and Anders. In the meeting with Brooke, the Poles made the case that Anders should be in control of all Polish Forces in Europe as the Poles wanted to form a united force in France with Anders at its head. Anders claimed that he did not want to return with Polish forces via Vienna as they might clash with the Soviets which surprised Brooke, judging by his use of an exclamation mark in his diary. The Polish plan was to advance through France into Germany and reinforce their number using Poles who they came across during this advance and, if necessary, take part in the occupation of Germany. Brooke was somewhat cautious about this as he saw straight away that it was to be difficult politically and consulted with Eden on the matter.[27] Of course the real prize was Poland, while the circumstances of Anders' visit pointed towards his ambition for political power there after the war.

The presence of the apolitical Kopański was an attempt by the Poles to pull the wool over British eyes. His presence suggested that the gathering was a professional meeting concerning the future of the Polish armed forces as described in Brooke's diary – but the British were not fooled. Brooke made it quite clear in his diary that he had qualms about the entire Polish concept of how they wished to proceed and was to report the conversation to Eden. The British response was immediate; although not made public, a minute from the Foreign Office makes their reaction to the Polish plan clear. According to the Foreign Office, it was all about creating a strong Polish Army for any future 'argument' with the Soviet Union. The Polish plans were immediately rejected by the British, the reason cited was that it did not fit in with their immediate war aims. Furthermore it was suggested that there could be no question of Anders or any other Polish commander proclaiming himself as Army Commander at the present time, but there was no objection to Anders, as senior Polish general, regarding himself as Army Commander as long as it was done discreetly with no outward or visible signs. The British did add that if the climate changed at some date in the future this post would be confirmed.[28] This was a major problem for the London Poles: the British government may have agreed in principle with them on many points but could not say so in public for fear of offending the Soviets and, to a point, the American government, while rarely did Polish plans ever coincide with what was necessary to complete the war against Germany. The logic behind this decision was unclear and some objected, citing that Anders was unlikely to be discreet.[29]

Even after the British intervention, or so they had thought, Anders' plan became clear almost immediately when General Maczek, Commander of the First Polish Armoured Division, was called away from the fighting in north-west Europe and told to report to Anders in London. At the same time General Kluchowski, General Officer commanding Polish forces in Scotland, was also summoned to London. The arrival of such eminent senior Polish officers suggested that no matter what the British government had requested, Anders' promotion was going ahead and it was unlikely to be discreet. It seemed that something was 'in the wind'.[30] The Foreign Office was thrown into a panic and suggested that Eden should see Anders and, if at all possible, also see Maczek and Kluchowski in order to avoid 'discussion of politics'. Eden's marginalia proves that Mikołajczyk considered that this must happen, while Warner was most anxious that Anders should be seen by the Foreign Secretary and headed off before he had time to promote his anti-Soviet agenda to the other Polish generals.[31] Eden need not have worried about Maczek who throughout his entire career had been apolitical, something that he maintained into his long retirement at a great cost to himself. Maczek was a very independent man; fiercely loyal to Poland he waged war in an often unorthodox manner, but with great skill on the battlefield which did not translate into success outside of the military. In his immediate retirement period he was forced to accept work as a barman in a hotel belonging to one of his former sergeants. The men of the First Polish Armoured Division loved Maczek and whenever they dropped into the bar, they always stood to attention before Maczek in recognition of his rank and honour before ordering their drink.

Anders continued with his anti-Soviet rhetoric. He maintained the view that even though the Polish Army was fighting Germany, the 'real enemy' was the Soviet Union and continued his demand that the Polish Army should be kept together as a single entity, ready for the day when it would have to fight the Soviet Union. It was Anders' contention that eventually a Polish Army would be given to a 'united Polish Government'.[32] Even though Anders' agenda does seem to have been rather unpalatable for the British government and the Foreign Office, it should be noted that often, as can be seen in the last reference given here, it was Anders' enemies such as Kot who were given full rein by the Foreign Office in their criticism of him. Often senior British and American officers serving with Anders on the Front in Italy had sympathy for him and his men. As ever it was politics before deeds and damn the truth – whatever that might have been. Even so, it was equally obvious that Anders was following his own political agenda for personal power in Poland, and by maintaining his anti-Soviet stance he was endangering the cohesion of the Alliance against Germany. His view that a future war against the Soviet Union was necessary, even though this attitude could only be damaging for his own country as its future was discussed at Yalta and elsewhere. It was certain that Stalin and the Soviet government would not accept a hostile neighbour on its western frontier, which was also part of the traditional invasion route from the West into Russia. Therefore Stalin would only accept a Soviet-friendly Poland and there was simply nothing that the Allies could do about this, even if they disagreed with him.

A problem for Anders was that Stalin was sending mixed messages despite the actions of his security services in Poland in the wake of the Red Army advance across Polish territory. In March 1945 Stalin remarked to Tito that 'today Socialism is possible even under the English [sic] monarchy. Revolution is no longer necessary everywhere.' In May 1946, speaking to leaders of the Polish Government, Stalin mused further and this time considered that:

> In Poland there is no dictatorship of the proletariat, and you don't
> need it there. ... The democracy you have established in Poland,

in Yugoslavia and partly in Czechoslovakia is a democracy that is drawing you closer to socialism without the necessity of establishing the dictatorship of the proletariat or a soviet system.[33]

These are all weasel words as Stalin knew what he was about – the dictatorship of the proletariat was largely about smashing the pre-revolutionary state as given out by Marx himself, but most of the pre-war east-central European states were already smashed by warfare, deportation and genocide, thus leaving a vacuum into which stepped the Red Army and the Soviet ideal. Milovan Djilas, vice-president of Yugoslavia and close colleague of Tito at the time, noted that Stalin never recognised the British Labour Party as being Socialist.[34] Therefore Stalin's words about revolution and change in the UK are irrelevant; he never meant them. But all the same any attempt, externally such as Anders, or internally such as the AK and its successors in the Polish example, to prevent a Soviet takeover of east-central European territories was ruthlessly snuffed out by the Soviet security forces.

Anders continued in his disregard for British wishes and warnings. On 26 February 1945, as his Order for the Day, Anders promulgated very publicly his appointment as Commander-in-chief, Polish armed forces in 'Poland's direst hour'. This was posted to every Polish unit in the West.[35] Sir Orme Sargent minuted that it was too late to prevent the Polish presidential decree appointing Anders as Commander-in-chief but hoped to prevent its publication until Anders had had a meeting with Churchill and CIGS. At the Foreign Office, Sargent warned that if the appointment was made public via the press, the British government must disown it and make it clear that this was a unilateral decision made by the Polish government in London.[36] Recording in his diary on 26 February 1945, Brooke wrote that he had heard that Anders had been appointed acting commander-in-chief of the Polish Forces. Brooke's attitude was that it was 'just one more nail in the coffin of the Polish Army'. He was also disappointed in Anders as he had been more or less assured by him that such a situation would not arise.[37] Anders continued to make unnecessary enemies in his rush to try to get what he wanted. Ultimately, he failed in everything. Sargent suggested to Churchill that a scheduled meeting with Anders on 28 February should be cancelled as it might suggest that the British government were in agreement with the Polish Government-in-Exile about Anders' new appointment. Furthermore the meeting with Churchill, if it went ahead, might serve to enhance Anders' authority with Polish troops and thus serve as a fillip to the Polish anti-Soviet campaign.[38]

An official British rebuff to Anders and the Polish government in London might have served as evidence that he and his government were acting alone and without British authority to pursue the course they were, but Anders went even further in his defiance. As the war in Europe was being seen as nearly over with Germany continuing to crumble on all fronts, Anders announced that Polish objectives had not been met and said 'that there cannot be an honest or just world order without a great, strong and independent Poland'.[39] This may have been true if the text had been confined to an 'independent Poland'; the rest was merely antagonistic, but by this stage of the war Anders should have learnt that it would be best to confine his words to the private ear of those that mattered where he still had friends and allies, rather than broadcasting and reducing his circle of allies even further.

Mikołajczyk was very unhappy with Anders' appointment because he feared he would use his new post and influence to undermine the Polish Army with a 'whispering campaign' against the Yalta Treaty. Much of Anders' strategy, according to Mikołajczyk, was to assert that Polish soldiers would find it impossible to return home to Poland after the war and would have to wait until Poland was free of Soviet domination. Anders was more-or-less correct in this assertion as many Poles found life fraught with danger under the Soviet occupation. It was not just those who had served in the West, but also those who had fought in the Warsaw Uprising who were liable to Soviet recriminations.

Mikołajczyk had meet Anders a few days previously and was struck by Anders' confidence that a war of liberation would be fought against the Soviet Union. Mikołajczyk indicated to the British government that they should not pursue the idea that Polish armed forces should be allowed to settle within the British Empire because this was just what Anders needed for propaganda purposes.[40] Anders was deluded enough to believe that the Soviet occupation of Poland was merely transitional and that once Germany was defeated, the British and Americans would round on the Soviets.[41] There was even more critical comment from within exiled Polish circles as a leading article in a London based Polish journal *Jutro Polski*, correctly argued that Anders' appointment as Commander-in-chief was the formal liquidation of Sikorski's work. It was claimed that as Commander-in-chief, Anders was able to educate the Polish Army in an anti-Sikorski spirit and of course Anders' antagonism towards democracy was highlighted, often presenting Sikorski's and Mikołajczyk's governments as 'unhealthy manifestations of party spirit'. This was frequently expressed by Anders in telegrams to Raczkiewicz and his disloyalty was rewarded with the post of commander-in-chief. *Jutro Polski* considered such an appointment unnecessary and unhelpful, especially for the Polish armed forces. But most of all Anders' appointment was dangerous and guided only by political calculation and the journal attacked it as such:

> There are political considerations at the back of this appointment the political consideration of men who know that they cannot return to power in Poland [and] have decided to remain abroad. They naturally wish to retain around them as many Poles as possible, especially the armed forces, so they may hide under the toga of heroism and patriotism the faults that they have committed before the war. They know that the Polish army by its own merits became an object of interest to the British and they wanted to increase their own importance by maintaining control of it. This is the reason why the Commander-in-Chief was appointed without consulting the Allies who are responsible for the military operations as a whole.[42]

Quite a blunt and direct criticism of the Polish military politicians who were unwilling to relinquish power, even if they were forced to live in exile; they just wanted a measure of power – even to the point of absurdity and falsehood. In anticipation of any attacks for its assault on Anders, *Jutro Polski* stated that the (Polish) army was 'the blood of our blood, the property of the nation for which we are responsible and must not be exposed to danger in order to forward the political aims of individuals'.[43] One might say 'busted' in modern parlance, but Anders was not: *Jutro Polski* had failed to understand the collective experience of Anders and his men, which was the very reason why they were so hostile towards the Soviet Union and this was the very reason why Anders could continue to count on the corporative support of his army – they knew and understood how the Soviet Union functioned and that Stalin was just as bad as Hitler. The war was basically about freedom, but half of Europe was about to embark on nearly fifty years of subservience to the Soviet Union and Anders and his men knew this and were not about to go quietly.

After Anders' death in 1970, Leon Mitkiewicz, who had been a Polish Army colonel and had served as the Polish representative on the Allied Combined Chiefs of Staff Committee, asserted in 1971 that the first mistake that the exiled Polish government made was to allow for the withdrawal of Anders' Army from Russia (Soviet Union) to Persia (Iran). Mitkiewicz argued that if Anders had been made to remain in the Soviet Union and his army had fought alongside the Red Army, then the fate of Poland might have been different.[44] This was wishful thinking and a complete misunderstanding of Anders and his men who knew the Soviet Union and its government, as well as having suffered from its cruelty. These men could never have served under Soviet command, which was something that the Polish Government-in-Exile never understood about Anders and his men. Mitkiewicz mused that an Anders' style army alongside the Red Army might have made a difference to a post-war Poland; this might have been true, but it was unlikely because the knavery of Stalinist rule would have without doubt kept a large Polish force away from Poland – unless it was considered somehow 'Soviet friendly'.

It can be argued that Anders, in his belligerent stance against the Soviet Union was his own and Poland's worst enemy. Perhaps if he had returned with his army to Poland with Mikołajczyk, given that partisan fighting continued in Poland until at least 1948, it might have proved difficult for Soviet forces and their allies to have taken over Poland if they had had to deal with thousands of trained Polish soldiers arriving in Poland between 1945 and 1946. Without doubt the Soviet government would have had to find a different formula for annexing Poland.

Chapter 9

Europe and Poland:
Immediate Post-War Problems

The ability of the Soviet Union to evade any censorship by the UK and the US government after June 1941 was easy as long as the Soviet government kept its country in the war against Germany; it more-or-less had a free hand in east-central Europe, aided and abetted by the Western Powers. This situation was furthered after May 1945 when the Soviet government was encouraged to declare war against Japan and to later raid the Japanese backdoor via Manchuria, thus giving the already beleaguered Japanese yet another front to defend. By this time the Americans were bombing the Japanese mainland more-or-less at will while the US Navy and land forces – notably the United States Marine Corps – were banging on the Japanese front door. The war against Japan was to be kept up as intently as the war against Germany had been. This process of favouring the Soviet Union had begun on paper in 1941 and became *Realpolitik* during 1943 as the war turned against Germany.

Even if the German invasion of the Soviet Union during June 1941 was to be the catalyst that gave rise to 2nd Polish Corps, it was a false dawn for Polish independence and freedom. The heady days of August 1941, which saw Anders proclaiming that the formation of a Polish Army on Soviet soil was to help defeat the only enemy of Poland – Germany – alongside the Allies including the Soviet Union, all involved in fighting against Germany. In the summer of 1945 there were three apparent Polish fronts, of which one was a fighting front. The fighting front was the civil war in Poland as Polish Nationalists tried to prevent a complete Soviet takeover of Poland, while in Western Europe the Polish First Armoured Division, which had grown out of Polish 1st Corps, had been given the task of occupying the Wilhelmshaven area in Germany, the only part of Germany to be occupied by Polish armed forces. Anders and his men remained in Italy which had become a hotbed of intrigue as Italian communists, aided and abetted by Yugoslav communists led by the legendary partisan leader, Tito, in turn encouraged by Moscow, vied for power within Italy, while the city of Trieste became a bone of contention between Yugoslavs and Italians of any political hue. It was considered by some that perhaps only military intervention would convince Tito's people to leave Trieste alone.[1] Indeed shortly after the war had finished in Europe, Churchill was forced to complain to Stalin about Tito's forces entering Italian towns in the Italian province of Venezia Giulia. Churchill recognised that the governance of this area was to be settled at a future peace treaty owing to the fact that the majority of the population in the region were actually Yugoslavs and that the area was occupied for the United Nations by British armed forces until a settlement was reached. Tito's actions were not helpful as Churchill made clear to Stalin.[2] On 2 May 1945 a New Zealand division accepted the surrender of the Trieste area and moved in to find that Yugoslav forces were occupying much of the city of Trieste, as well as extending their occupation into parts of Austria, which had been allocated to British administration. In Venezia Giulia, especially in Trieste, the Yugoslavs were carrying out executions and deportations of Italians. These measures were directed not only against Italian ex-fascists, but also against those Italians who might oppose a Yugoslav annexation of the area. Yugoslav forces also began to steal all manner of property in Venezia Giulia as well as the Austrian territory they had entered. These illegal actions led to heightened relations between British and American troops and the Yugoslav forces.[3] At the time, Tito was an ally of Stalin and willing to aid the world revolution; within a few years the two men would fall out and cracks in the Communist world would start. Stalin's attitude – as he wrote to the American president Harry Truman – was that Tito's forces had driven the Germans from the disputed area and therefore they had every right to claim it for themselves. In a note to Churchill, Stalin referred the British premier to the fuller message sent to the American president.[4] It would seem that Stalin had the measure of Churchill's importance in the post-war alliance. Of course this did not bode well for Anders or his compatriots, as their main sponsor was already diminished in the eyes of Stalin.

The presence of Polish troops in the west became a source of agitation between London, Warsaw and Moscow. However there was a tiny flaw in Stalin's plan to introduce Communism to Poland and that was the fact that he had been responsible for the destruction of the pre-war Polish Communist

Party. This meant that the entire structure had to be rebuilt, which no doubt suited Stalin as he wished to return Poland as a vassal state of the Soviet Union by using figures loyal to him and slavish to the Soviet system. Quite simply, traitors and collaborators; something still to be acknowledged by most Poles. Ironically, a potential Polish enemy from within Communist ranks, Władysław Gomułka, survived the war as he had been in a Polish prison when Stalin was having the Polish Communist Party slaughtered at the end of the 1930s. Therefore at the time of the attempted Sovietisation of Poland, there were a number of organisations ranged against the Soviets and renegade Poles supporting the Soviets; the opposition included Gomułka, to a certain extent, Stanisław Mikołajczyk, who been a Polish prime minister in exile and, of course, Anders and his force. There was enough opposition in Poland to ensure Stalin realised that taking over Poland was not going to be a walk-over as he might have thought; these were the ingredients for the Polish Civil War. The object of Soviet policy was world domination as set out in the Marxist-Leninist text and the work of Stalin, simply the world revolution; Anders had long warned the Western Allies about this but was ignored during wartime because the Soviet Union had to be kept in the war against Germany, and later was instrumental in the defeat of Japan. A further problem was that by July 1945 Winston Churchill was out of office, replaced by Clement Attlee and a Labour administration, which is often touted in Polish circles as being pro-Soviet. This may have been true at grassroots level but not at government level. However, lasting damage was to be done to Anders and his cause.

The case of Gomułka is interesting, if under-researched. He ruled Poland from 1956 until 1970, when he was ousted from power as a result of his failed economic policies and general intertia and little interest has been taken of him since his death in 1982, even in Poland, where he acquired a reputation of being a bore. However, Gomułka was responsible for ensuring that a Communist system of government was introduced into Poland after 1945. Unlike most of the other Polish Communist leaders being touted between 1945 and 1946, Gomułka was not a Stalinist and was not loyal to Stalin or to Moscow; he had no reason to be. The other leading Polish Communists owed everything to Stalin, including their lives. It was Gomułka's soft soaping and badgering of the Polish population, which was in flux as land was redistributed and borders reaffixed and nationalities redefined, which no doubt had the effect of ensuring that Communism was introduced in Poland. It was Gomułka who would eventually out-manoeuvre Mikołajczyk, one of the few senior London Poles to return to Poland at war's end, in order to take part in the intermediate Polish government before elections were held in 1947. Mikołajczyk was more or less abandoned by both the American and British governments as relations with the Soviet Union became frostier and frostier while Gomułka, within a month of the war ending in Europe, claimed that a new Poland was being built and everybody was working eighteen hours a day to ensure the success of this project. Gomułka isolated Mikołajczyk and his supporters by claiming that the London Poles had made many mistakes and that it was only by being in step with the Communists that the émigré Poles would have any chance of sharing power in Poland.[5]

Great changes were afoot in Poland as the country totally rebranded itself with more than a guiding hand from Moscow, which was still hidden from many unless you were part of the opposition. As one can imagine, the country had been ransacked not only by the Germans but also by the Soviets, while the fact that several cities had been besieged during the fighting had taken its toll. Furthermore, the mass extermination of the Jewish population, not to mention the high tally of Poles – especially the educated and skilled – murdered by both the Germans and the Soviets was to leave its mark as these were the very people needed to rebuild Poland. Other areas of concern were the new frontiers with land being annexed from Germany in the west, but land being lost to the Soviet Union in the east, while the German population, or those deemed to be German, were ruthlessly expelled from Poland and herded towards the west and to British and American occupied Germany. This was a brutal act but quite understandable given how Germans of all hues had treated the Poles; ironically the Germans who survived expulsion were to benefit in the 1960s from the economic success of West Germany, while Poles remaining in Poland were not to enjoy such an economic benefit and largely lived in poverty until the collapse of Communism in east-central Europe during 1989. There were two major concerns running through post-war society: one was the question of land reform which excited many Poles still wedded to the land and following largely agricultural lives; the other was the fixing of the Polish western frontier. Questions relating to these matters were to be addressed by a plebiscite which was entitled 'three times yes' or *'trzy razy tak!'* Prażmowska notes that land reform was extremely important to the Soviets as they needed peasant support to ensure that their agendas were carried, and that they did not starve because a food supply of sorts needed to be maintained. Without peasant support the entire Soviet programme for Poland would have been doomed.[6] Even with the use of terror by the NKVD it was unlikely that Poland could have been subdued if the populace had risen against it; partisans were still in the forests and if a general uprising had broken out the British and Americans could not have prevented Polish troops in the west from joining their compatriots. Simply, the majority of the Polish population between 1945 and 1948 were, at best, apathetic to the subtle Soviet takeover of their country as many still believed that Poles would continue to rule Poland albeit under a different system of governance, while others were downright greedy and assumed they would do well out of any such arrangement.

As Poland was rebuilt at breakneck speed, if one takes Gomułka's word, there was at least a facade of democracy in the country during the summer of 1945 as Mikołajczyk shared the deputy premiership with Gomułka. Even so, the senior positions went to Polish Stalinists as Bolesław Bierut was to be president of Poland and Edward Osóbka-Morawski was to be prime minister. While these decisions were being made, a trial of sixteen ex-AK commanders was being held in Moscow which indicated that even though the provisional government was going through the motions of transforming Poland into a democracy, it was becoming obvious to those who cared that Poland was never really going to be a democracy – at least in the short term – and as a result would have to be Soviet friendly. The outcome of the Moscow Trials was that the sixteen AK leaders were sentenced to various terms of imprisonment, none of which exceeded ten years. The West was delighted that nobody had been sentenced to death and put the London Poles on notice that they did not support any anti-Soviet activity in Poland, at least publicly. For the London Poles the sharing of the office of deputy Polish prime minister was a disaster as Gomułka easily dominated Mikołajczyk while overall the Moscow Agreement awarded Mikołajczzk's party, the Peasant Party, a third of the power in the provisional government, but it was all window dressing by the Soviet-backed Poles and ultimately Stalin and Moscow – and of course all of the key appointments were held by Moscow loyalists.

A further problem for Western Poles was that in the eyes of the British, Americans and even the French governments, the Poles in exile tended to label anything from Poland with which they disagreed as 'red' – basically Communist – despite the occasional merits of some of the cases. This perceived unflattering image embarrassed the Western governments while it further convinced those in the West – such as communists, trade unionists and ordinary people in the UK, especially in the industrial north and Midlands, Scotland and Wales – that those Poles still in the West were extremists, fascists, anti-Semites and reactionaries.

The fact that Churchill was also on the verge of losing power as the result of the British general election of July 1945 did not help. Churchill's power had been on the wane for some time by then, while his age and health were also against him. Roosevelt's successor Harry S. Truman was still finding his feet. It was only Stalin who, by the summer of 1945, felt secure in his position. While the Soviets remained all-conquering and still necessary (owing to the need to complete the war with Japan), the insecurity in the West allowed the Soviets to do as they wished in east-central Europe and especially in Poland. Much of this was to do with the western frontier of the new Poland which was to run along the river Oder/Neisse. It was a good idea for Poland to have an immediate geographic obstacle on its western frontier with Germany because in 1939 the Germans, attacking from the north and the west, had overrun almost half of Poland before they came across any form of natural obstacle such as a river. At that time, owing to three years of drought, rivers and other water obstacles had been easily forded.

Churchill had not foreseen that the new Poland would run as far west as it did, but there was little he could do about the situation because by the time agreements were signed on the matter, he was no longer in power. However, what was more important was that Poles and the Red Army were already in possession of what had been Breslau (now Wrocław), Polish farmers were already harvesting the fields abandoned by the ex-German population and Polish miners were mining coal in abandoned ex-German mines. This was all part of the luck that the Communists in Poland enjoyed – to the despair of their compatriots left stranded in the West. A further problem, as Bethell discusses, is that the London Poles did not have the luxury of being able to practice democratic politics as seen in the West in one form or another, but seemed unable to undertake the gangster politics of those of the Communist ilk. Furthermore they did not have the support of the majority of Poles living in Poland. And of course they had already lost the recognition of the Western Allies and had not ever really been recognised by the Soviet government and its cohorts. To embarrass further any remaining supporters of the London Poles, some of the unrecognised exiled government began to demand the return of eastern Poland, which historically was largely devoid of Poles and rejected the richer lands annexed from Germany. It made life very difficult for those who might have sought to establish a non-Communist government in Poland, but made it all too easy for those who wished to establish a Communist government, especially with the campaign for 'three times yes'.[7]

The campaign for 'three times yes' was to be crucial for trying to establish legitimacy for the establishment of a Communist government, even if the coming election returned such a method of governance. Prior to being ousted from power Churchill had spoken to Bierut about the future of Poland and how democracy would be restored there. Churchill was quite anxious about how Poland was descending into violence and anarchy. Bierut reassured Churchill that this was not the case and that the new Poland was to be an inclusive society with chances for all. He was lying and Churchill was out of power within days and Clement Attlee and the Labour Party formed a new government. As Bethell noted, with the war won in Europe, Churchill was able to feel less restrained by the presence of the Soviets and with the recent news that the Americans had an atomic bomb, perhaps he should have been more determined in trying to ensure that Poland was returned to democracy. For the previous eighteen months however, Churchill had operated from a point of ignorance regarding Poland and nothing had changed. Attlee was to prove even more ignorant and so the Soviets were allowed to get way with everything they wanted to in Poland, aided and abetted by Polish collaborators while the local population on the whole were indifferent to the fate of their homeland. They seem to have been both traumatised and mesmerised as new plans for Poland were laid out by Moscow – with the real agenda hidden from view, and this was where the 'three times yes' campaign played its part.

The famous British historian Norman Davies once described the 'three times yes' campaign as being a campaign in which the question of 'do children like ice cream' was posed in three different ways. Of course the answer had to be 'yes'. The three questions posed in the referendum were: 'Are you in favour of the abolition of the Senate?', 'Are you in favour of making permanent the land and nationalisation reforms?' and 'Are you in favour of the fixing of the Polish western frontier on the Oder-Neisse Line?' The obvious answer, as Davies suggested, was 'yes'. There was nothing blatantly pro-Communist in the questions because the inter-war Polish Republic had been one of misery and privilege: misery for most industrial workers and peasants as they were either poorly paid, treated badly and unfairly, or were expected to live off poor land which could hardly keep a family. At the same time there was a minority elite that totally despised its workers and peasants, more-or-less treating them as something subhuman while living on huge estates, oblivious to the poverty of those around them. It was not surprising that people voted for land reform and nationalisation of industry. It should also be noted that much of the land in the new western Poland had been vacated by the former German minority and so it was an obvious target for reform and redistribution. Furthermore many industrial complexes had been owned by Germans or Jews who were either dead or in exile, while in 1945 Polish industry was more-or-less wrecked and the Soviets were looting what was left, both from Germany proper and the new Polish lands. The question of the new western frontier went without saying but the Polish population were not asked whether they approved of the new eastern frontier with the Soviet Union. They were not asked because, without doubt, the answer would have been 'No'. Of course many would have preferred to have returned to their former homes in what had been eastern Poland and was now part of the Soviet Union. This is what Anders and his men raged about – there seemed to be no understanding or sympathy from either the British or American governments regarding their situations. Many of Anders' men had lost their homelands in former eastern Poland and the West could not see that the Soviet government was yet to finish its imperialist policies of expansion as far as possible in all directions. It did not suit the British or American governments to look at what Anders was saying and once the decision had been taken by Western governments to recognise Stalin's Poles as the new power in Poland and remove recognition of the exiled Poles in the West, it was more or less game over for Anders and his followers. The first question posed was more-or-less an irrelevance.

The problem was that the Western Poles did not know how to respond to this referendum and knew that if they recommended that all three questions should be answered with a resounding 'yes', then this could and would be interpreted as being a vote of confidence in the provisional government and its plans for a Communist Poland. Mikołajczyk knew that his supporters living in Poland would support the 'three times yes' campaign, therefore he suggested that members of the Peasant Party should vote 'no' in answer to the first question posed in protest against the violence and anarchy let loose in the country at the hands of the Communists as they tried to seize control of Poland. Of course this was a futile act and if needs be the Soviets, using the NKVD, would have terrorised the Polish populace into whatever answers were needed to secure Soviet rule in Poland. It should be seen that the security agencies in Poland did indeed carry out a reign of terror to ensure compliance by its population and that people did vote against question one. The official figure was given as thirty-eight per cent voted against the abolition of the senate, the least important of the questions posed, but Mikołajczyk claimed eighty per cent and invited Western journalists to understand his reasoning. Western diplomats had already witnessed how the Communists were conducting themselves and terrorising Poles and Western protests quickly followed as the Soviets and Warsaw government violated the Potsdam and Yalta treaties. The Communists once more branded Mikołajczyk a 'traitor' as he had invited outsiders to intervene in Polish domestic affairs. Even so the British and Americans did not welcome those who questioned the legality of the Polish-Soviet frontiers. Gomułka declared that any Pole who disputed the western frontier was a traitor; he was clearly aiming at the friendless western Poles.

Gomułka managed to link Mikołajczyk with the two underground armed groups, the fascist leaning NSZ, which was clearly of a dubious persuasion and had at times during the war joined German forces in fighting the Soviets and the other group, WIN, a manifestation of the now defunct AK, which was probably more in tune with ordinary Poles, but so many people were tired of fighting and uncertainty and just wanted peace. Therefore it should be seen that neither group enjoyed real support among Poles, while Gomułka made sure that the two groups were isolated within Polish society.

Meanwhile British and American diplomats reported to their governments that it had become impossible to investigate and report at all on activities within Poland. The Western diplomats had the ear of all the wrong people, including Mikołajczyk and Cardinals Hlond and Sapieha, (who was also a 'Prince' – of what, one cannot be sure). The fact that the British Ambassador,

Cavendish-Bentinck, used an airplane which he dubbed his 'peering machine' as he reconnoitred Poland and saw what he considered 'disturbing scenes' meant nothing to the Polish or Soviet authorities. He and the American Ambassador, Bliss Lane, may have complained and reported their concerns, but the Communists no longer saw any reason to humour the Western allies.

Sir Orme Sargent at the Foreign Office noted that once the war in Europe was over, Anders and the Polish Government-in-Exile were trying to obtain the number of Poles released from the German Army for service in the Polish Army. Under Polish law it was interpreted that such personnel were already members of the Polish armed forces.[8] It quickly became obvious however, that this was not going to be practical as there was a fear that Wehrmacht trained Polish troops, even though they were beyond doubt 'excellent fighting material', and hated the Soviets, were 'dangerously pro-German in sympathy'.[9] Anders suggested that he could provide Polish labour for civil work in the UK. Churchill, as optimistic as ever, considered this to be a brilliant idea as he informed Eden and the British Secretary of State for War. In Churchill's view there was no need to involve politics, but merely to move these men to the UK where such labour was in great demand as the British sought to rebuild their shattered country. Churchill considered that as the Soviet government had never considered it necessary to inform the British government when it deported a 'few hundred thousand people to Siberia', he might deploy 128,000 troops in a Corps for occupation purposes in a part of the British zone of occupation in Germany, but away from the Soviets.[10] This idea was also short lived because by the end of June 1945 the recruitment of Polish troops from the ex-Wehrmacht was halted owing to their attitude of being quite anti-Soviet and very pro-German.[11] And this was the genius of Gomułka as he successfully divided Mikołajczyk from any sense of popular support within Poland as it became obvious that the London Poles were not considered by Poles in Poland to be the legitimate successors to the pre-war Polish regime; they could not shake off the suspicion that Poles in London had sat out the war in the relative luxury of Kensington flats and drawing rooms. Maisky, back in 1941, had been very critical of the Polish Government-in-Exile and its excesses regarding expenditure and servants and basically 'puttin' on the Ritz'.[12] Up to a point this was unfair criticism, but equally there were many who had plotted to regain power in Poland once the war was over, while the London Poles had made an all too easy target for the Soviets and Polish Communists to criticise with their perceived 'easy war' and being out of touch with those who had remained in Poland and suffered the Nazi occupation.

By the summer of 1945 many mistakes had been made regarding Poland, especially by leverage in the new post-war world which was seen by Stalin as a chance to extend his empire and spread the international revolution. The annexation of Poland meant more territory for the Soviet Union as well as a buffer area protecting the Soviet Union from any attack from the West. Stalin was careful how he constructed his thoughts regarding Poland when he spoke to representatives of the Western world. When asked about Soviet actions in Poland in a post-war interview, he quoted the words of Bolesław Bierut, the Stalinist president of the Polish Peoples Republic and puppet of the Soviet Union:

> the great help which was rendered by the Soviet government was a decisive factor which inspired the Polish workers to crush the foundations of capitalism in Poland and to establish the regime of a people's democracy. After the war, the first and foremost task of the Polish working class was to ensure their independence against the attack of Anglo-American imperialists. The masses of the [Polish] people must be grateful for the possibility given us to use the wide experience of the social construction work of the Soviet Union which helps to consolidate the people's democracy that carries out the functions of the proletarian dictatorship with ever increasing efficiency and promotes the growth of the socialist elements in the economic life of the country.[13]

Beirut of course would have had very little to say about what happened in Poland unless it was the pursuit of Stalinism and close ties with the Soviet Union, which basically placed Poland into Soviet bondage.

Stalin did not trust the West at all and considered that eventually a resurrected Germany might be part of an invasion of the Soviet Union – it was to take the West a little longer to work out Stalin and the Soviet Union, even by 1945, and certainly during his lifetime, Stalin went unchallenged on the whole and duped many Western observers. It was not until 25 February 1956 when the Soviet leader Nikita Khrushchev, who eventually replaced Stalin following the latter's death in 1953, denounced Stalin's rule when Khrushchev made the so-called 'Secret Speech' at the 20th Congress of the Communist Party of the Soviet Union. Even then it was only a partial denouncement because, despite having mellowed during the war years, throughout the 1930s Khrushchev had been an enthusiastic Stalinist. Anders meanwhile continued trying to brief the Western allies against Stalin and the Soviet Union, observing in December 1945 that the policy being followed by the Soviet government had two lines: the continuation of the former imperialist line of gradually moving westward, and the continuation of Lenin's work in the policy of Stalin which was twofold. The first phase of Lenin's policy was the takeover of Europe and then later the world – basically a 'Sovietisation' of the world, or the world revolution.[14] But as we have seen, Anders and his men were lone voices crying in the wilderness as the West, tired and ravaged by war, were not interested in further instability and the possibility of renewed warfare against an ally, which the Soviet Union still was at the time. However, Anders had correctly anticipated the Cold War, which never developed into fighting in Europe, but was fought in Latin America, Africa and Asia, notably Korea (1950-53) and Vietnam, that long running war which began before 1966 when the USA became openly involved and more-or-less ceased in 1973 with the American withdrawal from South-East Asia.

Anders was often accused of sending elements from Second Polish Corps into Poland to assassinate enemies and spread terrorism. Naturally he denied these charges. The problem for historians is that the two sources claiming and counter-claiming are unreliable because it involves the Communist Polish government, and Anders and his people. We have already seen that some within Anders' entourage were capable of plotting against General Sikorski, the Polish prime minister and commander-in-chief, and probably assassinated him. Therefore it was not beyond the wit of members of Polish Second Corps to enter Poland with ill-intent. Even so, there are traces of Anders and his people being involved in intrigue if not actually planning and working towards the eradication of Sovietization in Poland, with some limited connivance of both the UK and US governments, but all of this conspiratorial work was supposed to have ended on 4 September 1945. It is likely that Anders secretly continued in his actions because evidence is available that points towards intelligence gathering still being conducted by Polish Second Corps, firstly in Italy between July and December 1945, and then into Poland itself between December 1945 and May 1947. The suggestion is that Anders was trying to establish an intelligence network in Poland.[15] While in January 1946, working against Anders and his army's presence in Italy, the Polish government in Warsaw launched a campaign of negative criticism of Polish 2nd Corps. Molotov went further and asserted that 'Anders' bands were endangering peace', while claiming that dozens of men from Polish 2nd Corps had been arrested by the Allied authorities as they had been influenced by the 'Fascist General Anders' to work and plot against the Soviet Union as well as disrupt and destroy the new democratic powers in Poland.[16]

The historian Anita Prażmowska notes that the work of exiled Poles continued in spite of British disapproval of the Communist regime in Poland. This is known because in 1952 it was learnt with shock among the exiled Polish community in the UK that the military organisations preparing and training men to eventually destabilise Poland had been infiltrated by Communists. An investigation revealed that funds allocated to some military commanders to finance plans to recover Poland had been diverted and their use had not been sanctioned by exiled community leaders.[17] Indeed *The Manchester Guardian* reported in August 1946 that since the beginning of that year, 2,800 people had been killed in Poland as a result of the insurgency going on in that country. Whether Anders' men are involved is unclear, but it was suggested that 'agents' were sent aboard with the aim of disrupting elections in Poland.[18] During December 1945 Mikołajczyk was very clear that Anders and his men were responsible, with others, for murder and assassinations of Polish political figures of all persuasions if they opposed Anders. Mikołajczyk was particularly incensed when his own deputy, Bolesław Scriborek, Secretary General of Mikołajczyk's own party, the Peasant Party, was shot dead in Łódź. This shooting and its location is significant. Łódź is often dismissed by Poles and others as an ex-textile city full of slums, but in 1945 it served as the Polish capital owing to the destruction of Warsaw during and after the Warsaw Uprising of 1944. Scriborek was playing a significant role in the resurrection of Poland at this time.[19] Indeed, in a press release for 29 October 1945 in the Łódź area, Polish Nationalists, described as AK in the report, claimed that during the period of 15 September and 15 October 1945 they had had their activities 'liquidated'. It asserted that 1,369 AK fighters had been identified and registered and their weapons and equipment taken.[20] This does suggest significant Nationalist activity in the Łódź area alone and who was supplying arms and equipment to Polish nationalists fighting against the Communists was forever the question – with suspicion lying largely with Anders.

The end of November and the beginning of December 1945 had been a very bad few weeks because scores of people were murdered in Poland. These murders, over a three-week period, were seen by Mikołajczyk as being 'political murders' and he blamed partisans from the NSZ and 'people from General Anders' who were trying to provoke an armed intervention in Poland by British and American armed forces.[21] It is interesting to note that Mikołajczyk does not lay the blame at the doors of either the Soviet/Polish Communist security services, or of the successor groups of the Polish wartime military underground movement, the AK now reborn as either NIE or WiN. Clearly Mikołajczyk was seeing the murky hands of Polish fascism involved in these attacks against even moderate Poles such as his party and his colleagues. And of course Anders and his supporters were gravely mistaken if they seriously considered that either the British or Americans would get involved in another war, far less one against a former ally and a powerful one to boot. Europe was tired of war and the Americans were sick of Europe and the Europeans and had already indicated that they were ready to leave the continent as many of their immigrant ancestors had done in the past.

However, Anders should not be dismissed as being unrealistic because Churchill had planned that the Western Allies could strike against the Soviet Union should the Soviets not comply with agreements such as Yalta. As we have seen, the Soviets had promised that there would be free and unfettered elections in the lands they had supposedly liberated. The idea was that local populations would be free to decide how they wanted to be governed. Poland was to be the touchstone for this as Poland, at least in the eyes of Churchill, was the very reason that the UK and the British Empire went to war – ruining itself in the process. If Poland was to be annexed by another dictatorship, albeit a wartime ally, despite being one of the original aggressors, what was the point in the sacrifice made by the British people? It was to this end that Churchill, no doubt to the shock and horror of his military advisors, had a plan drawn up with the purpose of striking out at the Soviet Union in the case of its non-compliance with treaties regarding the future of Europe, especially its conduct in Poland.

As it became increasingly likely that the Soviet Union had no intention of fulfilling its promises, the plans were examined as the war in Europe drew to a close and before the war against Japan had been concluded. Churchill's exasperation with the Soviets reached its zenith when, as Victory Day in Europe was being celebrated on 9 May 1945, Soviet paratroopers seized the Danish island of Bornholm in a lightning raid. There were other concerns such as the situation in Trieste where a dangerous face-off was developing between British troops under Field Marshal Alexander and Tito's Communist partisans. The situation in the circumstances surrounding the Italian port was unclear as it was not certain whether Tito was acting unilaterally, or whether Stalin's hand was behind it all. Churchill suspected that Stalin was behind the Trieste situation. To this end Churchill ordered that the plan for a strike against the Soviet Union, known as Operation UNTHINKABLE, should be examined.[22] It is interesting to note that according to Corti, Italian Communists in the Emilia area were mostly former fascists and had sensed that Polish troops in Italy were essentially anti-Communist and so in red paint on the walls of the Via Emilia these 'Communists' proclaimed that Polish troops were fascists. Amazingly the Polish troops failed to react to this jibe.[23]

It is also interesting to relate that there was another action on 9 May 1945 when WiN members ambushed the NKVD 2nd Border Regiment in the Galician villages of Kuryłówka and Sepl in former eastern Poland and left fifty NKVD troops dead. A further WiN action happened on 21 May 1945 when its troops attacked an ex-German prisoner-of-war camp in Rembertów in east Warsaw where 50,000 Poles were held and it was probable that they were destined to be sent to Siberia. Attacking as the Soviet guards were drinking away their Saturday night, WiN troops stormed the camp and within thirty minutes had released 500 Poles. The émigré Polish newspapers in the west lauded this action as the beginning of a national uprising while Radio Warsaw under Soviet control urged Poles in the West to return to Poland.[24] This was the fevered and uncertain atmosphere that Poland and its people endured as peace was declared. It did not feel so to many Poles and those still in the West were uncertain if they should risk returning home or not.

The British military chiefs reviewed the situation, were not impressed and were indeed alarmed. However, the ability to do anything about the situation between the Western Allies and the Soviet Union was limited, and UNTHINKABLE was not the vehicle for retaliation as it was too blunt an instrument and failed to look at the ability of the Soviet Union to react to any measures taken by deploying this plan. UNTHINKABLE called for a pre-emptive strike against the Red Army on 1 July 1945 in order to impose the will of the USA and the British Empire, as Churchill chose to refer to the British, in order to 'get a square deal for Poland'. His service chiefs were somewhat shocked at such an audacious idea, let alone a plan to try to cut down to size an ally which was largely responsible for the defeat of Germany – even if it had also helped to start World War Two. Churchill was hugely concerned with the fact that the Soviets had extended a lot further west than had been originally envisaged.[25]

The somewhat startled British service chiefs looked at their options and in reply wrote a document: *Russia: Threat to Western Civilization.* In this paper British generals pointed out that the Red Army had two-and-a-half times more divisions than all the Western armies combined. Taking the central front around Dresden, the Soviets had superiority of 2:1 in armour and 4:1 in infantry. It was also noted that even if the Western armies had some initial success, the Soviets would no doubt take the long-term option and wage total war against the West over a protracted length of time as had been the case against Germany. Furthermore it was unlikely that the Americans would be interested, let alone participate in such an action for any length of time. As Field Marshal Brooke noted, the whole idea was 'fantastic' and 'unworkable'.[26] It was all part of Churchill's makeup – mad ideas with flashes of genuine brilliance and insight. Churchill may have been morally right in the case of Soviet intransigence, but he had to face reality.[27]

It was Field Marshal Alan Brooke who often had to drag Churchill back to reality and he did so in this case. Much of Brooke's inner thoughts, as with many people, are to be found in his private diary, one which should have never been kept during wartime and was never intended for publication. On 24 May 1945 Brooke recorded that he had looked that evening at the Planners' report on the possibility of attacking the Soviet Union. Brooke concluded that the entire enterprise was impossible and that from there on, the Soviet Union would be the most powerful force in Europe. Brooke also revealed that the COS and the Foreign Office had been at loggerheads over the Soviet Union since at least 2 October 1944. On this date the COS discussed a paper which they had released previously and which noted that in the future the Soviet Union might indeed become unfriendly towards the West. The Foreign Office refused to accept this and so in October 1944 the COS sat down to discuss the attitude of the Foreign Office regarding the Soviet Union.[28] The case of UNTHINKABLE, the clue was in the name, was quite a farsighted gambit of Churchill, however reason should have told him that an unprovoked attack on Soviet forces by the West was never going to happen. It had nothing of the Realpolitik necessary to prevent a premature shooting-war beginning between the Allies; senior British commanders knew this and made sure that UNTHINKABLE didn't go any further than that of the planning stage.

The major problem regarding UNTHINKABLE was that it called for an unprovoked attack on the Soviet Union. The consequences would have been dire and also would have played into the hands of the Soviet Union as Stalin strained to unleash the world revolution. It was during this period of heightened tension as the European war ended that Stalin remarked to Harriman, who thought the Soviets had done so well getting to Berlin, that Tsar Alexander I had got to Paris during the Napoleonic Wars.[29] This remark clearly illustrated Stalin's line of thought. Therefore, if UNTHINKABLE had been implemented, it would have been a gross folly by the British as the Soviet Union would have been seen as the aggrieved party in spite of Soviet shenanigans in east-central Europe, notably of course in Poland, and could have legitimately responded with its full arsenal claiming self defence – which of course it would have been. However, once the Red Army, or the Soviet Army as it had been rebranded at war's end, began to move further westward into the Western Allies' sectors of occupied Germany, the Soviets would not have stopped.[30]

The British COS realised that any attack on the Soviet Union was impossible because not only were the Allies outnumbered, but the question arose of just how far would an attack on the Soviet Union penetrate Soviet territory? It was considered that if one took the German campaign of 1942 as an example and studied just how far the German armed forces had made their way into the Soviet Union, it had been to no avail. The COS was not even interested in going as far. It was realised that any attempt to subdue the Soviet Union militarily was open-ended and just too risky. Not only would it have taken a long time to defeat the Soviet Union, assuming that this might even happen, there were by-products of Allied aggression against the Soviet Union. It was feared that the Soviets would stir up trouble in the Middle East, notably in Iraq and Iran, fuel anti-British sentiment in India, while in the Far East it was seriously considered that the Soviets would go over to the Japanese and overturn Allied gains in its war against Japan. Another problem was Yugoslavia, which was already bad enough as Tito and his forces did their best to seize Trieste. If the Soviets openly interfered in this dispute between Yugoslavia and Italy, with the Allies taking the side of Italy, it was thought that a Soviet offensive against Austria was also possible.[31]

Field Marshal Brooke was disturbed at what he was forced to examine because he was trying to focus on the war against Japan and how to proceed after the capture (or recapture) of Singapore, but was also being forced to consider the Soviet Union as a hostile force and what could be done about it. All that Brooke could divine was that, at best, the Western Allies might achieve a limited advance into the Soviet Union before coming to a halt and probably being driven back.[32] Brooke was well aware of other problems in Europe and in the Middle East, notably Syria and Lebanon, while Tito continued in his stance against Italy. The French Government was also trying to re-establish its authority in the Middle East but was learning that the German defeat and occupation of France had caused it to lose status in the eyes of its former colonial subjects, who now strove for independence – and were willing to fight for it. These were the many things that disturbed the COS while Brooke was more concerned about de Gaulle than he was about Stalin.[33] Brooke was concerned mainly about events on the Italian frontier and in the Middle East as they were things that affected British policies. British as well as Polish troops were still in Italy, while Syria and Lebanon were too close to the British Mandate of Palestine for comfort. European Jews who had survived the horrors of the Nazi genocide were making their way to Palestine and demanding a Jewish homeland and an independent state. The British government realised that the Muslim population in the Middle East would not welcome large scale Jewish migration far less an independent Jewish state in the centre of the Middle East and so sought to prevent Jewish migration there. The entire area was ready to explode into warfare and the French government's actions were not helpful and so the COS tried to prevent bloodshed. Regarding Stalin, the Soviets, Poland and east-central Europe, Brooke realised there was little that could be done and so the area had to be abandoned on the whole. That is why he advised that Operation UNTHINKABLE should be shelved – it was 'unthinkable', as he wrote on 31 May 1945.[34]

In the case of Poland, which would have been the cause of any hostilities breaking out between the Allies and the Soviet Union, the Soviet Union had considerable internal security units within Poland but was struggling. It was believed that the vast majority of Poles were 'violently anti-Russian' (rather than anti-Communist or anti-Socialist) while the Berling Army, which was supposed to be pro-Soviet, was unreliable as far as the Soviets were concerned. By the summer of 1945 this Polish force numbered some ten divisions and in the case of conflict between the Allies and the Soviets it was not clear if the Berling Army would even remain neutral, let alone support the Soviets. It was more probable that they would side with anti-Soviet forces.

Meanwhile Churchill wrote a memorandum to General Ismay of the COS; he was actually beginning to think his own 'unthinkable': that there was little that the British could do to tame the Soviet Union and its appetite for land. It had dawned on Churchill that the Americans had little interest in Europe and, at best, the USA was likely to remove itself back to its occupation zone in Germany. Furthermore, the bulk of US forces were likely to be returned from Europe to the USA or to the Pacific to continue the war against the Japanese. In the face of an unprovoked attack from the west and with little or no support from the USA, it was indeed possible that the Soviet Army in response could overrun Holland, Belgium and France and then – as was the case in 1940 – the defence of the United Kingdom would have to be studied with the enemy in occupation of the channel ports on the French coast. The British may have had a maritime and air superiority compared to the Soviets, but even Churchill realised that warfare had changed since 1940 and now rockets could make nonsense of British defences as he contemplated just how the Soviet Union might invade the UK if war broke out with the Soviets.[35] It was all very discouraging and the very reason why the British finally realised that there was nothing they could do militarily to try to persuade the Soviet government to stick to the promises it had made during the war concerning the future of east-central Europe, especially Poland. The Allies could only use diplomacy and economic leverage to try to contain Soviet imperialist ambitions, but the reality was that only Stalin's death would moderate this. Even today, Russian neo-imperialism continues its pressure.

Anders could have known nothing of Operation UNTHINKABLE; if he had, he would have worried at it like a terrier after a rat and done his best to make it happen. Brooke had a 'difficult lunch' with Anders on 8 June 1945. Anders had just resigned his post as Deputy Commander Polish armed forces and was on the way to Italy to resume his command of 2nd Polish Corps in Italy. Brooke remarked that Anders was 'as fanatical as ever in his outlook on Russia'. Anders was also still trying to increase the size of his force in Italy. Brooke noted that Anders had no real plans and just hoped to find a way of fighting his way back to Poland. In Brooke's opinion, Anders was capable of anything at that time and could have been quite dangerous and so needed watching closely.[36] This more-or-less proves that Anders had no idea about UNTHINKABLE and why should he have done so? He was only a minor ally, but also a major political embarrassment. Brooke's words of him speak volumes about how the British regarded Anders who, just over a year previously, had been feted by the British government and King George VI himself. How politics had damned the warrior.

The fact that there was a plan such as UNTHINKABLE shows that Anders was not as unreasonable as many people try to make him out to be. Of course, he was his own worst enemy, but the unfortunate thing was that both he and Churchill were both right at times when it was politically inconvenient or embarrassing to those who might be their allies. But of course Brooke, at times, doubted the sanity of Churchill and wished that he might go away. Even so, practically it might have been useful if Anders' forces could have been used clandestinely in Poland with the British government holding the whole thing at arm's length, but the risk of being caught was extremely high and the state of peace in Europe was perilous so even this was too much of a gamble – and the British government were not fools.

Before Churchill was voted from office he continued to worry about Soviet expansion into Europe; it was more than he had bargained for and it made him uncomfortable. He claimed that the situation in Europe was the most worrying he had ever experienced.[37] Churchill was not the only one concerned about Soviet hegemony spreading deeper into Europe than had been anticipated. At least three diplomats, Christopher Warner and Frank Roberts of the Foreign Office, experienced observers of east-central Europe and the Soviet Union, and the American, George Kennan, a seasoned diplomat with an extensive knowledge of the Soviet Union, tried to alert their respective governments to the danger that the Soviet Union presented for any meaningful peace. There would be a definite curtailment of freedom in east-central Europe if the Soviets were allowed to continue in their programme of absorbing the region. All three were gently rebuffed because their arguments and views were inconvenient. Roberts remarks that in the absence of their ambassadors it was very difficult to advise their governments, but he and his American counterparts maintained a barrage of messages, missives and papers all pertaining to how the Soviet government was behaving and what they considered to be the next moves by the Soviets – and none of them were friendly moves. Roberts noted that Kennan had a more difficult time as the Truman administration, which succeeded Roosevelt's, still tried to maintain a pro-Soviet policy. The two diplomats worked together closely but still maintained their independence of each other in their approaches in trying to deal with the ever-expanding influence of Soviet ideology across Europe and elsewhere.

Kennan's approach resulted in the appearance of the 'The Long Telegram', which was eventually published as an article in *Foreign Affairs* during 1946 over the signature '*X*'. Kennan, drawing on his extensive knowledge of Russian history and Soviet ideology, considered that the Soviet Union could not be treated as any other country, hostile or friendly, and that it should be treated as an enemy because its long-term aims were inconsistent with democracy. Even so Kennan argued that with intelligent handling, fortified with strength and realism, it should be possible to at least exist in peace alongside the Soviet Union. Kennan noted that this would have been impossible with Nazi Germany, which he put outside of the realm of reality. Roberts was in agreement with Kennan's findings but wanted to take a more positive view of the Soviet Union by looking at past Anglo-Russo relations. As was noticed by Roberts, historically, the relationship between the UK and Russia had always been one of hostility but had rarely ended in war – the exceptions being the Crimean War in the mid-1850s and the Allied intervention against the Bolshevik Revolution at the end of the First World War. Overall there had been cooperation in major world conflicts ranging from the Napoleonic War and the two world wars.

Roberts' advice to the Foreign Office and to the new Foreign Secretary, Ernest Bevin, was well taken. There may have been some slight differences or nuances as Roberts and his colleagues were able to observe Stalinism in action from Moscow, with its executions and the sending of people to concentration camps. Even so Roberts considered that on the whole there was still room for limited cooperation in certain fields, even if some in London refused to see this. Over all though, the differences were slight and did not harm his career and Bevin sent for Roberts to serve as his Principal Private Secretary. In this position Roberts was able to influence Bevin, thus giving him a more level-headed approach towards the Soviet Union and how to deal with it in good times and bad. Thanks to Roberts' influence the West was able to react with caution in ameliorating circumstances after the death of Stalin in 1953.[38] However, in 1946 the West was beginning to understand how to deal with Stalin and his government, but with changes in administration in both the UK and in the USA it was down to civil servants such as Roberts to provide consistency in policy, at least in the UK, while Stalin had nothing but death to consider. Of course decisions being made did not suit all, especially Anders and the Poles in London.

There was another problem as the American and British governments withdrew their recognition of the Polish Government-in-Exile in favour of that of the temporary government in Warsaw which was pro-Soviet while elections in Poland were in the offing. This was something that the British military chiefs, among others, were aware of before the decision was made public. It was a situation which sat uncomfortably with Brooke because on 2 July he faithfully recorded in his diary that difficulties lay ahead concerning the future of the Polish armed forces. He noted that in a few days the British government would be officially recognising the Polish government in Warsaw and letting the Polish Government-in-Exile go. Once this was promulgated the Polish forces in the West faced a serious problem which the Foreign Office had been ignoring since May despite frequent requests to reach a decision of how the Polish armed forces in the West were to be disposed of as hostilities ended in Europe.[39] And so we have it – little if anything had been prepared by the Foreign Office of what to do with the Polish Army once peace returned to

Europe. This was more to do with Second Polish Corps because First Polish Corps, which was more-or-less the Polish First Armoured Division, was in the short term engaged in occupation duties in Germany. Anders' people were not to be entrusted with such duties owing to their naked hostility towards the Soviet Union. Meanwhile the coming elections in Poland were to be a bone of contention as the Soviet authorities, namely the NKVD, assisted by Polish Stalinists ensured that the result of this election would be totally favourable towards the Soviet Union and to Stalin; not even partially, but totally.

Despite Anders being somewhat side-lined by political events in the UK, not all was lost because even though the Labour Party had been elected to govern in Britain, at the top of the party there were those who sympathised with the predicament of the Poles in the West. One of these was Ernest Bevin, an unlikely champion for Poland, even if he did so indirectly, he did so because he had seen through Stalin's Russia and knew it for the evil and corrupt empire it was. Roberts noted that Bevin 'understood Marxism-Leninism' and was a realist. Bevin may not have agreed with everything that Roberts put before him but he had the ability to get policy changed where it needed changing – and in sensible and measured steps.[40] This of course included not attacking the Soviet Union militarily as this was already a rather dead duck after UNTHINKABLE had been mauled by British service chiefs during the summer of 1945. A policy of containment and accommodation rather than of aggression or appeasement seemed to be the order of the day and became the trademark of the Cold War in Europe at least. Containment and accommodation obviously had to be tempered with reality – perhaps something learned from the Soviets as the world revolution was based on being able to advance in good times but withdraw or stop at a point when it was not to the advantage of the Soviets, and wait until it was possible to do so once more. During the summer of 1946 the Soviet government even made a claim on Libya (Tripolitania) as part of Soviet war reparations.[41] Of course the Red Army had not fought in Libya nor taken part in the North Africa Campaign which had been a straightforward struggle between Western Allies, including Polish troops, against Germany and Italy. There was no Soviet involvement at all.

By 1946 Anders and his men were deeply unpopular with the general public in the UK as propaganda often purveyed by the British trade union movement claimed that these men were fascists and anti-Semites.[42] Therefore, an extract from the Polish prime minister's speech to the National Home Council (Warsaw), to whom the Polish Government-in-Exile had lost British and American recognition during July 1945, was easily believed by many in the West, as well as in Poland, because it suited their views. The Polish prime minister alleged that,

> great difficulties have been experienced in carrying out the demobilisation of Polish troops abroad. There are people who would like to profit from the blood that has been lost by Polish soldiers. Consequently, the return of these troops to Poland has been a very slow affair. They came back even without the arms with which they fought. On the other hand, the adherents of Anders who were active in the underground movement attack the peaceful population and are equipped not only with new uniforms but also with automatic arms of excellent quality and first class wireless for spying purposes and communications. For obvious reasons, the Polish Army had to engage these political gangsters directed by Anders from abroad whose activities constitute a danger for the sovereignty and independence of the state. In their newspapers published for foreign money these gentlemen enlarge on the alleged dissatisfaction of the population with the Government policy. They expose, however, their true intentions by terrorising the people in order to prove the correctness of Anders' allegations. History has taught us the lesson that terror has always been the weapon of the weak and has never achieved its object. Polish troops fighting political gangs perform their difficult tasks as honourably as they did against the Germans. Our army is bravely fighting the elements who would lead their country to anarchy and civil war. The Polish soldier has not shed his blood for six years to allow political speculators to ruin the fruits of his victories. The Polish Army does not serve any political party but it should be realised that it would continue to serve the state authorities in their actions intended to strengthen the democratic regime in Poland. The Polish soldier defends the people against political banditism and actively helps the peasant.[43]

Of course the entire document is riddled with hypocrisy and lies, but Anders had to compete with such words. The entire question of there being a Polish

Army in Poland was nonsense; at best it was a Soviet colonial army or perhaps a militia with all senior officers being Russian or Soviet citizens. It had the autonomy of the British Indian Army or the African regiments raised by the French during the days of the French Empire. If terror was the weapon of the weak, then the Soviet Union was an extremely weak regime and of course a civil war and anarchy had already broken out in Poland as Bolshevik theory demanded as the fruits of victory had been snatched away from the Polish soldier by Stalin and the Soviet Union. It is all too painful to read – and for Anders and his men to have to swallow and possibly digest. There was little they could do about such propaganda expect issue denials and perhaps observe that there were two other Polish armies in the West, the First Polish Armoured Division occupying German territory and of course Polish Second Corps in Italy.

Indeed an earlier statement issued by Warsaw reported that the Polish perpetrators were, on the whole, personnel arrested from, or repatriated elements of, Polish Second Corps. This was 'confirmed' later and the type of people arrested, according to the authorities, seemed to have been every enemy of the Polish people and included personnel from Polish Second Corps, mainly a group of 'reactionary' officers who had served at the siege of Tobruk, a famous and heroic incident in the North Africa Campaign. Those arrested also included Volksdeutscher, Polish fascists, SS men, Ukrainian nationalists and Yugoslavs loyal to Michailović, Tito's deadly enemy.[44] Of course this list is a work of fantasy, those listed could never have worked together no matter the circumstances. However, the situation in Poland in 1946 was abnormal as the population was traumatised by war and the horrors which had come with the German occupation. Despite the denials issued by Warsaw relating to the use of terror, it was widely used in Poland in order to enforce the Sovietisation of Poland upon an unwilling population largely too terrified to ask questions relating to official information. With Polish collaborators, the Soviets were winning the propaganda war in 1946. As Bethell observed, the electoral campaign for what became the 1947 elections blurred into a civil war.[45]

Was there a civil war in Poland between 1944 and 1948? It very much depends on who one asks, as the distinguished veteran Polish military writer, Jerzy Ślaski observes. Ślaski, a survivor of both the Gestapo and the NKVD as he fought for a truly free Poland, notes that some historians claim a low figure for those opposing the Soviet takeover of Poland while others clearly exaggerated the numbers involved. It all depended on one's political viewpoint and, at present, there is still too little information to decide on what happened in Poland during this period. Ślaski writes that there was never a civil war, or any kind of war at all, but a 'gigantic hunt for small groups [of resistors] armed only with light infantry weapons who were doomed and isolated. These weak forces were confronted by the Communist powers with an army numbering more than a quarter of a million.' Ślaski observes that this huge Communist force was made up of UB (Polish Security Service) and MO (Polish citizens' militia), soldiers of the Polish Army and KBW, members of paramilitary Communist formations, armed Communist party members supported by armoured vehicles, artillery and aircraft. Furthermore, this large and well prepared force was supported by Soviet armed forces which at that time were stationed all over Poland and from time to time undertook operations against Polish Nationalists on their own initiative. However, despite this seemingly overwhelming strength arrayed against Polish resistors it seemed that the Polish Communists may well have been defeated but for support from the Red Army as KBW (*Korpus Bezpieczeństwa Wewnętrznego* [Internal Security Corps] Major General Włodzimierz Muś admitted in an interview with journalists in 1989 that the Polish resistance was better organised and had better tactics for fighting in towns and in the forests as well as enjoying popular support. Muś claimed that the resistors had 'better people' as well as being better trained.[46] It was an odd admission to make but by 1989 it didn't matter because Communism was collapsing in east-central Europe anyway. What does matter for this narrative is what was happening to Anders and his men against this background of a Soviet takeover in their homeland.

Anders had a very hard time with the Western media. In an interview in New York he was asked difficult questions such as why Poles in Poland were not as free as Germans now under Anglo-American occupation. He was also obliged to deny that his troops were involved in actions in Italy as notes from both the Soviet and Yugoslav governments were alleging, and he confessed to having been happy with how the British Foreign Secretary, Ernest Bevin, was defending Polish troops against charges made by various Soviet backed governments or by the Soviet government itself. Anders also denied that Polish troops were 'flexing their muscles' in Italy and questioned why the Soviet government so disliked the presence of Polish troops in Italy while the Soviet Army was occupying entire European countries. He also denied that he or any of those under his command had any terrorist links in Poland and demanded proof from the Soviet government rather than allegations.[47]

During the same month, February 1946, Anders was also interviewed by *The Guardian* and the reporter took a less favourable line towards him. Anders claimed that six or seven Polish troops had been killed in Italy by Communists. This was not what the reporter wanted to hear and then Anders pressed on for once with his agenda and asserted that he did not want to go to war with the Soviet Union (which was not strictly true) but that he just wanted Poland clear of Communism and that without Soviet support, Communism would not last in Poland. He also claimed that the 'Germans in five years of occupation have not ravaged Poland as much as the Bolsheviks have these past months'. Eventually the journalist, fed up with Anders, cut the interview short.[48] It was probably true that Polish troops had been killed by Italian communists as there was a state of near anarchy in Italy post-war and Polish troops had been identified with fascism. Anders had long hankered after war against the Soviet Union and was aghast that the Western Allies would not turn against Stalin; no matter the provocation while it was pure hyperbole to suggest that the Red Army had behaved worse than the German occupying forces. The Red Army and the NKVD were many things, but they did not commit genocide and did not murder around twenty-five per cent of the population of Poland. It should be noted that a Polish plan dated 11 August 1944 anticipated war between the UK and the Soviet Union sometime before 1954 and this was the very reason why Anders wanted to maintain Polish armed forces in the West with the highest possible numbers ready to fight the Soviet Union and regain Poland for the Poles.[49]

In another interview with Associated Press on 20 February 1946 Anders noted that Warsaw had demanded the return to Poland of all Polish troops in Italy. He also had to issue more denials concerning Polish troops in Italy. Anders observed that there were no Polish troops in the disputed Venezia Giulia region and that Polish troops were not being recruited under the slogan 'fight against Communism in Yugoslavia'. He also addressed the claims made in the Italian Communist press that Polish troops were conducting a violent anti-Communist campaign in Italy. Anders said that should be investigated and if true, those doing so would be punished. He also made the point that so many did not want to hear and that was that all of his troops (including Anders himself) had seen Communism and had no sympathy for it. Anders suggested that all Italian Communists should go to the Soviet Union and see it with their own eyes.[50]

The views of Anders were also those of a great many of his troops, as can be seen from the archives of 1st Carpathian Brigade. In June 1945 it was noted that the defeat of Germany in the minds of the soldiers of the brigade had not brought about Polish independence because Poland was now occupied by the Soviet Army and the Soviet political police and many soldiers were left unsettled and worrying about their futures. On 6 July 1945 Anders tried to put heart into his men in an Order of the Day when he addressed the problem which both he and his men faced. He knew that the situation looked terrible and could understand that his men were downhearted and concerned for their families and their futures. However Anders considered that the situation could not last indefinitely and that one day Poland would be free and independent. Even so, in the short term life did not look promising because between August and September 1945 relations between Italian civilians and Polish troops deteriorated. The major problem was that while local Italian civilians were being radicalised and sponsored by Moscow, Polish troops remained anti-Soviet while there were calls for Poles to be removed from the Cesenatico region. On 11 August 1945 there was a fight between an Italian civilian and a Polish soldier which left the Italian dead of knife wounds. *Unita*, the Italian Communist Party daily newspaper cranked up the rhetoric over this incident and tried to make it worse than it was. It should also be noted that there was a Soviet mission whose members were wearing either Soviet Army or NKVD uniforms present in Cesenatico. The tense situation between Italians and Poles continued right through to the end of 1945 with problems between Poles and local Communists. To make matters worse, Poles in German uniforms were also captured in Italy. However, during the spring of 1946 it was noted that Polish troops and Italian civilians were becoming closer and forming relationships.[51] It would seem that eventually humanity and nature will always triumph over social engineering and politics.

It was not only the Soviets who made trouble for Anders because the British, especially at the War Office, also harboured their suspicions about his activities during and after the war. In a statement issued on 11 February 1946, Anders was clearly furious when he said 'in recent months numerous accusations mounting both in frequency and ferocity have been directed against myself and at times, the troops under my command.'[52] Anders was also forced to deny being pro-German and a fascist. He claimed that he was not a traitor and had no allegiance to any political party. Anders also issued a furious denial that he was responsible for the death of Sikorski or as he put it, 'it is preposterous that I should be accused of being morally responsible for or in any way connected with the death of Poland's great war leader, General Sikorski.' He also denied supporting the Polish underground which was now fighting the Soviet takeover or aiding terrorism in Poland.[53] However, as we have already seen, if well respected and senior Polish figures such as Mikołajczyk were willing to go on record – as he did in a newspaper interview in December 1945 – and publicly state that people from Anders' circles had entered Poland during the period of November–December 1945 and carried out scores of political murders, it is difficult to accept Anders' denials that he had anything to do with the chaos in Poland. It was not credible, and even if it was true that the Soviet Union was taking over Poland, Anders' method of trying to deal with it was totally flawed and irresponsible and only strengthened the hand of the Soviets and Polish Stalinist allies. If one accepts that he was correct in his assumptions about how the Soviet Union would take over east-central Europe, Anders' frustration must have been immense, and frustration can make for some quite irrational decisions. Anders was not a criminal, but an extremely thwarted man.

It is without a doubt that Anders shed crocodile tears over the death of Sikorski and continued with these false tears over the memory of his former leader and his failed legacy; very soon the British government learned, via Kot, what Anders was really up to. Kot had told the British Ambassador in Warsaw that Anders was indeed collaborating with 'subversive elements' in Poland, was receiving couriers coming from Poland and was in radio contact with the Polish military underground. Most damning was that, according to Kot, in spite of British requests not to do so Anders was still recruiting men to Second Corps as if trying to replace the 12,000 men who had returned to Poland. By May 1945 the Poles, especially Second Polish Corps, were seen as a political embarrassment and it was clear that they could not remain under arms forever. As for Anders, he was seen as being a law unto himself (as Sikorski had found) and was merely waiting for the appropriate moment when he would be able to seize Poland using armed intervention.[54] The last piece of information was hardly a revelation because the British government had known since 1943 that both Kot and Anders sought power in post-war Poland, and neither would have been too fussy how they gained this – or how they held on to it. Neither could be considered to have been democratic in the Western sense of the word. The problem lay with the fact that even if Anders was not going to secure democracy for his homeland, whatever he might have imposed it would not have been as bad as annexation and the tyranny Poland was experiencing as the Red Army, with their Polish Stalinist collaborators, set about systematically destroying any vestige of Polish independence. The Polish historian Andrzej Chmielarz, while denying that there was a civil war in Poland, insists that the situation was one where 'liberation' turned out to be annexation. The fighting in Poland was a popular rejection of the imposition of a Communist government on Poland in order to 'create a state with no sovereign authority'. Overall, the Soviet security services in their various forms outnumbered the local Polish security forces and so the country was, beyond doubt, occupied.[55] This occupation lasted until 1993 in the sense that the Soviet Army was still in the former East Germany, Czechoslovakia and Poland until then. This underlined the dependence on the Soviet military of Communist rule in these states.[56]

Once again there is suggestion that perhaps Anders and his men might have had a role to play in the immediate post-war situation in Poland as Poles were not totally against at least the notion of socialism coming to Poland, or a more egalitarian society rather than the scriptures of the pre-war Polish Republic. What Poles were not willing to endure was another occupation by another state. Soviet rule may not have been as murderous as German rule, but all the same it was not a Poland ruled by the Poles for the Polish people. Furthermore, the Soviet Union was merely the former Russian Empire reasserting itself.

The Poles in Italy never lost an opportunity to try to muddy the waters post-war with the Soviet government and the Warsaw government, and during the autumn of 1945 the British military authorities had to issue yet another warning to Anders concerning Polish attitudes towards Moscow and Warsaw. It appears that Polish Second Corps had had a concert party entitled the 'Atomic Bomb'. Major-General A.D. Ward, in a letter to Anders, admitted that the standards of the show were high but he was surprised and concerned at the element of propaganda in some of the acts. Ward complained:

> I feel that little good can be done by the suggestion that the atomic bomb provides the solution to your difficulties with Soviet Russia, by ridiculing those who opt to return to Poland or by the satire of the San Francisco Conference in the final act of the Concert Party.

Ward told Anders that there had been large numbers of complaints about political and 'propagandist activities' in Polish Second Corps. The complaint ran further:

> On my return I found further protests about the attitude of your newspapers to the Polish Provisional Government in Warsaw and protests from our Ambassador in Warsaw that men are being invited to leave Poland and come to Italy to join the Corps. These matters will be dealt with separately by the branches of the staff concerned; I merely quote them as justifying my concern over items in the programme of your Concert Party.[57]

This incident and its repercussions, especially from the British Ambassador, rather proves that Polish Second Corps was indeed recruiting from inside of Poland and that is a short step from subversion inside Poland and a headache for British, and no doubt American, diplomacy.

Anders dismayed the Western Allies further during November 1945 when he wrote a long memorandum of the general military situation at that time. His opening salvo was to criticise the Allied war aims which had been formulated in September 1939, as he saw it, but had not been achieved in 1945. As he put it, Germany and Japan may have been 'smashed', but real peace had not been achieved. According to Anders ten countries in Europe (over 100 million people) had lost their freedom. He also commented that the situation in China was serious (civil war) and that the situation in the Middle East was very disturbing, and wrote that 'it therefore seems to me that quiet and peaceful work throughout the world is not at present possible.' Then Anders dropped his bombshell as he stated quite clearly that the single reason for this was the expansion of the

Soviet Union which on the European and Asiatic continents in 1945 was the only power. This was not strictly true, but it was the only power willing to flex its muscles and while the Western powers tried at least to repair Europe, the Soviets were definitely looting the wrecked continent as far as they could.

Anders continued with what should not have been said, that the Soviet Union or Russia had far-reaching imperialist plans and did not hide them. In Anders' opinion it was not just small states that should feel menaced but also larger states. He observed that the Soviet Union had expanded its borders further than the former Russian Empire and these newly acquired states were merely springboards for further expansion and invasion. Areas under threat according to Anders included Germany, Austria and the Italian-Yugoslav frontier, while the Soviet Union held an unusually favourable position in the Balkans which threatened Greece, Turkey and the Middle East. He also commented that the latest developments in China were consistent with Soviet policy in Asia.

Then Anders gave full vent to his ideas and wrote that Russia pays complete homage to the principle that war is the furtherance and most realistic continuance of policy.

> Moreover, Russia, in agreement with Clausewitz, believes that "war exists more for the defender than the conqueror; after all it is only aggression that results in defence and conjunction with it, war. The conqueror is always the lover of peace. (This was Bonaparte's view too). He would rather seize foreign territory by a policy of peace!!!" And in the margin alongside this argument, underlining it five times, Lenin wrote – "Ha! Ha! War is the tool of politics, the continuation of foreign relations in conjunction with the use of other means." To sum up, Russia, like Germany, looks on aggression as a logical furtherance of policy in order to achieve the aims of that policy, whereas the defender makes it into war by attempting to frustrate that achievement. In fact they deny the right of others to oppose their desires, and thence accuse the defender of making war. She has not only taken over the old imperialist policy from Tsarist Russia but she has strengthened it. For this purpose also she is better placed, having officially adopted the ideology and the character of a communist state.

Anders wrote of how the Russians or the Soviets relied on surprise and could wait for the right time to launch an attack after investigating its potential prey, especially democratic states. Russia, according to Anders, knew a lot about other states, not only through its diplomatic and military missions and agents, but also through the use of local Communist parties. On the other hand it seemed that the West knew little about the Soviet Union such as there was little knowledge of Soviet military strengths in northern Finland and the Baltic states. Anders estimated that there were between 2 million and 2.5 million Soviet troops in Germany and Poland and that reports show that numerous convoys of equipment and troops were moving across Poland to the West.

Regarding Poland, Anders stated that despite official statements from the Soviet government it was not true that Soviet garrisons had withdrawn from Poland during August 1945. What had taken place were inter-unit movements which did not extend beyond the Polish frontiers. Their only purpose was to deceive and to convince outside observers that they had returned to the Soviet Union. Indeed, in a statement published in October 1945 Soviet garrisons were established in Poland in a response to the Polish government's request to do so. This was an attempt to legalise the Soviet presence in Poland. The nascent Polish People's Army, now termed the 'Zymirski Army' consisting of 400,000 men, was commanded almost exclusively by Soviet officers from the rank of captain upwards. Anders noted that the borders in the new territories belonging to the Soviets had been tightened, Eastern Europe had become an armed camp in many ways, and that the Soviet Union was on a war footing. Anders seemed to underline this by stating:

> All people coming from Poland or other occupied countries state unanimously that not only the ordinary soldiers, but also the Soviet officers stress at every opportunity that the war had not ended yet, that today they defeated the Germans and tomorrow they will defeat the English. In view of the regime in Russia it is clear that such expressions of opinion are the result of internal propaganda spread for a definite purpose.

To add to the misery of the countries liberated/annexed by the Soviet Union, according to Anders, Soviet troops were living off these countries and taking all foodstuffs they could lay their hands on. If this continued the local populations might well have faced starvation. In Soviet propaganda it was always stressed just how countries such as Poland and Germany were immensely wealthy and could support such behaviour. Anders also spoke of how the Soviet Union was stripping these countries and others of their means of production, especially heavy war industries as machinery and other assets were shipped to the Soviet Union. Anders observed that all of the material taken to the East would increase Soviet war potential.

Anders continued with his theme that the war was not over until the Soviet Union had been defeated and made to release east-central Europe from its grasp. He noted that the last phase of the war was conducted almost entirely using American tanks and equipment, while the Soviet war industry was running at 'full pressure' and was yet to stop. He also pointed out that the Soviets were quite capable of using 'fifth columnists', or the enemy from within. This included the internal problems of Greece and its civil war, Italy in the grip of the Trieste question as it tussled with Yugoslavia over whom the city belonged to, and recent industrial strikes in both the UK and the USA; according to Anders, these were all Soviet attempts to paralyse these countries. This was part of the Soviet plan: attack at a place and a time of its choosing, but overall Anders did believe in the final victory of Western democracy.

A document was produced to reinforce Anders' words. Its origin was that of a Soviet document taken by the AK from a wounded Red Army political officer who had been rescued by Polish fighters in August 1944. The document, labelled 'top secret', was an instruction issued in April 1944 for Colonel-General Bogolbov, commander of the 1st Ukrainian Front and the 2nd Byelorussian Front, and concerned future Soviet planning. This document made fascinating reading as Soviet objectives were so clear. The Soviet Supreme Council had realised that many Red Army troops considered that the war was nearly over and looked towards demobilisation, but this sentiment had to be squashed even if the men were tired of the present war which had been long and bloody, it was only a stage in the overall plan. The war was to be in three stages. The first stage was to obtain the state boundaries of 1939-41 (eastern Poland and the Baltic States); the defeat of Germany and the struggle against 'our eternal enemies – the plutocratic countries – England and America'. There was to be an interval between stages two and three which was to be used by the Soviet Union to establish Soviet-friendly governments and the strengthening of Communist influence within the areas of Soviet influence. It was realised that there would be opposition to this and the UK was singled out as a state most likely to try to counter any pro-Soviet activity; action needed to be taken, ranging from disturbances and even civil war. The overall aim was to establish a 'European Union of Soviet Republics.'[58] Anders' critique should have been devastating but it seemed to have been ignored as it was embarrassing; in many ways it still seems as relevant today, even if some had hoped in 1991 to wish away the Cold War. Even so, much of Anders observations were very accurate and at times chilling.

What is important is that Anders had had this information for some time and sat on it; perhaps even he didn't want to rock the Allied boat in such a way until his hand was forced. An earlier report by a junior officer concerning the relationship between the Poles in the West and the British government at a time when the British had just withdrawn recognition of the Polish Government-in-Exile, pointed to a number of things which were finally revealed by Anders in late 1945. Again the report noted that the Soviet Union had achieved its open war aims with the complete cooperation of its Anglo-Saxon partners at Teheran and Yalta, but the overall plan was world revolution and the Soviet government was willing to take its time over this, proceed with caution and act when it needed to. To counter this, it was argued by the report's author that the Polish Constitution must be retained as it was a symbol of the ideal of a free Poland, but most importantly the Polish armed forces in the West must be kept intact as it was the 'genuine and living strength of Poland and the Polish nation'.[59] It is a matter of opinion which constitution was meant: the democratic 1921 constitution, or the illegal 1935 constitution, while the need to preserve the Polish armed forces in the west is notable because Anders was no real democrat and even though he genuinely wanted to see a free and independent Poland, he sought to command it. Anders' statement must have been like a bombshell because a military mission from Warsaw, which of course was Soviet friendly, had recently visited London. It did him no good however, because correspondence between General Kopański and Brigadier W.A.M. Stawell at the War Office at the beginning of November 1945 reveals that Stawell denies the Poles two things: a visit by Anders to London, and a visit by Kopański to Italy. Stawell observed that the situation at that time was 'delicate' and after the recent visit from Warsaw the British government were unwilling to do anything that might provoke suspicion of British intentions by the Warsaw authorities.[60] This made it clear that the London Poles were of no relevance to the British, and that Warsaw had the lead concerning Anglo-Polish relations.

Once the fighting finished in Europe the problem in Poland, as Prażmowska observes, was that the state of insecurity persisted post-war longer than in other European countries.[61] The main reason for this was that neither the Communist authorities nor the, by now weakened, underground movement had the ability in 1945 to completely impose their will on the country. The situation was different in Yugoslavia, where Tito's partisan movement was able to assume power; or in France where, for a transitional period, the French were able to rally around the exiled wartime leader General Charles de Gaulle and the pre-war administration was able to return to its former position; the pre-war Polish administration was unable to return.[62] A further problem was one for the émigré communities who had failed to understand that Poles who had endured the rigours of war and occupation in Poland had a different world-view; they were basically tired of war and struggle and just wanted to be left alone to resettle and bring back an element of normality to their lives. It was unthinkable to Poles in the West that Poles in Poland actually considered some of elements of the Communist plans appealing, while those such as Anders feared, quite rightly, that the NKVD would root out and destroy the Polish Underground, which was waiting for a chance to remove the Soviets and their Polish allies from Poland.[63] A further consideration should be that the Polish Second Republic was a shambles and was merely a Poland which suited elites, especially the military. To have been a peasant or an ordinary worker in Poland between 1918 and 1939 was a miserable existence and of course Poland was a dictatorship after 1926. Even the collective experience of war and occupation failed to close the gap in the attitudes of the elites, as witnessed during the Warsaw Uprising when the surprisingly incompetent General Bor-Komorowski caused the AK to rise up against the German garrison in Warsaw during the summer 1944. The Warsaw Uprising led to disaster, death and destruction, especially among non-combative civilians and then once the uprising failed Bor-Komorowski was taken into genteel captivity by the Germans while his compatriots were subject to illegal captivity, slave labour and death.[64] The old guard had learnt nothing, still took ordinary people for granted and cared nothing for their lives but merely sought a return to power at whatever cost.

Despite the problems faced by the minority of Poles actively opposed to the Soviet takeover in Poland, it should be recognised that Poles still loyal to London and to Anders post-war had been quite effective in penetrating the Soviet-backed Polish internal security forces. Members of NSZ and ex-fighters of the AK had successfully been placed within the ranks of the police (MO) and the Secret Police (UB) and so were privy to secrets and future operations against the Polish underground movement.[65] This led to a total communisation of the MO and UB as purges were undertaken and only members of the PPR and PPS would be members of these two forces.[66] Once the Polish Underground lost the ability to penetrate the Polish security services, fighting – in what is perceived by many to be the Polish Civil War – began in earnest. Despite the attempts to improve the internal situation in Poland from the Communist point of view, Radkiewicz, the Communist minister for public safety told Eugenio Reale, the Italian ambassador to Poland, a Communist and ex-prisoner of war with sympathy for the new regime, that 'common and political banditism' was a major problem for public order in January 1946.[67] Two observations should be made here: the Communists really had no patience as they seemed to think that things could be sorted almost immediately, while Reale, given his background and loyalties, was a disaster for Western Poles, especially as they were largely operating via Anders from Italy.

Radkiewicz declared that there were still 15,000 active 'political bandits' of whom the NSZ were the most active and dangerous (to the Communists that is). Further accusations were made by Radkiewicz as he claimed that the Polish Government-in-Exile and Anders were involved in causing dissent, with the PSL recently becoming involved. What was most disconcerting for Warsaw and for Reale was the allegation that much of the support for the underground came from Polish forces which were stationed in Italy, especially given that there had been undiminished agitation between Anders' troops and Italian Communists and Socialists. Radkiewicz was particularly vicious in his assertion that the NSZ was particularly supported by Anders.[68] This was a particular problem for Anders and his men as the NSZ were considered to be fascist not only by the Soviets, but also by many in the UK and other places as well as having a bolthole in the West. In a press conference Radkiewicz claimed that

1,424 members of the security services had been killed in action while fighting underground forces, or bandits as he preferred, while another 2,000 members of other parties had been victims of attacks by the same people. The NKVD in Poland disagreed with the Polish report considering it an underestimation. Declaring that the attacks were more numerous than admitted by the Poles and that the attacks were largely carried out by AK-WiN or NSZ, according to Prażmowska, was an unveiled attack on PSL which had declared itself to be the official opposition. It was also alleged that there had never been an attack on PSL members or property.[69] This is not true as it is recorded that Mikołajczyk's deputy was murdered and it was claimed at the time that Anders' people were responsible.[70]

Even so, Prażmowska admits to remaining uncertain how the Communists managed to secure the upper hand and confidence to defeat their opponents.[71] I would suggest that the answer was unbridled terror, confusion and the ability of Soviet agitators to whip up the local population to find other targets such as the Jews – those that survived the Nazi attempt to exterminate them – with the Soviets and local Poles quite determined to finish the diabolical project in the name of nationalism and Polish Catholicism, but all the time manipulated by the NKVD and its various agencies. To whip up a pogrom in Poland was the easiest thing in the world once a frightened, superstitious and ignorant people were provided with a target to explain away problems, and so people died in Kielce in 1946 as a diversion to what was really going on in Poland – the complete annexation of the country by the Soviet Union. The Kielce pogrom is the most notorious pogrom of Polish post-war history but is largely unknown even within Poland. It began once a rumour spread that Jews had kidnapped a child as a sacrifice in a Jewish rite and a mob of Poles quickly grew and attacked a building sheltering Jews coming from the Soviet Union en route to Palestine. Forty of them were killed in the ensuing violence. As Ascherson observes, responsibility for the violence and murder was mixed as sides competing for power in Poland blamed each other. Mikołajczyk blamed Communist police provocation; others saw it as yet another manifestation of Polish anti-Semitism, while the Communists blamed right-wing Nationalists. An interesting observation is that Nationalists and several bishops responded to the Communist allegation by insisting that many Communists, especially those in the secret police, were Jews – as if the two were dependent on each other.[72] On investigation, *The Manchester Guardian* discovered that despite the recent horrors visited on the Jewish population in Poland and elsewhere by the Nazis, and notwithstanding the fact that millions of Poles were also murdered by the Nazis, many in Polish society – especially the clergy – were still unwilling to accept surviving Jews returning to their homes in Poland and only wished them harm.[73] This was a feature that continued throughout the Communist period and continues to this day, both in Poland and in the émigré circles of Poles, the so-called Polonia. Of course there is no evidence at all of Jews ever sacrificing Christian children for their blood; it is just the result of ignorance and intolerance among an uneducated people. Whoever caused the pogrom in Kielce on 4 July 1946, it illustrates just how a mob can be stirred up to commit mass murder if a despised minority is the target, while the attitude of senior Polish clergymen is appalling and speaks volumes about what may have happened that day. Even so, it is quite clear that many Poles in the Kielce area had also been involved in killing Jews, even during the German occupation. These killings can only be described as bestial as the Polish peasants slaughtered their Jewish neighbours without mercy, caring nothing for age or gender. They were just Jews and there appears not to have been any input by the occupying Germans as the Jewish victims were often slaughtered using farm implements or anything to hand.[74] The reading of this episode is hard, while the actions of those at Kielce remained damned forever and made it more difficult for moderate Poles trying to find a decent settlement for post-war Poland to overcome accusations of anti-Semitism and fascism.

Another area of intrigue was the historical antipathy between the Poles and the Ukrainians. During the war this had been ramped up by the Germans who had used Ukrainians against the Poles and stood back while both sides slaughtered each other, notably during 1943. Eventually Ukraine had managed to provide Ukrainian volunteers for the SS Ukrainian Division. Ukrainians, not necessarily serving with the Galicia Division as the Ukrainian SS Division was known, served in Warsaw during the 1944 Warsaw Uprising and swiftly acquired a reputation for brutality, rape and mass murder. This division in what could have been a united front if Poles and Ukrainians had managed to work together was exploited by the Soviet security apparatus while the recent legacy of slaughter could not be overcome. Even so, there is evidence that the Ukrainian underground, UPA, was beginning to cooperate with the

Poles in a common struggle against Soviet occupation. Eventually the joint Ukrainian-Polish actions, as limited as they were, became undone as the Soviet authorities enforced a policy of removing Ukrainians from the new eastern Poland, notably the Rzeszów region. The assassination of General Karol Świerczewski, the Deputy Minister of National Security, by the UPA, ensured a hardening of the resolve by the Polish government to remove Ukrainians from Polish territory. The Polish Army and the UB were put in charge of the deportation of Ukrainians and with Czech and Soviet assistance, over 18,000 soldiers were deployed in this work. This had the effect of removing Ukrainian identity from Poland and the removal of a possible ally for those Poles resisting Soviet domination in Poland. By the end of 1947 the Communist regime, with the removal of the Ukrainian minority from the 'new Poland', had perhaps not achieved what they had intended: the creation, as near as possible, of a 'nation-state', that is a state where the populace is made up of almost entirely a single ethnic group and not what politicians and journalists think it means i.e. simply a state. After 1947, the population of Poland was more or less made up of Slavic Poles and not its former mishmash of Poles, Germans, Jews and Ukrainians. However, a state dominated by the Soviet Union had also been created.[75] The Soviet plan to ensure that Poland became a Communist country, and one that had a Soviet-friendly Polish government, had worked just as Anders had feared. The West was outwitted, but equally the British and American governments had no interest in Poland as a single unity, although they were becoming more alarmed at the rate that Soviet influence was spreading across Europe, threatening France, Italy and Greece. It was quite clear that Communism or Stalinism was making its influence felt in Asia, notably China, which was engaged in a struggle between Mao's communists and the Nationalist regime. Indeed with the Japanese withdrawal towards Japan and subsequent defeat in September 1945, political vacuums opened up across south-east Asia as it was clear that many of the liberated countries were unwilling to allow their former European colonial masters, notably the UK, France and Holland, to return and take up where they left off in 1941 and 1942. Communism threatened to fill these vacuums and all roads led to Moscow and to Stalin. It was all as Anders had predicted and the West had tried to ignore this matter.

The British government wondered how to best dispose of Anders and in March 1946 even considered detaining him indefinitely in London if he proved to be uncooperative. This was at a time when Anders and several other Polish commanders were interviewed by the British authorities to try and gauge how the Polish commanders were thinking. Luckily Anders proved to be cooperative and saved the War Office a lot of embarrassment.[76] In July 1946 Brigadier Firth, a friend of Anders, went to Robin Hankey at the Foreign Office and asked:

> what are you going to do with Anders? If you put him on one side – the Poles will be furious and accuse us of lack of gratitude to a successful Commander; if you banish him to some country – the result will be the same; while if you leave him in the UK, out of a job, his influence will still be used, his advice taken – but without suitable control on our part; it will be more dangerous still.[77]

It would seem that Sikorski's great fixer, Jozef Retinger, once more rose to the occasion and interceded on Anders' behalf at the Foreign Office and a suitable line was taken.[78] This may explain why the British government decided to award a pension to Anders rather than to a man such as Maczek, who was the victor at Normandy but ended up a barman by 1950. He was politically too quiet and did not embarrass the British. For shame!

Anders was clearly going to be a problem for any British government because even though he was unlikely to have restored democracy to Poland, his views on the Soviet Union and its terrorist methods of ruling in east-central Europe, especially in Poland, were valid but embarrassing for the British and American governments. Even though the Soviet Union was one of the victorious Allies in the war against Germany and was about to join the British and the Americans in the war against Japan, it was also a running sore in the Alliance as senior Western figures were quite aware of the horrors that the Soviet Union using the NKVD had visited on those countries which had fallen to them. Anders used every occasion after the defeat of Germany to air his views on the Soviet Union. At Bologna, for example, at a time when General Mark Clark, the American Commander, was decorating Polish troops from Polish Second Corps with American decorations, Anders observed that Polish troops had made great sacrifices in Italy only to be denied freedom because many Polish troops could not return home due to the Soviet occupation of

Poland and annexation of eastern Poland.[79] Within a week Anders spoke out once more about a return to Poland, but to an independent Poland and certainly not a Poland which was the seventeenth Soviet republic. Anders noted that the reports which were coming out of Poland were not only Polish but also British, American, French and Italian and they all pointed towards a worsening situation in Poland. Indeed Anders claimed that there was no Poland as it had been destroyed by the NKVD while the Red Army conducted a reign of terror carrying out mass arrests and deportations. Furthermore Anders claimed that the National Unity Government, which was a sort of transitional government representing all political hues ranging from London Poles to Soviet-friendly Poles, was merely a sham as fifteen of the twenty representatives were actually agents of a foreign power: the Soviet Union.[80]

Anders continued in this vein and in a speech which was published in *Gazeta Żołnierza* said again that Poland was not free and that the Soviet Union was destroying Poland. Anders claimed once more that the NKVD were carrying out mass arrests and deporting Poles to the Soviet Arctic where no doubt they were used as slave labour. He pointed out the number of Soviet prison camps and concentration camps being re-established as well as reminding his men that they need not think that the NKVD would spare them if they returned to Poland because it was not only political figures and fascists who were being apprehended; the methodology being used by the NKVD was once more mass arrests as had been the case between 1939 and 1940 when all of Polish society living under Soviet occupation were affected. Anders also noted that any resistance put up by Poles associated with the military underground would be deemed as 'fascist' as of course Soviet propaganda was a vast, outrageous smear campaign.[81] It should be remembered that much of the British press at that time was also depicting members of Polish armed forces as 'fascist', especially those serving in Second Polish Corps. Furthermore the British authorities had been put on notice just after the Yalta Conference as they were issued a notification of Polish intentions which read

> The intention of the Polish Armed Forces is to fight the Germans as the interests of Poland demand and to remain at the side of Great Britain until the end of the present world war. Should Poland at that time not be a free and sovereign country and the Polish people be unable

to live in that country according to their own will, the Polish Armed Forces now fighting will be unable or unwilling to return to their country. The necessity will then arise of finding the Polish fighting men with work and such settlements as may ensure their freedom and the conservation of their language, traditions and culture.[82]

This top secret document, which made clear reference to the terms of the Yalta Agreement or as the Poles preferred the 'Crimean Talks', certainly put the British government on notice of Polish post-war intentions if necessary. Of course this became reality.

Anders was not going to drop the matter of the Soviet annexation of Poland and became more vocal as time passed. On 11 September 1945 in the format of an 'Officers' Order', Anders once more raised the crimes of the Soviet Union committed against Polish people since 1939, with a complete condemnation of the mass deaths of Polish men, women and children through starvation and ill-treatment while in Soviet captivity. Anders, as ever, observed that despite huge Polish losses while fighting in the West, Poland remained occupied by the Soviet Union and that there could not be any talk of the demobilisation of Polish armed forces as long as the situation continued and that the struggle must go on. Anders also mentioned that the Italian Communist Party and its press had been attacking Polish Second Corps as directed by Moscow.[83]

The problem for Anders was that he may have been morally right, and he was definitely correct about what was happening in Poland, but the reality was that not enough people cared. Elements of the British press and the entire Soviet press were very skilled in convincing people that the Poles in the West were indeed fascists, while Anders made a fatal mistake in never really recognising the huge numbers of Soviet war dead. How the Soviet Union suffered so badly during the Second World War was not only due to German aggression, but also the effects of Sovietisation and neglect. When the British general, Sir Mike Jackson, was visiting the Soviet armed forces Museum in Moscow decades after the Second World War, he noticed that the Soviet Union considered the Western war effort as being of little importance once measured against that of the Soviet Union.[84] Therefore it is not surprising that the Soviet view of the Polish contribution in the Second World War was that the Poles were more-or-less irrelevant – unless they served a Soviet purpose of course.

No matter how Anders complained about his and his countrymen's situation, there was always a rebuke from the British very close to hand. Anders' problem was that Polish Forces in the West, even though the war was over, remained under British command and therefore subject to British foreign policy objectives. As the Allies sought to put the world to rights according to their own vision and not to that of Anders, Polish hostility towards the Soviet Union was not welcomed, as evidenced in a note to Anders from Lieutenant-General William Morgan, Chief of Staff at the Allied Force Headquarters, sent during July 1945. Morgan had been directed by Field Marshal Alexander, who was in Potsdam helping to devise policy to defeat Japan with the use of the Red Army. Alexander had been approached, presumably by the Soviets who had concerns about various criticisms of the Soviet Union by Anders, particularly an 'Order of the Day' for 6 July 1945 which seems to have been more objectionable than usual. Alexander liked Anders and sought to deal with the matter himself; he sent the following message via Morgan: 'As a friend I must sincerely advise you not to repeat anything of this nature and as your Commander-in-Chief, I insist that, in future, all statements by you which might be politically controversial be passed to me for approval.' Morgan requested that as Alexander was away at present, Anders would refrain from doing anything which 'might' be politically controversial without first submitting it to Allied Forces Headquarters for approval.[85] Basically Anders was being told to grow up – he had lost the argument and was being expected to deal with it. Anders should have known by 1945 that he and his corps were no longer needed and his petulance would cut no ice with the British as they would remove both him and his corps at the drop of a hat. Anders simply failed to realise this – even if he was correct in his assumptions concerning Soviet conduct in east-central Europe.

The problem vis-à-vis Polish Second Corps and the Allies, especially the British, was the decisions taken at the Yalta Conference which basically handed east-central Europe over to the Soviet Union as the Red Army was already in possession of these lands; the Western Allies were not about to undertake another war with the Soviet Union especially as Germany was yet to be totally defeated. In a meeting with Field Marshal Alexander during February 1945, Anders made it very clear how the Poles fighting in Italy felt about the conclusions of the Yalta talks. Anders said that Yalta was a major tragedy for Poland 'and that in spite of much thought [he] was completely at a loss to find a solution to his problem of what to tell his troops and how to maintain their morale'. It was during this period that the Poles were complaining that their role in the war against Germany was being understated. The Polish Military Attaché in London, Major-General Regulski wrote to Major General J.A. Sinclair at the War Office on 5 February 1945 complaining that on the BBC programme *They Fight with Alexander*, broadcast on 5 January 1945 graphically depicted the taking of Cassino town by the British Army yet hardly mentioned the Polish role, just a mention of the raising of the Polish national flag over Cassino Abbey 'as if this were the result of the fall of Cassino town'.[86] Sinclair claimed that the oversight of the Polish role in Italy was deliberate because there was a need to avoid mentioning Polish troops in Italy at this time, however, there was soon relating to the role of the First Polish Armoured Division (FPAD) in Holland as well as Polish troops in Italy.[87] This was a good idea from the British point of view as the FPAD had been making good progress as it advanced across Europe and was popular with the Dutch people following the liberation by the Poles of the city of Breda. The fact that the city was liberated without being wrecked was a bonus and the citizens of Breda remain grateful to their Polish liberators to the present day. Furthermore, FPAD did not cause any concern for the Soviet authorities while the Polish presence in Italy was a source of irritation for the Soviet government. Anders remained hostile towards the Soviet Union while he considered that the British and American governments did not do enough to support the Poles in the West.

The Soviet-friendly Polish government-in-waiting, the so-called 'Lublin government', was not considered respectable in the opinion of Anders, who believed its leader, Bolesław Beirut had been an OGPU (Soviet security police) agent for five years and had helped to organise the mass deportations of Poles while its military leader, Rola-Zymirski, had been cashiered from the pre-war Polish Army and imprisoned for five years. Anders told Alexander that in the eyes of the Soviets and the Lublin Government, all Poles who had served in the West or in the Polish Underground were fascists and that was why they could not return safely to Poland. Anders said he did not believe Stalin would stick to the terms of the Yalta Agreement, which in theory should have returned democratically elected governments throughout east-central Europe. It was Stalin's aim, according to Anders, to conquer all of Europe – and later the world. It was all in Stalin's writings as it had been in Hitler's, but few in the West had ever read either.

On learning of the terms of Yalta, Anders wrote to General McCreery and requested that Polish troops should leave the line but as there were no replacement troops Anders kept Second Polish Corps in place and gave orders for complete calm. To Anders, Soviet actions were like those of a blackmailer whose demands are never satisfied. Alexander had sympathy for the Polish plight and asked which was the gravest point for the Poles: the alteration of the pre-war Polish frontiers, or the possibility of the imposition of a Soviet Polish government? Anders said that it was the problem of the Lublin government as it affected the Polish oath of honour and allegiance. The signature of the 'Big Three', that is the UK, US and Soviet governments, legalised the Soviet actions through the medium of the Lublin government. Anders observed that despite five years of war with Germany, the Germans had never been able to form a Polish puppet government.[88] Anders' point here is not relevant as the Germans never really tried, while the Soviets very quickly found Poles who wished to betray their country. Power is power.

Some Allied military commanders may have had sympathy for Anders and his men but Churchill did not. Even though Anders was furious at the decisions made at Yalta, Churchill was not fazed by Anders' anger and bluster in February 1945 and told him bluntly that he should have tried to work with the Soviet government while observing that the UK had never guaranteed the Polish frontiers – but had guaranteed Polish independence back in 1939.[89] This may have been Churchill trying to deny responsibility for what seemed to have been craven behaviour at Yalta, but he had a point. Anders did not try to work with the Soviet government, but whether this had been realistic is a matter of opinion; the Red Army had swept all before them and committed atrocities against the Polish Underground military, so it seems unlikely that Anders would have found common ground with the Soviet government. However unlike Mikołajczyk, Anders found himself isolated from legal involvement in Poland and, along with other Polish military figures, quickly found himself exiled and stateless once the war was over and a Communist victory more-or-less assured in post-war Poland. Churchill's point was that Anders had given the Soviets every reason to allow them to exile him and to outlaw him. Perhaps he should not have done so and, with Mikołajczyk, achieved something worthwhile for Poland and its people – but this is mere conjecture and not history. And of course Mikołajczyk was also forced into exile in 1947 even if he was convinced that Poland and the Soviet Union could work together; he was not a fool and on learning during January 1947 of his impending arrest, trial and execution even he fled Poland under Stalinist rule.[90] It should be noted that there was no question of Mikołajczyk not being arrested and tried, and he had no chance of being acquitted – no, he was to be executed, there was to be no question about that; such was Soviet justice – as events in Hungary and Czechoslovakia in the late 1940s were to prove. Perhaps Anders was the most realistic of all of those senior figures who dealt with the Soviet government and Stalin during the Second World War. Anders was unique because he understood the country well, spoke Russian fluently, understood Leninism and Stalinism and had suffered the cruelty and lack of humanity of the Soviet system. No other senior Allied figure could have made such a claim.

The greatest heartbreak for Anders, and for all Poles in the West and serving in the Polish underground loyal to the London Poles, was the announcement of the recognition by the British and American governments of the Lublin government which, by July 1945, had the working title of the 'Provisional Government of National Unity'. At the same time recognition of the Polish Government-in-Exile was withdrawn. Anders said that it was 'a terrible blow, the more so in that it is entirely unmerited'.[91] The problem for Anders and the Western Poles was that the Polish Government-in-Exile was also operating on extremely dodgy ground as it took its legal basis from the 1935 Polish Constitution that had illegally overthrown the 1921 Polish Constitution which had provided for Polish democracy. The 1935 Polish Constitution was merely tailor made for the illegal rule of Marshal Piłsudski. A further consideration should be the 1940 coup d'état by renegade Sikorski-ite officers who turned August Zalewski out of office at gunpoint. Zalewski had been chosen as prime minister by President Raczkiewicz; he was in power for about twenty-four hours but his removal suited the British as they wanted to see Sikorski back in post as Polish Prime Minister. The entire affair is highly questionable and open to charges of illegality. Typically it was the Soviet government who objected to the use of the 1935 Polish Constitution while shedding crocodile tears over the fate of Polish democracy.

A consequence of the British government's recognition of the Warsaw Polish government was that Anders was no longer permitted to recruit for Second Polish Corps.[92] In a further meeting Anders was told that Second Polish Corps was to be wound down. Naturally Anders was against this as Poles everywhere looked to Second Polish Corps as a Polish Army – and what was to become of his men? Anders wanted to maintain a body of 100,000 men in Italy but it was pointed out that the British Army would soon only have 75,000 men in Italy. Therefore it became clear that the Poles would have to scale back. Anders was also told that eventually there was to be no Allied troops in Italy – and then what were the British to do with Second Polish Corps? Anders simply said that he and his men could not just go home because they had no homes to return to.[93] And that was the point; most of Second Polish Corps came from eastern Poland which had been annexed into the Soviet Union proper, rather than occupied Poland. These men were now Soviet citizens in the eyes of what passed for law in the Soviet Union and if they returned home their futures were uncertain and subject to the tender mercies of the Soviet legal system. In a further meeting with his British Allies, Anders lay before them his problems with the press as the British authorities remained opposed to censorship but advised the press using liaison officers to put the record straight; the Poles, however, remained victims of propaganda which was pro-Soviet and anti-Western Polish. Often figures such as Generals Anders and Sosnkowski and the Polish president, Władysław Raczkiewicz, were depicted as traitors and not having the interests of Poland or the Polish people at heart, while the greatest Polish victory of the Second World War was Lenino.[94] By the end of 1945 Anders was beginning to understand the situation of the exiled Poles in the West, but not what needed to be done to make the situation better. He wrote to Raczkiewicz noting that the Polish Goverment-in-Exile was no longer recognised by any country that mattered and to this end Anders suggested that maybe the government might be reconstructed as well as the appointment of an Inspector General of the Polish armed forces.[95] No doubt Anders had his eye on the appointment of Inspector General, but what could he seriously do with it? The Poles in the West had lost all their influence, as limited as it was. The Soviet Union was all conquering and the Polish armed forces in the West were about to become history.

This situation had been one that had vexed Anders ever since the withdrawal of British and American recognition of the Polish Government-in-Exile. Anders' belief was that the Soviet government had achieved all of its 'open' war aims with complete cooperation of the British and American governments owing to the conclusions reached at the Tehran and Yalta conferences. Anders divided Soviet war into two parts:- the 'open' policy, simply the defeat of Germany and later Japan, but the real agenda was, as ever, the world or international revolution which the Soviet government was willing to take its time over and pursue when opportunity arose. Anders considered that the Western Poles had a duty to oppose this policy even in the most fraught conditions of unrecognised exile. A major symbol of a free Poland was the retention of the (questionable and regrettable) 1935 Polish Constitution, while the presence of Polish Armed forces in Italy and in Germany held great symbolism to many Poles. However it was accepted that the withdrawal of the recognition by the major powers of the Western Poles was a huge handicap.[96]

A Staff Report made in November 1945 pointed towards the vexatious and complicated picture that was Poland and its relationship with its former Allies. Despite what the Polish Community believe today, in 1945 it was noted that there was no real relationship or love lost between the Soviet government and the Labour government in the UK. Indeed Ernest Bevin, the British Foreign Secretary, who is often touted by Poles as being an arch-Stalinist, was a great enemy of the Soviet government. What was clear though was that the grassroots Labour party did support Stalin and the Soviet government, although that support was divided. A clear picture of events in Poland was also impossible for Anders to divine; the only thing that was certain was that the Soviets were annexing the country and settling it in the manner that the Soviet government saw fit at the expense of everybody else. Reports were made of terrorist actions and of fighting between Polish nationalists and the NKVD, while a pogrom had been organised in Krakow by the NKVD. The Polish underground military was hampered by deportations and other Soviet measures, while the Soviet backed 'Zymierski Army' was totally dominated by the Soviets.[97]

In a meeting between the British prime minister, Clement Attlee and Anders, it was considered by Attlee that a debt was owed by the UK to the Polish armed forces but time had come to 'take stock' of the whole situation. Attlee was taking a realistic view of 1946; the war was over and armed forces throughout the world were being reduced and disbanded as there was no longer any need for them. The same applied to Second Polish Corps whose work in Italy, as far as the British government was concerned, was nearly finished. Attlee said of

Second Polish Corps 'it was becoming politically, an embarrassment and once the treaty with Italy was settled it must leave that country'.

Attlee shrewdly placed all of the decisions concerning the return to Poland on the shoulders of the Polish commanders. The British government had been in negotiations with the Warsaw government and now it was time for the Poles to decide whether to return to Poland or not. In Attlee's opinion there was no reason why the Poles should not return to their homeland if 'the conditions were right'. However even Attlee was aware that not everything was perfect in Poland as he admitted that the British government realised that not all Poles could return home and they would not be pressurised to do so and the UK would do its best to provide a future for these people. At the same time, he instantly crushed Churchill's idea of a Polish Foreign Legion to be employed in the British Army, although a few men might be retained for their specialist skills. Overall Attlee considered that all of the Poles should return home. Attlee requested Anders' support for the British initiative and the result of the outcome of the talks between Warsaw and London. He also asked that Polish troops should be allowed to choose freely 'without propaganda, pressure or obstruction'.

Anders expressed his gratitude for the 'kind references to the services of the Polish forces'. He also said that he had been asked by his colleagues to act as a spokesman and present their point of view and so began his critique of the policies already made. Anders was obviously annoyed at not being kept in the loop regarding these negotiations, it seemed to be a continuation of a policy developed by the Allies during the war of discussing Poland among themselves and reaching a conclusion without really involving the Poles at all. Anders remarked that he had received the Warsaw terms the previous morning, 14 March at 10 am, and Bevin's statement later that evening. This meant that he had had time to discuss the former but not the latter; all the same he wished to give his opinion as a soldier.

The most obvious drawback as far as Anders was concerned was that the decision of what to do about Polish Second Corps had had such an 'air of secrecy' over it, while the lack of time to prepare and issue any statements to his troops was another handicap which reduced his room for manoeuvre. Anders also complained that because everything had been a secret, when the edicts of Warsaw and London were made public he had little time to prepare any response because it was physically impossible for some Polish commanders to return from wherever they were in order to play their part in any negotiations.

Anders said that terms from Warsaw were nothing new to what had been broadcast from both Warsaw and Moscow, and did not promise any sense of a warm return, but spoke about punishment. There was some talk about those returning to Poland being treated 'equally', but the reality was already well known and many did not fancy going back to Poland. Anders said that he understood the difficulties of the British government, but considered that the Polish armed forces and about ninety per cent of the Polish nation wished to remain linked to the West at a time when they had been thrown to the Soviet Union. Therefore it seemed to many Poles that the disbanding of the Polish Armed Forces was a sign that the British government had lost interest in the Poles in the West. Anders complained that he was faced with a *fait accompli* and as a result he did not know how to present the situation to his men. He could understand that his men had to be moved from Italy, but not why he was being presented with agendas already set.

Bevin told Anders that the conclusions drawn were the 'logical outcome of the negotiations at Potsdam'. It was never made conditional on the election (to be held in Poland) but rather that the men should go back (to Poland) to take part in the elections. Anders said that he understood that but his men had a different view. Bevin replied that he had often made his position clear in the House of Commons, the Poles should return to Poland, help reconstruct their country and take part in the elections. Bevin observed that the demobilisation of Polish armed forces was in line with a general policy throughout the Allied armed forces: the oldest and those with the longest service being released first. The British policy was to encourage Polish service personnel to return to Poland and to encourage others to do the same and arrange their demobilisation. Bevin asserted that these two points must be accepted, but there was to be no question of compulsory repatriation.

Anders repudiated the entire notion of the most experienced men returning to Poland. He doubted that under the present conditions in Poland many would return, and he would not interfere one way or the other. He would even try to convince the 'waverers' to return to Poland as he did not want to keep them. Anders simply cut Bevin's argument to pieces by stating that of the 16,000 men who had returned to Poland, most of them had only enlisted towards the end of the war. Of the 60,000 men who had fought at Cassino, only 310 had returned to Poland.[98] Another consideration was that Anders had already condemned the coming elections in Poland as likely to be fraudulent, with the NKVD controlling them and ensuring a Soviet-friendly outcome.[99] For the British it was all wishful thinking that the Poles might just go away as if by magic, but these men had no intention of doing so. What was rarely mentioned in the negotiations however, was that the British security services did not trust the members of Second Polish Corps and wanted any that were to arrive in the UK to be vetted to weed out those who still harboured fascist sympathies.[100]

Within weeks though, Anders and his men were thwarted in any ambitions they may have harboured regarding keeping a Polish force together in the West, or of any war with the Soviet Union, as the British government formed the Polish Resettlement Corps (PRC). The PRC was to be a non-military organisation whose purpose was to reintegrate de-mobilised Polish servicemen back into civilian life. It was still hoped that most would return to Poland, but it was increasingly obvious that this would not be the case.

Anders was told of the proposed formation of the PRC in a meeting with British officials at the War Office during May 1946. He was told that camps to house Polish servicemen and their families had already been set up in the UK. It was anticipated that 160,000 service personnel plus their families were to be aided in this way. Naturally the Polish commanders had questions. Anders asked what military equipment should be brought back to the UK; he was told nothing, personal weapons only. General Kopański asked what would be the position of a man who refused to work in civilian life – the reply was that he would be kept in the PRC for the full term of his enlistment and then might be in a difficult position, having refused entry into civilian life, which suggested a job being offered. Kopański also asked what the position would be of Polish officers who were over age or unemployable. The reply was certainly not satisfactory, merely that difficult and complicated matters would be addressed later.[101]

In a letter from the exiled Polish politician, Tytus Filipowicz, Attlee was warned of the consequences of the unilateral decision by the British government to demobilise Polish armed forces. Filipowicz argued that the British government was not qualified to disband the Polish Army and only the legitimate Polish government could do so. He also made the old observations that the British and American governments had allowed the Soviet Union to annex all of east-central Europe.[102] No doubt Filipowicz was morally correct but exiled governments recognised by nobody that matters lack political strength and influence. The Poles on the western side had been one of the victors in the war against Germany, but had lost the war and their country to the Soviet Union. In 1946 the reality was that it was all over for the London Poles and their armed forces. They would have to wait for another era to dawn before they could gain influence once more; few lived to see that day dawn but incredibly, Edward Raczynski and General Maczek both did as very old men in 1989.

Anders also had to deal with the fallout from the British decision to demobilise Polish armed forces and made his feelings known in a meeting with the SAC in June 1946. Anders said that his corps was going through a difficult time and the British decision 'entailed breaking down the work of six years'. Like his men, Anders said he faced great difficulties as 'the soldiers [and in this term he included officers, NCOs and men] had always hoped that the Corps would be kept together until the elections in Poland, and they now wondered if in fact any elections should take place'. Anders said that he had to deal personally with parts of his corps because he had to explain the situation in which they found themselves, as well as maintain morale. Amazingly it was the soldiers who had served six years or more who seemed the most understanding. However Anders said that people who were leaving Poland (for the West) brought bad news from Poland as the Soviets began to Sovietise Poland. More people were being sent from the Soviet Union to Poland and fortifications were being added. Furthermore along the former eastern border with the Soviet Union, the 'Curzon Line', all civilians had been evacuated for a forty-mile belt each side of the line while there was unending anti-British and anti-American propaganda. As many of the troops serving in Polish Second Corps understood Russian, they could understand Russian radio and 'sense the spirit of belligerence being spread'. Overall the members of Polish Second Corps had a sense 'that Russia will start trouble soon'. Anders considered that this might happen in 1946 or 1947.[103] Anders was further incensed because, despite the Polish war record, the Poles were not even invited to the 'V' day celebrations held on 8 June 1946. As Anders observed there was not a 'V' day in Poland as it remained occupied by the Soviet Union.[104] Of course despite the best efforts of the Polish émigré community, Polish armed forces in 1946 were no longer the London-backed forces, as indeed the Polish Government-in-Exile was no longer the legal government of Poland, and therefore neither could realistically be invited to the victory celebrations a year after the German surrender. The Western Poles may well have had a moral right to be there, but politics and reality will always overtake morality. An apology seventy years later is meaningless and is no victory – just another cheap political shot to shut people up.

Anders embarrassed both the War Office and Foreign Office in his address to Myron Taylor, the Personal Representative of President Truman to the Pope. He told Taylor that Poland was yet to regain her freedom and had fought both totalitarian powers, Germany and the Soviet Union. In the opinion of Anders, Poland was ruled by 'servile agents of Moscow who have nothing in common with the Polish Nation'.[105] Anders was told on 24 June that he had embarrassed the British with his address to Taylor. On 1 July Anders was informed by Lieutenant-General Morgan that his remarks only caused harm to Poles, especially in the UK, as people tried to help them with resettlement. Furthermore, it did no good politically with the Soviet government or with the provisional Polish government if Anders maintained his anti-Soviet stance. Morgan told Anders that he was to make no further political statements without prior reference to him.[106]

In a meeting with Lieutenant-General Morgan at the end of July, Anders was dismayed at changes made to the PRC because he had thought it might be a military organisation but it was actually to be a 'quasi-civil formation'. Anders said that as a soldier he could not take any responsibility for it. He stated that he understood the political difficulties of the British government, but, as a Pole, loyal to his country, his duty was to do all he could for his men; but in his mind he could not do anything to help them at that time. Even so, he pledged that he would stay in Italy until the end in order to see the transformation of his corps as it was transferred to PRC. Morgan told Anders that AFHQ had had no foreknowledge of the War Office's decision concerning Second Polish Corps' future and observed that if Anders resigned before his work was done in Italy, the Soviet government and the Polish government in Warsaw would consider it to be a major victory.[107] Before the end of September 1946, Anders suffered his greatest defeat as he lost his Polish citizenship. On 28 September 1946, the Council of Ministers in Warsaw decided that Anders and seventy-five other senior Polish service officers serving in the West were to do so. The reason given for the deprival of their citizenship was their failure to return to Poland.[108] Of course Anders could not return to Poland, nor could his fellow commanders. It would have been highly likely that after some form of kangaroo court, he and his compatriots would have been executed.

The problem with Second Polish Corps was not one of their own making but they were impossible to be deployed in the manner of the Polish First Armoured Division which was used as an occupation force in Germany until 1947, but the British rejected the use of Anders' men as an occupying force because of their 'unrivalled talent for intrigue and propaganda against the Russians', and that they, the Poles, 'could use their occupation position to get support for the rearmament of Germany against the Soviet Union'. In other words it was feared that the Poles might agitate from Germany for the arming of Germans against the Soviet Union. It was also feared that in Germany the Soviets might be antagonised with the presence of Anders' men.[109] A further problem was that Kot and Anders continued to hate each. It was known that troops from Second Polish Corps had beaten up Kot's Staff in Rome.[110] Anders had to explain to some of his men that it would be impossible to return to Poland and wage war against the Soviets as the men and officers of 5th Division did not want to go to the UK but to return to Poland. Anders met with the division and told them that even if Second Polish Corps had 1,700 vehicles, including tanks, they lacked the fuel to get even to the Austrian Alps. On 10 June 1946 Second Polish Corps began to leave Italy for the UK. This process continued until the end of October. Anders left on the last day of October. His work was far from done but Polish service in Italy was finished.

Chapter 10

The End: 1947–1970

Anders may have misunderstood the position of Poland in the world ranks – it was nowhere as it was occupied by the Soviet Union with unsettled borders; the western border was not really accepted until 1970. However he was correct in his thinking as we have seen all along, Polish independence was not truly restored until 1989 when the Communist system collapsed across east-central Europe. Between 1944 and 1989 everything to do with Poland had to be approved by the Soviet government with the Soviet Ambassador in Warsaw acting as a quasi-High Commissioner. During this period it must be noted that Polish interests did not necessarily concern the Soviet government and were often contrary to what the Soviet government wished.

As we have noticed, Anders' approach towards all things Soviet was hostile while Sikorski and Mikołajczyk, often under the most impossible conditions, tried to find ways that would satisfy the British, American and Soviet governments and hopefully their own people. A tall order which often failed, especially when trying to please their compatriots. Anders' high-handed attitude towards the Soviet government caused offence not only among the Allies but also among Poles who were loyal to the government in London, but notably not the Polish president, who at times seems almost treacherous towards his own government when he was in cahoots with Anders – Sikorski's death was a great boost for Raczkiewicz. Anders also angered people such as the normally apolitical General Maczek who, shortly before the war in Europe ended, criticised Anders' attitude at a time when the future of the Polish Army in the west was in the balance. Maczek wanted to get the war finished and politics left to the politicians; Polish troops should be concerned with finishing off the enemy and then worry about the future once peace was declared. At the same time Anders, on his return to Italy, had had a 'stormy interview' with Field Marshal Alexander, the Supreme Allied Commander in Italy. It would seem that Anders may have been trying to remove Maczek's armoured division from the frontline in north-west Europe, but had agreed to keep them in place – this no doubt would explain Maczek's anger while Anders insisted that his own troops were to be kept in reserve.[1] A likely explanation was that Anders looked to the 2nd Polish Corps as his basis for power in post-war Poland as much as Piłsudski looked to the First Brigade in 1918 and after as both men realised that they did not necessarily have support from the entire Polish Army, which then raised the question of factionalism within the Polish Army. Maczek certainly had his faction, the Polish First Armoured Division, whether he wanted it or not. He was certainly apolitical, but was returned to Scotland in May 1945 just after the fighting in Europe was over. Maczek had no reason to love the Soviets and did not – they had annexed his homeland and even though he lived to the ripe old age of 102, dying in 1994, he could not return to his home. Partly because he was too frail, but also because Lwów and the surrounding area from where he came, had been annexed back in 1939 by the Soviet Union and fifty years on was part of Ukraine. Poland has never recovered these territories and shows no signs of wanting to do so. Perhaps if Maczek had fallen into Soviet captivity he might have supported Anders, but he did not so we can only speculate, but the differences between the Polish First Armoured Division and Anders' Army is telling. Maczek kept his men training and eventually landed in Europe during July 1944 – Anders' allowed his officers to plot and intrigue, often on the fringes of treachery at best.

However, the situation in the Polish Second Corps had been unsatisfactory for a while, even before the Yalta meeting. In December 1944 it was reported that a 'level headed' Polish officer had described the situation in Anders' Army as 'exactly like a woman on the verge of a hysterical breakdown'.[2] There lies the difference between Maczek and Anders; Maczek kept his men busy and did not harp on about the political situation – Anders and his men had a fixation on the politics rather than the fighting. This did Anders no favours at all.

Even so, the question of what was to happen at war's end was a live one in 1945. The British historian Martin Kitchen makes more observations of how the Poles were thinking as the war reached its climax in Europe. In mid-April 1945 a British report noted that evidence gained from the daily reading of letters from Polish troops suggested that there were 'three fatal tendencies in the thinking of Polish forces'. Two of these were an uncompromising hostility to the Soviet Union, and anything connected to the Lublin Committee. The situation regarding these two points got worse over a six-month period. The third matter seriously disturbed the British government as it suggested that members of 2nd Corps would continue in their uncompromising resistance to any settlement with the Soviet Union in the belief that there would be a war between Britain and the Soviet Union. It seemed that Anders was not alone in this belief as the Foreign Office was horrified to learn at the beginning of 1945 that there was great ferment at the Polish Government-in-Exile owing to reports on both Anders and Maczek. These reports suggested that even Maczek and other senior officers in both Italy and north-west Europe were minded to believe that once the war against Germany was over, the war would continue against the Soviet Union. The Foreign Office poured scorn on these reports and refused to believe them, but noted 'this is bad; and those who have given the Poles this advice bear a heavy responsibility.'[3] It is unlikely that Maczek would have supported such action in January 1945 and he gives no idea of what he thought in his autobiography of his fighting career – he never mentions politics but is clearly upset that he cannot return to Poland in 1945. Like Anders he was to lose his Polish citizenship and it should be noted that Maczek never recognised the Polish Peoples' Republic and even returned letters from their authorities unopened when they tried to reach out to him once the Communist regime was in tatters in the 1980s and returned to a hybrid communist-military junta led by General Wojciech Jaruzelski.

Of course Anders doggedly supported the Allies, notably the British, in the final months of the war in Europe as it was only his personality that could keep Polish troops in the line during the Italian Campaign. However, it was this very quality of leadership that made him dangerous; he could be quite irresponsible when it came to his dealings with the Soviet Union. By the end of 1946 his dreams of raising an army against the Soviet Union to fight for Polish independence were in tatters. The plan for using Polish ex-Wehrmacht troops to reinforce this army came to grief as it was quickly discovered that they were certainly anti-Soviet, but also pro-German in sympathy. Their recruitment was swiftly halted.[4] Anders' plan to recruit former Polish prisoners went against his original belief before 1945 when he considered that those who had served in the German Army for any length of time could not be trusted. Perhaps it suited him in 1945 to accept such men, but it certainly cut against the grain of the Allies – they sought out Nazis with the view to prosecute for war crimes, while Anders appeared to be trying to recruit them. This is not to overlook the fact that the Allies recruited Nazis for their own plans, such as the use of rocket technology; but they could, and Anders was in no position to do so. Another obstacle to any plans that Anders may have held for the recruitment of ex-German Army Polish troops was that many of the Polish prisoners-of-war were sent to the UK. This was highlighted when Anders wrote to General Sosnkowski, the Polish Supreme Commander, asking about the probability of establishing a third Polish Brigade.[5] There was also a consideration made by the Polish government in London during September 1944 when it was anticipated that the Germans were about to abandon Greece. It was estimated that from this quarter about 10,000 Poles might come into the hands of the Allies.[6] This question was put before Lieutenant General Scobie of the Royal Marines by Lieutenant General Stefan Kopański, Chief of the Polish General Staff. Kopański told Scobie that many of these Poles had been fighting against the Germans alongside Greek guerrillas but were not interested in Greek civil disturbances. Anders was told to prepare a group of officers to help assemble Polish troops in Greece and evacuate them to Italy.[7]

Other ideas for the use of Anders and his men were floated such as using them as civilian labourers. This was a better idea than Churchill's who considered that there might be a 'Polish Foreign Legion' in the manner of the French Foreign Legion. He was told that the Poles would not make 'good mercenaries'.[8] Churchill positively beamed over Anders' idea of using Poles as labourers in the task of rebuilding the shattered infrastructure of the UK after the war. For Churchill it was not only a good idea, but no politics were involved; the Soviets had never bothered to consult the British government when they had shipped hundreds of thousands to Siberia as slaves.[9] Another idea mooted was that Polish troops might be used for occupation duties in Germany; for once CIGS was in agreement as it would release British troops for the ongoing war against Japan.[10] At this point it was still expected that the war with Japan might drag on for several more years yet and therefore it was a realistic prospect that most of the British armed forces would be deployed in that theatre of operations. By June 1945 some ideas had been forged regarding the future deployment of Polish troops and as we have seen most of it was not to the liking of Anders. The Polish First Armoured Division serving in the

British 21 Army Group in Germany was indeed used as an occupation force in the Wilhelmshaven district, but in the communiqué issued it was termed as 'somewhere in Germany'. It was also made clear that the Polish Army was not going to be used in the war against Japan.[11]

Several observations need to be made here. It should be considered that in giving the First Polish Armoured Division occupation duties, it removed them from the influence of Anders and his somewhat lazy obsessions. General Maczek, even though he had been removed from command of the division almost immediately after the fighting had finished in Europe, had raised the division up by its bootstraps in 1940, turning the defeated Polish troops from being a near-criminal rabble to a proud and efficient crack armoured division.[12] In August 1944, under the command of Maczek and in defiance of his own commander, Maczek had made a stand in Normandy which more or less destroyed the German withdrawal and ensured the success of the Normandy campaign. It would have been sad to have allowed the First Polish Armoured Division to have fallen under the malicious influence of Anders.

It was also noticed that the morale of Polish troops in Italy was poor and that was the main reason why Poles were not used against Japan, even though Poland had declared war on Japan in 1941. It was one thing for Polish commanders to keep their troops in line while fighting the Germans who had invaded their country and attempted to wipe out the Polish nation, but the war against Japan would have been different. Many Poles were furious with their American and British allies for their perceived pro-Soviet policies and there was further unrest over the arrests of sixteen AK leaders by the Soviet security forces, who were then taken to Moscow for trial.[13] In these circumstances it would have been very difficult to convince Polish troops to fight the Japanese, with whom they had had little if any contact, but it might well have been interpreted that in fighting the Japanese, Polish troops were fighting for British and American imperial interests with no benefit to Poland. Sikorski had warned Kopański not to fight for British imperial interests during the North Africa campaign.[14] There, Sikorski was being foolish, but if he had been alive in 1945 he might have had a point. It certainly would not have been lost on Anders.

This unsatisfactory situation continued into the summer of 1945. Not only was the Polish Government-in-Exile no longer accredited as the legal government of Poland by the Allies and others after July 1945, but during August 1945 the British government also withdrew its recognition of the President of Poland (in London) as the supreme authority of Polish armed forces, as well as withdrawing recognition of the appointment of Polish commander-in-chief.[15] Despite his problems with Anders, Churchill stood by him and referred to him as 'this gallant man'. In recognition of Anders' war service with the Allies, Churchill recommended that Anders should be honoured by having him made a Knight Commander of the Bath (KCB).[16] This was not enough to save Anders from a frustrated exile as he railed against his own misfortune and that of Poland.

What would Anders' legacy be? Within his own circle and those who had been imprisoned and enslaved in the Soviet Union, Anders was very much like Moses in the Old Testament leading the Israelites out of bondage in Egypt to freedom in the Promised Land. Anders ensured that as many Poles as possible were able to leave the Soviet Union. However there is another legacy which many of those who left the Soviet Union via Anders refuse to discuss, and that is his apparent treachery towards Sikorski.

The rumours concerning of Anders' disloyalty towards Sikorski came to a head in 1960 when a small émigré Polish publication, *Narodowice*, published allegations against Anders which were basically criticisms of his character and career. But there was one very serious allegation that Anders also had to face as *Narodowice* alleged that he had been an enemy of Sikorski and his government.[17] Anders won most of the case as many slurs against him were discredited, but he was unable to defeat the allegation that he had been an enemy of Sikorski and his government and thus a ruling was made in the London court that this was the truth.[18] It seems that Anders was not accused of treachery, but that is a matter of semantics as we have seen during the course of this work that he, often aided and abetted by the British government, worked against his prime minister and commander-in-chief. Whether Anders knew of the plots against Sikorski, which emanated from Second Polish Corps, will have to lie as unproven. But there is a lot of suspicion hanging around Anders' Army. Anders was an example in miniature of how a warlord in the Polish Army could undermine at every opportunity the legal authorities of Poland.

The *Narodowice* case caused dismay among the émigré community and unsurprisingly some were unhappy that Anders fought it. The suggestion being that it was unhelpful that the émigrés' dirty laundry was done in public.[19] A major concern was that the case was being tried in London before a British jury, so it was unlikely that Polish considerations would be understood because very few British people have any knowledge of Polish history – or had even given it a second thought. By 1960 the Polish cause was largely forgotten by many British people and the events of the Second World War were beginning to pass into folk memory. It was already ancient history and Poland was firmly behind the Iron Curtain, the mythical ideological barrier which divided the democratic West from the Communist East. Poland was in the enemy camp.

Anders however was perhaps more astute than his supporters as he had to defend himself against the charges made by *Narodowice*. If he did not he would have been admitting that he had no honour and was a criminal. The British jury, although there was an attempt to acquaint them with Polish history after 1863 and how it impinged on the Anders' case, looked at the facts rather than history and cleared Anders of most of the charges – which were quite absurd. The question of Anders' loyalty to Sikorski and his policies which had vexed the Polish community caused most dismay among émigré Poles because the British jury was not swayed by Polish history but judging the case looked on the facts instead, and decided that Anders had indeed been an enemy of Sikorski. This was a blow to Anders and his supporters. They were as near as damn it being called traitors and for a man who saw honour to be as precious of life itself, Anders no doubt felt the sting of this judgement.

Some Poles tried to lessen the verdict by disputing the nuances in the meaning of 'enemy' in the English and Polish languages and tried to make the term 'determined opponent' stick.[20] This might have worked, as Anders' was a determined opponent of Sikorski, but for the other elements of his opposition to Sikorski and his policies towards the Soviet Union. It was obvious that Anders allowed his troops to reach a near mutinous state and then knew just when to rein them in and thus prevent an all out *putsch*. Anders' major failure was to withhold his unreserved support for his prime minister and commander-in-chief. In many armies he would have been cashiered; one can immediately think of MacArthur being sacked by Truman during the Korean War. MacArthur may have been correct in his decision to chase Chinese forces further than required, but it went against Truman's wishes. In the case of Anders however it seems that the Polish president had also been working against Sikorski, and with Anders. But the main problem in 1960 was that the war had been over for fifteen years and memories were not as clear as they may have been, and there was time to conduct an official version of events surrounding Sikorski and Anders. By 1960 many Poles had wrongly blamed Churchill for their situation and the fact that Poland remained under Communist control. As we have seen, they could not have been more wrong; if any Western leader had betrayed Poland it was Roosevelt, who had conducted squalid hole-in-the-corner conversations with Stalin, but without Churchill, and between them betrayed Poland. Roosevelt needed the American Polish community to ensure his return to power in 1944, but he still betrayed Poland. Dobbs notes that Churchill announced at Yalta that Poland 'must be mistress in her own house and captain of her own soul', while Roosevelt declared that Poland has been a 'source of trouble for over five hundred years'.[21] Walter Reid writes that Stalin and Roosevelt had worked together against Churchill as early as 1943 because at the Tehran Conference Churchill was distressed to find that Roosevelt had deserted him and seemed to be siding with Stalin against him. There was no Anglo–Saxon block against the Soviet Union.[22] Therefore when Poles assert that Churchill betrayed them, they are wrong.

By 1960 the exiled Poles living in the UK hadn't changed much since 1945 – fanatical and unrealistic as well as thinking they could bully a British jury into accepting their version of the relationship between Anders and Sikorski. The problem was that nobody except interested parties knew what had really happened, especially in the Middle East where Anders had done some of his best conspiring against Sikorski. Of course once Sikorski was dead, Anders could do as he pleased and it was only the British authorities who could sit on him when necessary. The mysterious death of Sikorski and entourage on 4 July 1943 off Gibraltar obviously coloured the Polish picture of Sikorski, Anders and Churchill. With official papers being withheld in British archives until the 1970s there was little curiosity regarding the papers related to the previous incidents regarding Sikorski's air travel in North America, though it seemed unlikely that any blame could be laid at Anders' door for the air crash. But archival sources point towards rogue elements of Polish Second Corps being most likely responsible for the act. Anders was often frustrated that he was held as being responsible for acts of treachery against his own authorities and railed against this charge as the war progressed. Whether he was involved in working against the Communist authorities is not certain, but it looks likely as even Mikołajczyk makes this assertion.

Anders never applied for UK citizenship even though many of his officers, fearing being considered disloyal by Anders, did so in secret.[23] Anders was about to enter the final phase of his life – that of being a symbol of a free Poland. Even if he was living in frustrated exile with an army of phantoms, his and their presence, as well as the fact that a Polish Government-in-Exile still sat until 1989, passing laws and electing ministers and presidents – did not matter as nobody recognised them. They represented a Poland which had been invaded and illegally occupied and remained symbolic of the illegality of Soviet rule in east-central Europe as the legal seals of the office of the president of Poland were kept in South Kensington and not Warsaw. Anders' life from 1946 until his death in 1970 illustrated this. In 1990 Anders' won his argument when Lech Wałęsa was democratically elected President of Poland. For the first time in over fifty years the seals of that office were transferred back from London to Poland, having been kept in the west since 1939. Poland had returned to Europe as a free and democratic state for the first time since 1926. It was all part of Anders' dream but he was never allowed to achieve power in Poland in any form or shape.

Endnotes

Chapter One: General Władysław Anders, Origins and the Polish Army, 1892–1939

1. Zbigniew S. Siemaszko, *Generał Anders w Latach 1892–1942*, Warsaw, LTW, 2012, pp. 21–31, 607–609; Harvey Sarner, *General Anders and the Soldiers of The Second Polish Corps*, Cathedral City, CA, Brunswick Press, 1997, pp. xi–xii.
2. Marian Romeyko, *Przed i po Maju*, Volume 2, Warsaw, MON, 1976, p. 26.
3. Siemaszko, pp. 61, 607–609.
4. *Kawalerowie Virtuti Militari 1792–1945: Wykazy odnaczonych za czyny z lat 1863–1894, 1914–1945* (eds) Gregorz Łukomski, Bogusław Polak, Andrzej Suchcitz, Koszalin, Politechniki Koszalinskiej, 1997, pp. 22. 66. 76.
5. Siemaszko, p. 61.
6. Adam Zamoyski, *The Battle of the Marchlands*, New York, Columbia University Press, 1981, p. 4.
7. Andrzej Garlicki, *Józef Piłsudski: 1867–1935*, edited and translated by John Coutouvidis, Aldershot, Scolar, 1993, p. xiii.
8. Andrzej Garlicki, *Przewrót majowy*, Warsaw, Czytelnik, 1978, p. 239.
9. Sarner, pp. xi–xii.
10. Siemaszko, p. 79.
11. Ibid.
12. *General Władysław Anders: Soldier and Leader of the Free Poles in Exile*, (eds) Joanna Pylat, Jan Ciechanowski and Andrzej Suchcitz, London, Polish University Abroad, 2008, Papers from the Conference Organised by the Polish University Abroad, 15–16 June, 2007, p. 9.
13. Joseph Rothschild, *Pilsudski's Coup d'état*, New York, Columbia, 1966, p. 190.
14. Walter M. Drzewieniecki, 'The Polish Army on the eve of World War II, *The Polish Review*, 26, 1981, 54–64. Andrew A. Michta, *The Soldier–Citizen: The Politics of the Polish Army after Communism*, London, Macmillan, 1997, p. 26.
15. Siemaszko, pp. 607–609.

16. Michael Zurowski, 'British Policy towards the Polish Second Corps' *East European Quarterly*, XXVII, No.3, September 1993, 271–300.

17. Suchcitz, *General Wladyslaw Anders*, pp. 11–12.

18. TNA (The (British) National Archives, Kew, London) WO (War Office) WO 106/6238 Report on the Franco–British Military Mission to Poland, July–August 1920, Major General Sir Percy Radcliffe, KCMG, CB, DSO, Director of Military Operations, 1 September 1920.

19. Suchcitz, *General Wladyslaw Anders*, pp. 11–12.

Chapter Two: 1939–1941: The Division of Poland and Relations with the Soviet Union

1. Andrzej Suchcitz, *A Brief Survey of Military Planning and Preparation for the Defence of Poland, October 1938–August 1939*, MA dissertation, University of London, 1981, p.2. Suchcitz also notes that the dispersal of Polish war industries was more suited to war with the Soviet Union rather than with Germany. Ibid. p.7.

2. Jan Karski, *The Great Powers & Poland, 1919–1945. From Versailles to Yalta*, Lanham, University of America Press, 1985, p. 234.

3. TNA, PREM 1 (Prime Ministers' Office) PREM 1/331A, Roseway to Rucker, August 1939.

4. www.pism.co.uk B.I. Dispositions concerning the Polish 1939 Campaign, *passim*.

5. Lieutenant General W. Anders, *An Army in Exile. The Story of the Second Polish Corps*, London, Macmillan & Co, 1949, p.1.

6. Ibid, pp. 1–2.

7. PISM (Polish Institute & Sikorski Museum, Kensington, London) B.I. 23/A/1, '*Relacja Dowodcy Nowogrodekiej Brygady Kawalerii*', undated.

8. Suchcitz, *General Wladyslaw Anders*, pp. 13–14.

9. Anders, p. 3.

10. Ibid, p. 4.

11. Siemaszko, p. 101.

12. PISM, B.I. 23/A/1.

13. Ibid, Anders, p. 4.

14. Siemaszko, p. 101.

15. Ibid.

16. Jozef Beck, *Final Report*, New York, Robert Speller & Sons, 1957, p. 216.

17. Sarner, p.2.

18. Siemaszko, p. 101.

19. Catherine Epstein's study of Arthur Greiser, a German Nazi born in what was German territory prior to 1918 but which became part of post 1918 Poland is an illustration of the German resentment towards Poland after 1918. It should be noted that Greiser's case is probably one of the most extreme but it represents the hatred of Poles by many Germans at that time especially once connected to German territorial losses to Poland and the consequences to both parties. Catherine Epstein, *Model Nazi: Arthur Greiser and the occupation of Western Poland*, New York, Oxford University Press, Inc, 2010.

20. Anders, pp. 3–8.

21. PISM, B.I. 23/A/1

22. The Romanian attitude was already known by the British and French Governments as when French officials asked the Romanian Military Attaché to Paris what was the Romanian Government's attitude towards Poles who retreated into Romania, he admitted that they would more than likely be interned. TNA, CAB 85 Allied Forces (Official) Committee, CAB 85/1 MR (39) Meeting Anglo–French Liaison, 16 September 1939.

23. Evan McGilvray, *Man of Steel and Honour: General Stanisław Maczek. Soldier of Poland, Commander of the 1st Polish Armoured Division in North–West Europe 1944–45*, Solihull, Helion, 2012, pp. 83–84.

24. Beck, p. 180.

25. Evan McGilvray, *Days of Adversity: The Warsaw Uprising, 1944*, Solihull, Helion, 2015, pp. 74–75.

26. Charles Edward Lysaght, *Brendan Bracken*, London, Allen Lane, 1979. P. 243.

27. Ibid.

28. Anders, pp. 8–13. See also Suchcitz, pp. 14–16. Suchcitz notes that it was the 12th Soviet Army which Anders were trying to get to Hungary were captured and later murdered by the Soviet security service, the NKVD at Charkov and Katyń.

29. PISM, PRM.4, The USSR and the Soviet Occupation of Eastern Poland, September –December 1939, PRM.4/2, 28 November 1939.

30. Sarner, p. 29 & p. 36.

31. Siemaszko, pp. 654–655.

32. Ian Kershaw, *Fateful Choices. Ten Decisions that Changed the World, 1940–1941*, London, Allen Lane, 2007, p. 258.

33. Anders, pp. 13–37.

34. PISM, PRM.11/7, *Sztab Głowny Oddział II*, Paris, 6 May 1940.

Chapter Three: Amnesty and Evacuation

1. Anders, pp. 41–44.

2. Ibid, p. 44.

3. Evan McGilvray, *A Military Government in Exile. The Polish Government–in–Exile, 1939–1945. A Study in discontent*, Solihull, Helion, 2013, p. 78. Keith Sword, *Deportation and Exile. Poles in the Soviet Union, 1939–48*, Basingstoke, Macmillan, 1996, p. 31. Anne Applebaum, *Gulag. A History of the Soviet Camps*, London, BCA, 2003, pp. 403–404; 407. Golfo Alexpoulos. 'Amnesty 1945: The Revolving Door of Stalin's Gulag', *Slavic Review*, 64 (2005) 274–306. Edward J. Rozek, *Allied Wartime Diplomacy. A Pattern in Poland*, New York, John Wiley & Sons, 1958, p. 64.

4. McGilvray, *A Military Government in Exile*, pp. 65–68.

5. Ibid, p. 76.

6. PISM, PRM (Polish Prime Ministers' Office) PRM 35c/15, 24 August 1940; PRM–K.102 (Minutes of the Council of Ministers [Polish Government–in–Exile's Cabinet]) PRM–K. 102/28c, 24 August 1940.

7. *Armia Krajowa w Dokumentach, 1939–1945 Vol.1* (henceforth *AK1*) London, Studium Polski Podziemnej, 1970, pp. 88–89, 267, 272, 297–299; PISM, PRM–K. 102/21a, 2 December 1940.

8. McGilvray, *A Military Government in Exile*, p. 71.

9. PISM, PRM 42/2/1, 14 August 1941; PRM 42/8/1, 13 August 1941.

10. PISM, KGA (General Anders' Collection) KGA/1c, Order No.1 Moscow, 22 August 1941.

11. Ibid, 25 August 1941.

12. PISM, KGA/1c, Speech by Anders, 11 December 1941.

13. Anders, p. 52.

14. Tadeusz Felsztyn, *Dzieje 2 Korpusu*, London, Gryf, 1947, p. 10. A record of Felsztyn in Soviet captivity is found in Major General Jerzy Wołkowicki's papers in www.pism.co.uk Kol.212/3.

15. Zurowski, p. 272.

16. Anders, p.52.

17. Ibid, p. 53.

18. Peter Clarke, *The Cripps Version. The Life of Sir Stafford Cripps, 1889–1952*, London, Allen Lane, The Penguin Press, 2002, pp. 190–191.

19. Stanisław Kot, *Listy z Rosji do Gen. Sikorskiego*, London, Jutro Polski, 1955, p. 82. Anders, p. 61.

20. TNA, FO 371/31088/C11653, Hankey to Makins, 1942.

21. TNA, FO 371/3108/C130909, Memorandum by Hills, 29 October 1942. Kot, pp. 334–337; Sword, pp. 107–112.

22. Anders, pp. 61–62, 76. Kot later was to protest in print that he could follow what was being said owing to his knowledge of Old Slavonic. Kot, *Conversations with the Kremlin*, p.xi. Even if this was likely it should not detract from the fact that Anders at all times was more aware of Soviet intentions than any other Polish representative present at Polish–Soviet talks involving Anders.

23. Ibid, p. xiii.

24. PISM, KGA.1b, Polish General Staff in the Soviet Union, 23 September 1941– 30 March 1942, KGA.1b, entry, 22 November 1941.

25. PISM, KOL 1, Journal of Activities of the Supreme Commander, KOL 1/26, Kot to Sikorski, 22 September 1941.

26. PISM, KGA.1b, Talks between Kot and Stalin, 21 November 1941.

27. Siemaszko, pp. 294–295.

28. PISM, PRM. 41/4, Anders, Sikorski meeting with Stalin, 4 December 1941. Molotov indeed toasted Klimkowski as 'a representative of Polish military youth'. Stanislaw Kot, *Conversations with the Kremlin and Dispatches from Russia*, London, Oxford University Press, 1963, p. 164.

29. TNA, FO 371/34593/C4597/940/G, Baghdad to Minister of State, Cairo, 22 April 1943.

30. Siemaszko, pp. 294–295.

31. Eugenia Maresh, 'The Polish 2 Corps in Preparation for Action and its Disbandment 1943–1946' in *General Władysław Anders*, Pylat et al, pp. 34–35. See also TNA, FO 371/31089 C 11652, 'British Liaison with the Poles in Persia', 10 November 1942.

32. Jerzy Klimkowski, *Byłem Adiutantem Generała Andersa*, Warsaw, MON, 1959, pp. 134–135; Zygmunt Berling, *Wspomnienia 1, Z Łagrów do Andersa*, Warsaw, Polski Dom Wydawniczy, 1990, pp. 111–112. *Documents on Polish Soviet Relations,*

1939–1945 Volume 1, London, Heinmann, 1961, (henceforth: *DPSR1*) p. 159. TNA, FO 371/26760/C1090, Foreign Office to Moscow, 27 September 1941.

33. PISM, KGA/7f, Polish–Soviet Relations, KGA/7f, Letter from Eden to Sir S. Cripps, 26 September 1941.

34. PISM, PRM 41/3/26, Sikorski to Churchill, 17 December 1941; PRM 41/5/5, note of a conversation between General MacFarlane and General Szyszko–Bohusz, 21 November 1941; PRM 41/6/13, Ciechanowski (Washington DC) to Council of Ministers, 25 November 1941.

35. *DPSR1*, pp. 149–151, 187, 207.

36. Piotr Zaroń, *Armia Andersa*, Toruń, Adam Marszałek, 1996, pp. 151–153. PISM, KOL 1/27, Sikorski to Anders, 1 October 1941; Sikorski–Bogomolov Talks, 6 October 1941.

37. Anita J. Prażmowska, 'Poland's Eastern and Western Frontiers in General Sikorski's Foreign Policy' in *General Władysław Sikorski's Wartime Leader Conference Papers* (4 November 2003), Jan Ciechanowski and Andrzej Suchcitz (eds) London, Polish Institute & Sikorski Museum, 2007, pp. 106–122.

38. PISM, KGA/7b, Polish–Soviet Relations: Correspondence with the Soviets, 1939–1942, Declaration by General Anders to raise divisions of Polish troops in the Soviet Union, 12 September 1941.

39. PISM, KGA/7b, General Anders: Rebuilding the Polish Army from the Soviet Union, 20 October 1941.

40. PISM, KGA/7b, Brigadier–General Szyszko–Bohusz to Anders, 19 November 1941.

41. PISM, KGA/7c, Polish–Soviet Relations, 1941–1942, Minutes of a conversation between Brigadier General Panfilov and General Anders, 18 August 1941.

42. PISM, KGA/7c, Conversation between Sikorski, Stalin, Kot, Molotov, Anders, 3 December 1941.

43. PISM, KGA/7i, Polish–Soviet Relations – The Polish Army in the Soviet Union, 1941–1949, President Raczkiewicz to Anders, 1 September 1941.

44. McGilvray, *A Military Government in Exile*, pp. 53–55.

45. Zurowski, p. 273. Anders, p. 65.

46. *The Sunday Express*, 31 March 1940.

47. *The Maisky Diaries. Red Ambassador to the Court of St James 1932–1943*, Gabriel Gorodetsky (ed) London, Yale University, 2015, diary entry 3 November 1941 + editor's notes. pp. 399–401.

48. *Correspondence Between the Chairman of the Council of Ministers of the USSR and the Presidents of the USA and the Prime Ministers of Great Britain during the Great Patriotic War of 1941–1945. Volume 1. Correspondence with Winston S. Churchill and Clement R. Attlee (July 1941–November 1945*, Moscow, Progress Publishers, 1957, No. 14, Churchill to Stalin, 21 September 1941, pp. 33–35. Hereafter *Correspondence 1*.

49. Lysaght, p. 163.

50. Norman Davies, *God's Playground: A History of Poland. Volume 2: 1795 to the Present*, Oxford, Clarendon Press, 1981, p. 393–394.

51. Kot, *Conversations with the Kremlin*, p. 43.

52. Zurowski, pp. 273–274.

53. Anders, p. 81.

54. Zurowski, p. 275.

55. *The Times*, 29 September 1941.

56. *The Times*, 30 September 1941.

57. www.fdrlibrary.marist.org Box 1, Churchill to Roosevelt, July–December 1941, Vol. 3 part 1, Churchill to Roosevelt, 5 October 1941, assessed 28 October 2014.

58. *The New York Times*, 2 October 1941.

59. *The New York Times*, 1 October 1941; *The Times*, 11 October 1941.

60. *The Times*, 13 October 1941.

61. www.fdrlibrary.marist.org Box 1, Vol. 3 Part 1, undated message from Churchill to Roosevelt.

62. Ian Kershaw, *Hitler, 1889–1936: Hubris*, London, Penguin, 1999, p. 421.

63. Zurowski, p. 275.

64. Ibid.

65. Ibid, pp. 275–276.

66. Anders, pp. 117–118.

67. Zurowski, pp. 271–286. Also see McGilvray, *A Military Government in Exile*, pp. 77–97.

68. PISM, KGA/7d, Polish–Soviet Relations – Correspondence with the Allies, 1939–1942, 22 August 1942.

69. Ibid.

70. PISM, KGA/7e, Polish–Soviet Relations – Correspondence with the Allies, 1942. Notes of a discussion between General Anders and General Sir Alan Brook, 24 April 1942, War Office, 15:30 – 16:30. Signed off by Brigadier Regulski.

71. Sarner, p. 81.
72. Ibid, pp. 88–92.
73. PISM, KGA/7e, 24 April 1942.
74. PISM, KGA/7e, Report of conversation between British C–in–C, ME, (General Auchinleck) General Anders, Brigadier Elrington, Colonels Sherston and Hulls, 20 May 1942.
75. PISM, KGA/7e, Note of a conversation held at the British Embassy, Cairo, 22 August 1942.
76. Ibid.
77. PISM, KGA/7i, Polish–Soviet Relations – The Polish Army in the Soviet Union, 1941–1949, Minutes taken at a meeting, 23 April 1942.
78. PISM, KGA/21 Part 2, The Polish Army in the Soviet Union, Lieutenant–Colonel Ludwik Domon to General Michał Karszewicz–Tokarzewski, 15 July 1942.
79. Sarner, p. 56.
80. Ibid, pp. 151–152.
81. PISM, KOL 1/32, Kot to Sikorski, 21 March 1942; Władysław Anders, *Bez Ostatniego Rozdiału*, Newtown, Montgomeryshire Press, 1949, p.145.

Chapter Four: The Formation of Second Polish Corps

1. TNA, FO 371/31082/C3779, 2 April 1942.
2. Zurowski, p. 287.
3. TNA, FO 371/31080/C3251, C–in–C Middle East to WO, 22 March 1942.
4. TNA, FO 371/31080/C3293, 24 March 1942; 29 March 1942.
5. Leon Mitkiewicz, *Dokumenty. Z Generałem Sikorskim na Obezyznie (Fragmenty Wspomnień)* Paris, Kultury, 1969, p. 254. See also Bernadeta Tendyra, *General Sikorski and the Polish Government–in–Exile, 1939–1943. A Study in Polish Internal Émigré Politics in Wartime*, Ph.D thesis, The London School of Economics and Political Science, 2000, pp. 239–240.
6. Ibid, p. 241. PISM, KOL 1/32, I, Sikorski to Anders, Kuibyshev, 21 March 1942; Klimecki to Zając, 30 March 1942; KOL 1/33, I, Sikorski to Anders, 2 April 1942.
7. Klimkowski, pp. 255–257; Mitkiewicz, pp. 175–176.
8. PISM, KOL 1/33, I, 23 April 1942.
9. Zurowski, p. 293.
10. Tendyra, p. 243.

11. TNA, FO 371/31083/C4606, 22 April 1942; FO 371/31082/C4344, 23 April 1942.

12. PISM, KOL 1/33, I, Sikorski to Churchill, 24 April 1942.

13. *Polski Siły Zbrojne w Drugiej Światowej*, Vol. II, part 2, (hereafter: *PSZ II, 2*) London, Instytut Historyczny im. Gen. Sikorskiego, 1959, p. 305.

14. TNA, FO 371/31082/C4502, 28 April 1942.

15. Klimkowski, pp. 274–275, 279.

16. *DPSR 1*, pp. 373–374.

17. TNA, FO 371/31084/C6553, Clark–Kerr to FO, 30 June 1942; PISM, KOL, I, Sikorski to Kot and Anders, 2 July 1942.

18. Sarah Meiklejohn Terry, *Poland's Place in Europe. General Sikorski and the Origins of the Oder–Neisse Line, 1939–1943*, Princeton, Princeton University Press, 1983, pp. 239–244; Tendyra, p. 253.

19. Tendyra, p. 254.

20. PISM, KOL 1/37, I, 6 August 1942; Anders to Sikorski, 2 August 1942, 6 August 1942; Sikorski to Anders, 4 August 1942; 18 August 1942.

21. Tendyra, p. 256, PISM, PRM 73/4/148, Anders to Sikorski, 17 August 1942, 18 August 1942. TNA PREM 3/354/6, undated, *DPSR1*, pp. 421–424.

22. McGilvray, *A Military Government in Exile*, p. 87.

23. Ibid.

24. PISM, KOL 1/37, Part 2, *Dziennik Podroży Szefa Sztabu N.W. Gen–Brig. T. Klimeckiego na Śr. Wchód*, 20 August 1942–30 September 1942, (hereafter *Klimecki 1942 Report*) pp. 287–289.

25. PISM, PRM 73/1/38, 24 August 1942; *Klimecki 1942 Report*, p. 299. TNA, FO 371/31086/C7661, Sikorski to Churchill, 3 August 1942.

26. PISM, *Klimecki 1942 Report*, p. 284; KOL 1/38, Kot to Sikorski, 1 September 1942.

27. PISM, *Klimecki 1942 Report*, pp. 288–290; KOL 1/38, I, Kot to Sikorski, 31 August 1942. TNA, PREM 3/354/6, Rowan to Churchill, 26 August 1942.

28. PISM, *Klimecki 1942 Report*, p. 300.

29. TNA, FO 371/31686/C7661, Minute by Roberts, 6 August 1942, Sikorski to Churchill, 3 August 1942, Brown to Lawford, 4 August 1942.

30. TNA, FO 371/31085/C7214, C–in–C, Middle East to War Office, 17 July 1942, PREM 3/354/6, Redman to Lawford, 17 August 1942; PISM, KOL 1/37, I, *Komunikat Naczelnego Wodza Nr. 4*, 8 August 1942, *PSZ, II,2*, pp. 309–310.

31. Felsztyn, p. 19.
32. Tendyra, p. 259. PISM, *Klimecki 1942 Report*, pp. 293–299, 306, 308.
33. PISM, *Klimecki 1942 Report*, p. 299.
34. Anders always referred to Berling as 'Colonel Berling' as he never recognised his Soviet rank and in his memoirs made reference to 'the deserter Colonel Berling', Anders, p. 195. PISM, KGA. 39/1 Press cuttings from *Orel Biały Dziennik Żołnierz APW*, July – October 1944. An appreciation of Polish communists in 1944 notes Berling as being the Vice–Minister of war in the provisional communist backed Polish government set up in Lublin during 1944 with the rank of 'general' but this was a Red Army rank. His official Polish Army rank was that of Lieutenant Colonel. It was further noted that when the Polish Army was beginning the process of leaving the Soviet Union in 1941, he had been sentenced to death by a Polish court martial but escaped custody before the sentence could be carried out. Sarner considers that Berling was driven by ambition and that Anders refused to promote him to full Colonel. When it became quite clear that Berling would never become a General under Anders' command, Berling took up a Soviet offer of the rank. Sarner, p. 14. An earlier report in the Polish exile press noted that 'Colonel' Berling who had broken with Anders had joined the international revolution by becoming involved in propaganda against Poland and its army. See: PISM, KGA.36 *Kurier Polski*, 13 October 1943. A Polish radio news bulletin previously had announced that according to the Soviet press there were hundreds of thousands of Poles willing to fight but Anders was preventing them from therefore the Union of Polish Patriots (a stooge Polish government in waiting under Soviet control) were to form a Polish division. The *Pravda* article also alleged that the only Poles fighting the Germans at the time were serving in the Red Army. PISM, KGA.36, Radio Bulletin, Jerusalem, 19 May 1943.

Chapter Five: Anders and Sikorski, 1942–1943

1. Anders, p. 148.
2. Ibid, p. 196.
3. TNA, FO 371/31089/C13090, Report to Major C. Bryson on the British Army in the Middle East, 108, 25 November 1942. Zaroń, pp. 174–177. See also PISM, PRM.80/5, Kot to Sikorski, 22 August 1942.

4. TNA, FO 371/31089/C8428/74/55, Polish Political Situation, Minister of State, Cairo, 30 August 1942; FO 371/31089/C8428/74/55, Draft telegram (FO) to Mexico City, 14 December 1941.
5. TNA, FO 371/31089/C13090/74/55, Major C. Bryson on the Polish Army in the Middle East, 108, 25 November 1942.
6. TNA, FO 371/31089/C13090/74/55, Report by Major C. Bryson on the Polish Army in the Middle East, no. 2, 10 November 1942.
7. McGilvray, *A Military Goverment in Exile*, pp. 46–47.
8. See above FN 145.
9. Ibid, *Klimecki 1942 Report*, p. 320.
10. TNA, FO 371/31088/C11652, Hankey to Makins, 10 November 1942. PISM, KOL 1/39, I, Kot to Sikorski, 27 November 1942.
11. Kot, pp. 270–271. PISM, PRM. 80/17, Kot to Sikorski, 24 September 1942, KOL 1/38, I, Sikorski to Anders, 26 September 1942; KOL 1/39, I, Anders to Sikorski, 4 October 1942; Sikorski to Anders, 7 October 1942.
12. Stefan Kopański, *Wspomnienia Wojenne, 1939–1946*, London, Veritas, 1961, pp. 270–271.
13. PISM, PRM.107, The Middle East, 1943, PRM.107/13, Kot (Jerusalem) to Sikorski, 4 February 1943; PRM.107/15, Sikorski to Anders and Kot, 5 February 1943; PRM.107/28, Bader (Tehran) 12 February 1943.
14. PISM, PRM.107/22, Anders to Sikorski, 9 February 1943; PRM.107/14, Kot (Jerusalem) 4 February 1943.
15. PISM, PRM.107/31, Ambassador RP, Tehran to General Sikorski, 17 April 1943.
16. Piotr Potomski, *Generał Broni Stanisław Władysław Maczek (1892–1994)* Warsaw, Uniwersytetu Warszawa, 2008, p. 339. Teresa Torańska, *Oni*, London, Aneks, 1985, p. 340.
17. Information supplied to author by Antoni Położński, veteran of 10th Mounted Rifles, First Polish Armoured Division and personal friend of Skibiński, Dec 1998.
18. Sarner, pp. 29, 73, 155, 282.
19. Klimkowski, *Byłem Adiutantem*, pp. 340–344; p. 357.
20. PISM, PRM. 80, Karol Bader to Stanisław Mikołajczyk, 31 January 1942.
21. TNA, FO 371/31082/C3950/G, Sikorski to General Boruta, 7 April 1942.
22. TNA, FO 371/26760/C7402/G, 30 Military Mission, Moscow to WO, 27 July 1942.

23. TNA, PREM 3/354/2, Minister of State, Cairo to Foreign Office, 6 February 1943; FO 371/34563/C1723/G, Minute by Allen, 12 February 1943.

24. PISM, KOL 1/14, I, Lieutenant Colonel De Chair, No. 4 Military Mission, to Sikorski, 23 September 1940.

25. TNA, PREM 3/354/2, Minister of State, Cairo, to Foreign Office, 6 February 1943.

26. PISM, KGA/11, Klimkowski to Anders, 19 January 1943.

27. TNA, FO 371/34593/C4597/940/G, Baghdad to Minister of State, Cairo, 22 April 1943.

28. Sarner, p. 56.

29. TNA, FO 371/31089/C13090, Bryson Report, 25 November 1942; FO 371/31088/C11652, 25 November 1942.

30. PISM, KOL 1/40, I, 17 November 1942, Sikorski to Anders, 25 & 26 November 1942. TNA, PREM 3/351/11, 17 November 1942. See also Conrad Black, *Franklin Delano Roosevelt. Champion of Freedom*, London, Weidenfeld & Nicolson, 2004, p. 852.

31. *DPSR 1*, pp. 473–474.

32. PISM, KOL 1/41, I, Anders to Sikorski, 2 December 1942.

33. PISM, PREM 69/138, undated. Jan Ciechanowski, *Defeat in Victory*, New York, Doubleday, 1947, p. 122–123.

34. TNA, FO 371/34563/C910/G, FO to Washington DC, 7 February 1943.

35. TNA, KV, British Security Files, KV 2/516, Sikorski's Visit to the USA, 17 February 1943.

36. Sarner, pp. 110–113.

37. Ibid, p. 152.

38. TNA, FO 371/34593/C3742, Eden to Churchill, 11 April 1943.

39. PISM, PRM 107/12, received 9 February 1943.

40. PISM, PRM–K. 102/55a, 11 February 1943.

41. PISM, PRM 107/28; PRM 107/31. Both undated.

42. PISM, KOL 1/43, I, Anders to Sikorski, 18 February 1943.

43. TNA, FO 371/34593/C3375, Hopkins to Strang, 17 March 1943. Previously Hulls as a Lieutenant Colonel had been the Imperial General Staff's Liaison Officer to the Polish Commander in the Soviet Union and had liaised with Soviet officials, Żaron, p. 39. Hulls also spoke Russian.

44. TNA, FO 371/34593/C3375, Minute by Lambert, 8 April 1943; FO 371/34593/C3602, Minute by Roberts, undated.

45. TNA, FO 371/31088/C10946/G, WO to C–in–C Persia–Iraq, 3 November 1942; C11048/G, Minister of State, Cairo to the Undersecretary of State, FO, 12 November 1942, C9293/74/G, Minister of State, Cairo to FO, 20 November 1942.

46. Eugenio Corti, *The Last Soldiers of the King: Wartime Italy, 1943–1945* (translated by Manuela Arundel) Missouri, University of Missouri, 2003, p. 11.

47. TNA, FO 371/34593/C3623, Minister of State, Cairo to FO, 1 April 1943.

48. Tendyra, p. 285. TNA, FO 371/34593/C1938, Eden to Cadogan, 20 February 1943; PREM 3/354/2, 20 February 1943.

49. PISM, KOL 1/44, I, 15 & 17 March 1943.

50. TNA, FO 371/345593/C3742/G, (Prime Minister's Personal Telegram, M.2224/3) 3 April 1943.

51. TNA, FO 371/34593/C3742/G, Eden to Churchill, 11 April 1943.

52. TNA, FO 371/34593/C3623/G55, Minister of State, Cairo, to FO, 2 April 1943.

53. McGilvray, *A Military Government in Exile*, p. 118.

54. Foreign and Commonwealth Office Departmental Series of Eastern Europe and Soviet Department, The Butler Memorandum, DS 2/73, 10 April 1973, www.fco.gov.uk accessed 1 March 2004, p. 8, fn. 12. Hereafter *Butler*.

55. Janusz K. Zawody, *Katyń*, Lublin, Spotkania, 1989, p. 26. Kacewicz pinpoints 16 July 1941 as the date when the Germans captured Smolensk and the Katyń area. George Kacewicz, *Great Britain, the Soviet Union and the Polish Government–in–Exile, 1939–1945*, The Hague, Nijhoff, 1979, p. 160, fn. 83. See also *Butler*, p. 15.

56. Sergo Beria, *My Father: Inside Stalin's Kremlin*, London, Duckworth, 2001, pp. 90, 319, fn. 43.

57. Jacek Ślusarczyk, *Polityka Rządu Generała W. Sikorskiego Wobec ZSSR*, Warsaw, PAN, 1985, p.88; Norman Davies, *Rising '44 'The Battle for Warsaw'* London, Macmillan, 2003, p. 91.

58. Tadeusz Bór–Komorowski, *Armia Podziemna*, 3rd Edition, London, Veritas, 1967, p. 48.

59. *Butler*, p. 8.

60. PISM, PRM 96/10, Discussion between General Sikorski, Raczyński, Churchill and Sir Alexander Cadogan, 15 April 1943.

61. Bellamy estimates that in 1943 the Red Army was holding down 200 German divisions. Chris Bellamy, *Absolute War. Soviet Russia in the Second World War*, London, Macmillan, 2007, p. 601. It should also be considered that this does not include Germany's allies: Italy, Finland, Hungary and Romania, all of whom had troops serving to various degrees on the Russian Front.

62. Black, pp. 742, 830.

63. *Cadogan Diaries*, diary entry, 18 June 1943, p. 537.

64. TNA, PREM 3/354/8, Churchill to Eden, 28 April 1943.

65. *Dziennik Polski*, 21 April 1943.

66. TNA, FO 371/34571/C4828; C4778, Pownall to Anders, 29 April 1943.

67. G.A. Shepperd, *The Italian Campaign, 1943–45. A Political and Military re-assessment*, London, Arthur Barker Ltd, 1968, p. 267.

68. TNA, PREM 3/354/8, FO to Moscow, 30 April 1943.

69. Stalin to Churchill, 4 May 1943, *Correspondence Between the Chairman of Ministers of the USSR and the Presidents of the USA and the Prime Ministers of Great Britain During the Great Patriotic War of 1941–1945*, Vol. 1, Moscow, Progress, 1957, pp. 131–132 (Hereafter *Correspondence 1*) See also Stalin to Roosevelt, 29 April 1943, *Correspondence 2*, pp. 56–57.

70. TNA, PREM 3/354/8, Churchill to Stalin, 26 April 1943; Churchill to Stalin, 24 April 1943; 30 April 1943. *Correspondence 1*, pp. 126–127; 129–130. Roosevelt to Stalin, 26 April 1943, *Correspondence 2*, p. 56. Warren F. Kimball, *Churchill & Roosevelt. The Complete Correspondence, Vol. 2*, Princeton, Princeton University Press, 1984, pp. 203–205.

71. TNA, FO 371/34574/C5138, Churchill to Eden; Eden to Churchill, 10 May 1943. Churchill to Stalin, 12 May 1943, *Correspondence 1*, p. 134. Even so Churchill remarked that the Poles were not reasonable but the Soviets were impossible, TNA, PREM 3/354/8, Churchill to Roosevelt, 28 April 1943.

72. TNA, FO 371/345675/C5295, Eden to Clark–Kerr, 11 May 1943. Stalin had already told Clark–Kerr, the British Ambassador to the Soviet Union, on 6 May 1943, that he would not resume relations with the Polish Goverment–in–Exile until the Poles had reformed that government, TNA, FO 371/34574/C5189, Clark–Kerr, 8 May 1943.

73. *Documents on Polish–Soviet Relations, 1939–1945, Volume II, 1943–1945*, London, Heinemann, 1967, pp. 696–702. (Hereafter *DPSR 2*). Tendyra, pp. 295–296.

74. PISM, KOL 1/45, II, *Dziennik Podróży Szefa Sztabu Naczelnego Wodza Gen. Bryg. Tadeusza Klimeckiego na Śred. Wschód. Kwiecień, Maj, Czerwiec, Lipiec, 1943 rok.* (Henceforth *Klimecki 1943 Report*), *Notatka Nr. 270*, 27 April 1943.

75. PISM, *Klimecki 1943 Report*, pp. 171–173.

76. Ibid, p. 192.

77. TNA, FO 371/34593/C3742, FO to the Minister of State, Cairo, 13 April 1943; TNA, PREM 3/354/8, Churchill to Sir Alexander Cadogan, 3 April 1943.

78. PISM, *Klimecki 1943 Report*, p. 202.

79. Jerzy Klimkowski, *Katastrofa w Gibraltarze. Kulisy Śmierci Generała Sikorskiego*, Bielsko–Biała, Wydawnictwo Śląsk, 1965, p. 62.

80. Edward Raczyński, *In Allied London*, London, Weidenfeld & Nicolson, 1962, pp. 139–140.

81. TNA, KV 2/516, 'General Wladyslaw Sikorski – General Kazimierz Sosnkowski' Robinson–Scott to Captain Derbyshire, 19 April 1943.

82. TNA, FO 371/34577/C5843/910/G, Roberts to Moscow, 25 May 1943. Earlier Frank Roberts had minuted that Sikorski's visit to the Middle East was a matter of the highest political importance owing to the poor state of Polish–Soviet relations, a fact emphasised by German propaganda, TNA, FO 850, Foreign Office Communications, FO 850/84 Y2391/G, F.K. Roberts, 19 April 1943.

83. Tendyra, p. 304. PISM, KOL 1/47, I, 10 June 1943. TNA, FO 371/34594/C6892/G, Minister of State, Cairo to FO, 16 June 1943.

84. TNA, FO 371/34593/C3375/G, Hopkinson, Cairo to Strang, 17 March 1943; C3583/G, Minister of State, Cairo to FO, 31 March 1943.

85. TNA, FO 371/34593/C3623/335/G55, Minutes by Roberts and Allen, 2 April 1943. Roberts also observed that there was no alternative to Sikorski as Polish Prime Minister.

86. PISM, KOL 1/47, I, 10 June 1943.

87. TNA, FO 371/34593/C3375, Hopkins, Baghdad, to Minister of State, Cairo, 27 May 1943. Casey and Hopkins were local British officials in Iraq.

88. TNA, FO 371/34614 A/C5992, Minister of State, Cairo to FO, 27 May 1943. PISM, KOL 1/48, I, Report by T. Żaźuliński, 8 July 1943.

89. Tendyra, p. 305.

90. TNA, FO 371/34594/C6892, Minister of State, Cairo to FO, 16 June 1943. *PSZ*, Part 2, pp. 328–329.

91. PISM, PRM 66/31, Duff Cooper to Sikorski, 21 July 1942.

92. PISM, PRM 66/32, Sikorski to Duff Cooper, 23 July 1942.

93. David Irving, *Accident. The Death of General Sikorski*, London, William Kimber, 1967, pp. 155–156.

94. PISM, A.XII 3/81, 26 April 1943.

95. The Polish Government–in–Exile considered that the incident took place on 21 March 1942, PISM, A.XII 3/81, 26 April 1943. The British Government set the date as around 22 March 1942, TNA, PREM 3/354, 26 April 1943.

96. TNA, PREM 3/354/1, 26 April 1943.

97. Irving, p. 157.

98. PISM, PRM 69/138, undated. Jan Ciechanowski, *Defeat in Victory*, London, Gollancz, 1948, p. 134.

99. Robert Rhodes James, *Victor Cazalet. A Portrait*, London, Hamilton, 1976, p. 282.

100. Irving, pp. 157–163.

101. PISM, KOL 1/47, Sikorski to Raczkiewicz, 4 June 1943; KOL 1/48, 3 July 1943. TNA, FO 371/34594/C7463, Minister of State, Cairo, to FO, 3 July 1943.

102. Olgierd Terlicki, *Generał Sikorski*, Vol. 2. Kraków, Wydawnictwo Literackie Kraków, 1983, pp. 226–227. Stanisław Strumph–Wojtkiewicz, *Sikorski i Jego Żołnierz*, Łódź, Księgarni Ludowej, 1946, p. 66. Kopański, p. 282. PISM, PRM–K. 102/59f, 25 June 1943. Michał Sokolnicki, Polish Ambassador to Turkey and a veteran of Piłsudski's Legions, recorded in his diary, 12 May 1943, the eighth anniversary of Piłsudski's death, that the choir in Ankara sang '*Pierwszą Brygadę*' before Mass commemorating Piłsudski. Michał Sokolnicki, *Dziennik Ankarski, 1939–1943*, London, Gryf, 1965, p. 514. This incident illustrates the influence of Piłsudski and the First Brigade even after the death of Piłsudski.

103. TNA, CAB 122 British Joint Staff Missions, CAB 122/141, Eden to Halifax, 1 June 1943.

104. TNA, FO 371/34594/C6892/G, Minister of State, Cairo, to FO, 16 June 1943.

105. TNA, FO 371/34594/C763/335/55Pol/43/47, Minister of State, Cairo, to FO, 3 July 1943.

Chapter Six: Italy and Monte Cassino

1. PISM, KGA 1b, *Dziennik Czynności Gen. W. Andersa od 30/X/42 do 14/III/44*. General Sir Henry Maitland Wilson in a letter made reference to Anders' illness, KGA. 3a, Wilson to Anders, 17 July 1943.

2. PISM, KGA. 3a, Kenny to Anders, 17 July 1943.

3. Kot, *Conversations with the Kremlin*, B17. Sikorski meets Stalin, 3 December 1941, pp. 140–160.

4. PISM, C.88/1, *Kronika 3. Brygady Strzelców Karpackich* (History of 3rd Carpathian Infantry Brigade) 30 March 1945.

5. PISM, KGA. 3a, Notes concerning the possible reorganisation of the Polish Second Corps, Cairo, 6 December 1943.

6. See McGilvray, *Man of Steel and Honour*, pp. 122–125.

7. TNA, WO 204/7761, Move of Polish Corps, December 1943–February 1944. Order dated, 13 December 1943.

8. Matthew Parker, *Monte Cassino. The Story of the Hardest Fought Battle of World War Two*, London, Headline, 2003, p. 8; Lloyd Clark, *Anzio. The Friction of War. Italy and the Battle for Rome 1944*, London, Headline, 2006, p. 8.

9. Special Collections, Brotherton Library, University of Leeds, Inverchapel Papers, 1942, Meeting at the Kremlin, 12 August 1942 (FO 800/300).

10. Parker, pp. xvii–xviii.

11. Alex Danchev, Daniel Todman (eds) *War Diaries, 1939–1945. Field Marshal Lord Alanbrooke*, London, Weidenfeld & Nicolson, 2001, diary entries, 14–18 September 1943, pp. 452–453 (hereafter *'Alanbrooke'*).

12. Ibid, p. 535.

13. James Holland, *Italy's Sorrow. A Year of War, 1944–1945*. London, Harper Press, 2008, pp.405–406.

14. Halik Kochanski, *The Eagle Unbowed. Poland and the Poles in the Second World War*, London, Allen Lane, 2012, p. 467.

15. Holland, p. 82.

16. PISM, KGA/28, Correspondence with the Allies, 1942–1943, Anders' Report on Polish Prisoners of War, 13 April 1943.

17. PISM, KGA 32/I/3, General H.R. Alexander, Commander–in–Chief, Allied Mediterranean Force to Major General Z. Szyszko–Bohusz, 2 Polish Corps, 16 January 1944. See Holland, p.429 & p. 493.

18. *The Alexander Memoirs 1940–1945. Field Marshal Earl Alexander of Tunis*, Barnsley, Frontline Books, 2010, p. 141.

19. Norman Davies, *Trail of Hope. The Anders Army, An Odyssey Across Three Continents*, Oxford, Osprey, 2015, pp.506–507.

20. Kochanski, pp. 467–468.

21. Fred Majdalany, *Cassino: Portrait of a Battle*, London, Longmans, Green and Co, 1957, p.84.

22. Shepperd, p. 233.

23. Kochanski, p. 468.

24. Majdalany, pp. 114–115.

25. Ibid, pp. 118–119.

26. Ibid, p. 194.

27. Ibid, p. 246.

28. Shepperd, pp. 266–269.

29. PISM, KGA 32/II/3, Notes for General Anders.

30. PISM, KGA 32/II/5, Notes for General Anders, 16 May 1944.

31. Ibid, 17 May 1944.

32. Shepperd, p. 269.

33. Kochanski, pp. 469–474; Shepperd, pp. 265–269.

34. Parker, p. 345.

35. PISM, KGA 32/II/8, Anders to Sosnkowski, 18 May 1944.

36. PISM, KGA 32/II/9, General Leese to Anders, 18 May 1944.

37. PISM, KGA 32/II/15, Telegram for Anders, 22 May 1944. *Dziennik Żołnierz APW* (Field Edition) 25 May 1944 reported Alexander decorating Anders.

Chapter Seven: Italy after Monte Cassino

1. PISM, KGA/32/II/14, Notes for General Anders.

2. PISM, KGA/32/II/ 19, Leese to Anders, 21 May 1944.

3. PISM, KGA/32/II/42, General Sir Oliver Leese, Memorandum to all Corps down to Companies, 5 June 1944.

4. F.K. Hałuszczak, (ed) *Koło Żołnierzy Pułku 6 Pancernego Dzieci Lwowskich*, privately printed, Leeds, 1966, pp. 16–23.

5. Andrew Roberts, *Masters and Commanders. How Roosevelt, Churchill, Marshall and Alanbrooke Won the War in the West*, London, Allen Lane, 2008, p. 509.

6. Olgierd Terlicki, *Poles in the Italian Campaign, 1943–1945*, Warsaw, Interpress, 1972, p. 96.

7. TNA, WO 204/8042, Report of 2 Polish Corps Operations on the Adriatic Sector, undated.

8. TNA, WO 204/7078, Polcorps Intelligence Summaries, 1 August – 28 September 1944. Intelligence Summary No. 61, 28 September 1944.

9. Hałuszczak, pp. 24–34.

Chapter Eight: 1945–1948: A New Poland and a Divided Europe

1. TNA, FO 371/4577 N1317/6/G55, Churchill to Eden, 25 January 1945.

2. Brotherton Library, University of Leeds, Map Room, Reel 5, Churchill to Roosevelt, 16 December 1944.

3. *Cadogan*, 20 February 1945, p. 719.

4. Ibid, 3–9 April 1945, pp. 726–727.

5. Fraser J. Harbutt, *Yalta 1945. Europe and America at the Crossroads*, New York, Cambridge University Press, 2010, p. 282.

6. Ibid, editor's note, p. 733.

7. Ibid, 4 May 1945; 5 May 1945, pp. 738–739.

8. S.M. Plokhy, *Yalta: The Price of Peace*, New York, Penguin, 2010, p. 397.

9. *Cadogan*, p. 765.

10. Ibid, 21 July 1945 and 22 July 1945, pp. 767–769.

11. Ibid, 31 July 1945, pp. 777–778.

12. Plokhy, p. 345.

13. *British Foreign Policy in the Second World War*, Volume III, (ed) Llewellyn Woodward, London, HMSO, 1971, pp. 244–245. (Henceforth known as *BFPWW2 (3)*.

14. *Correspondence 1*, No. 301, Secret and Personal From Premier J.V. Stalin to the Prime Minister, Mr. W. Churchill, 23 July 1944, pp. 245–246.

15. Plokhy, pp. 351–352.

16. TNA, FO 371/47574 N 146/6/55, Eden to O'Malley, 4 January 1945.

17. TNA, FO 371/47575 N 193/6/55, Statement of General Rola–Zymierski, 4 January 1945.

18. TNA, FO 371/4757, FO to Washington, Message from Stalin to Roosevelt, 30 December 1944.

19. McGilvray, *A Military Government in Exile*, p. 167.

20. A. Lemesis, *Stalin's Oath. A Talk with Stalin about Communist Aggression*, Stockholm, Latvian National Fund, 1951, p. 54.

21. TNA, CAB 122/920, T. no. 241, Roberts (Moscow) to Lord Halifax, 25 April 1945.

22. PISM, PRM 161/3 *Reports of the Situation in Occupied Poland, 1945*, J. 'Jur' Lerski to Mr. Hore–Belisha, 31 January 1945.

23. Ibid.

24. *Dziennik czynności Prezydenta RP Władysława Raczkiewicza, 1939–1947 Tom 2*, (ed) Jacek Piotrowski, Wrocław, Wydawnictwo Uniwersytetu Wrocławskiego, 2004, pp. 423–429. (Hereafter *Raczkiewicz 2*).

25. TNA, FO 371/47660 N 1103 /123/G 55, Warner to FO, 30 January 1945.

26. Plokhy, pp. 370–371.

27. *Alanbrooke Diaries*, Diary entry, 24 January 1945, p. 649.

28. TNA, FO 371/47660 N/1398/123/G 55, 24 January 1945.

29. Ibid, Minute by Warner, 11 February 1945. Christopher Warner was Head of the Northern Department at the FO and was its resident Soviet and East European expert; he knew the risks that the British Goverment and the FO ran by not totally censuring Anders.

30. TNA, FO 371/47601 N 2102/123/G55, FO Minute, Mr Allen, 20 February 1945.

31. Ibid, Eden agreed to do so.

32. TNA, FO 371/47660 N 2026/123/ G55, FO Minute Mr Wilson – Conversation with Mr Deutscher (Close confidant of Stanisław Kot) [Confidant of General Sikorski] 24 February 1945.

33. Plokhy, p. 379.

34. Milovan Djilas, *Conversations with Stalin*, London, Pelican, 1962, p. 90.

35. TNA, FO 371/4766 N 2196/123/55, Anders' Order of the Day, 26 February 1945. *The Manchester Guardian*, 27 February 1945.

36. TNA, FO 371/47661 N 2585/123 G 55, FO Minute, Sir Orme Sargent, 26 February 1945.

37. Brooke Diaries, 26 February 1945, p. 666.

38. TNA, PREM 3/352/9, Letter from Sargent, 27 February 1945.

39. TNA, FO 371/47661 N 2585/123/G 55, FO Minute, Sir Orme Sargent, 26 February 1945.

40. TNA, PREM 3/356/3, Sargent Meeting with Stanislav Mikolajczyk, 27 February 1945.

41. Anders, *An Army in Exile*, p. 154.

42. TNA, FO 371/4766 N 2312/123/55, Minute by Savery on leading article in *Jutro Polski* (published 3 March 1945) 4 March 1945.

43. Ibid.

44. Leon Mitkiewicz, *W Najwyższym Sztabie Zachodnich Aliantów 1943–1945 (Combined Chiefs of Staff)* London, Katolicki Ośrodek Wydawniczy Veritas, 1971, p. 89.

Chapter Nine: Europe and Poland: Immediate Post-War Problems

1. PISM, C.340II 18 LBS (18th Battalion Lwow Rifles) Diary, 22–25 May 1945.

2. *Correspondence 1*, No. 467, Personal and Secret Message from Mr Churchill to Marshal Stalin, 15 May 1945, pp. 353–355.

3. British FP 368–369.

4. Ibid, No. 470, Personal and Secret From Premier J.V. Stalin to the President, Mr. H. Truman, 22 May 1945, pp. 357–358.

5. Nicholas Bethell, *Gomułka: His Poland and His Communism*, London, Penguin, 1972, pp. 98–99.

6. Prażmowska, p. 149.

7. Bethell, pp. 98–128.

8. TNA, FO 371/47665 N 6146/123/G 55, Polish armed forces, Minute by Sir Orme Sargent, 18 May 1945.

9. TNA, FO 371/47665 N 6300/G, Colville to Dixon, 31 May 1945.

10. Ibid, Churchill to Eden and Secretary of State for War, 31 May 1945.

11. TNA, FO 371/47665 N7260/123/G, June 1945.

12. *Maisky Diaries*, pp. 348–349. Entry 29 April 1941.

13. Lemesis, pp.52–53.

14. PISM, KGA.42, Information from the Cultural and Press Department, 2nd Corps (Polish), 20 December 1945.

15. Wiesław Jan Wysocki, *Rotmistrz Witold Pilecki, 1901–1948*, Warsaw, Rytm, 2012, pp. 198–200.

16. Jan Linowski, *Wielka Brytania w polityce zagranicznej Polski w latach 1945–1956*, Toruń, 2001, p. 78.

17. Anita J. Prażmowska, *Civil War in Poland, 1942–1948*, Basingstoke, Palgrave Macmillan, 2004, pp. 147–148.

18. *The Manchester Guardian*, 9 August 1946.

19. *Kształtowanie Władzy Ludowej w Łodzi i Województwie Łódzkim w 1945 Roku: Wybór Żródeł*, (ed) Genowefa Adamczewska, Mieczysław Bandurka, Edward Chobot, Maria Ojrzyńska, Warsaw–Łódź, Państwowe Wydawnictwo Naukowe, 1985, pp. 72, 74, 85, 116, 123, 133, 178, 180, 182.

20. Ibid, pp. 267–270.

21. *The Manchester Guardian*, 13 December 1945.

22. Michael Dobbs, *Six Months in 1945. From World War to Cold War*, London, Hutchinson, 2012, p. 211. Operation UNTHINKABLE, TNA, CAB 120/691/109040.

23. Corti, pp. 319–320.

24. Andrew Borowiec, *Warsaw Boy: A Memoir of a Wartime Childhood*, London, Penguin, 2015, p. 341.

25. Dobbs, p. 211.

26. Ibid, pp. 211–212.

27. Andrew Roberts, p.266.

28. Brooke Diary, 4 October 1944, pp. 598–599; 24 May 1945, pp. 693–694.

29. Dobbs, p.299.

30. TNA, CAB 120/691, May–July 1945.

31. Ibid.

32. *Alanbrooke Diaries*, Diary entry 24 May 1945, pp. 693–694.

33. Ibid, Diary entries, 28 May–31 May 1945, pp. 694–695.

34. Ibid, Diary entry, 31 May 1945, p. 695.

35. TNA, CAB 120/691, May – July 1945.

36. *Brooke Diaries*, Diary entry, 8 June 1945, p. 696.

37. Ibid, Diary entry, 11 June 1945, p. 697.

38. Frank Roberts, *Dealing with Dictators: The Destruction & Revival of Europe, 1930–70*, London, Weidenfeld & Nicolson, 1991, pp. 107–110. See also John Saville, *The Politics of Continuity. British Foreign Policy and the Labour Government, 1945–46*, London, Verso, 1993, pp. 47, 51.

39. *Brooke Diaries*, Diary entry, 2 July 1945, p. 701.

40. Frank Roberts, p. 110.

41. Alan Bullock, *Ernest Bevin, Foreign Secretary, 1945–1951*, New York, W.W. Norton, 1983, p. 263.

42. See Evan McGilvray 'General Stanisław Maczek and Post–war Britain' in Peter D. Stachura (ed) *The Poles in Britain 1940–2000. From Betrayal to Assimilation*, London, Frank Cass, 2004, pp. 59–68.

43. PISM, KGA.42, Political News Summary: Extract from the Polish Prime Minister's Speech to the National Home Council, 28 April 1946.
44. PISM, KGA.42/1, 1 January 1946.
45. Bethell, p. 129.
46. Jerzy Ślaski, '*The armed forces of the anticommunist resistance between 1944–1947*' in Andrzej Ajnenkiel (ed) *Wojna Domowa Czy Nowa Okupacja? Polska po Roku1944 – Civil War in Poland or New Occupation? Poland After 1944*. Warsaw, Rytm, 2001, pp. 253–261.
47. PISM, KGA.42, Interview with Anders, New York, 21 February 1946.
48. PISM, KGA.42, Interview with *The Manchester Guardian*, February 1946.
49. Prażmowska, pp. 145–146.
50. PISM, KGA.42, Interview, 20 February 1946.
51. PISM, C.8/II 1st Carpathian Brigade, Chronicle, June 1945–March 1946.
52. TNA, FO 371/56464, N 1669, Self Defence statement by General Anders to the WO, 11 February 1946.
53. Ibid.
54. Eugenia Maresh, 'The Polish 2 Corps in Preparation for Action and Disbandment 1943–1946' in Pylat et al, p. 51.
55. Andrzej Chmielarz '*Operations of the 64th Division of NKVD Armies of the Interior Against the Polish Underground*' in Ajnenkiel (ed) pp. 293–301.
56. Andrzej Ajnenkiel '*Conclusions*' in Ajnenkiel (ed) p. 416. The authors remembers travelling by train between Łódź and Warsaw during the summer of 1992 and seeing Soviet Army tanks on railway freight flatbeds in siding. This was a full six months after the demise of the Soviet Union.
57. PISM, KGA/5a, General Anders, Correspondence with the Allies, Major General A.D. Ward to Anders, 1 November 1945.
58. PISM, KGA/5a, November 1945, General Anders' Memorandum of the Present Military Situation.
59. PISM, KGA/5d, Miscellaneous Correspondence, 1945, Report, Lieutenant Bohan Podoski, 6 July 1945.
60. PISM, A.XII.1/48a, Brigadier W.A.M, Stawell to Lieutenant General S. Kopanski, 2 November 1945.
61. Prażmowska, p. 143.
62. Ibid.
63. Ibid, p. 145

64. McGilvray, *Days of Adversity*, pp. 144–146.

65. Prażmowska, p. 158.

66. Ibid.

67. Ibid.

68. Ibid. pp. 158–159.

69. Ibid.

70. *The Manchester Guardian*, 13 December 1945.

71. Prażmowska, p. 159.

72. Ibid, pp. 164,170,172–173,175. Neal Ascherson, *The Struggles for Poland*, London, Michael Joseph, 1987, p. 145. See also: *The Manchester Guardian*, 6 July 1946; 13 July 1946.

73. *The Manchester Guardian*, 17 July 1946.

74. Jan Tomasz Gross, *Golden Harvest*, Oxford, Oxford University Press, 2012, pp. 50–57.

75. Prażmowska, pp. 186–190.

76. TNA, FO 371/56468, N 3670, Interviews with General Anders and other Polish Commanders, 15 March 1946.

77. TNA, FO 371/56668, N 9024, Confidential letter written by Brigadier Firth to Robin Hankey, 13 July 1946.

78. Maresh, p. 54.

79. PISM, KGA.1g, Collected Speeches of General Anders, 1945, Bologna, 29 June 1945, reported in *Dziennik*

80. PISM, KGA.1g, General Anders, speech to Gryfów, Wrócimy *do Polski, ale Polski Niepodległej a nie do 17–tej republika sowieckiej*, 9 July 1945.

81. PISM, KGA.1g, General Anders, '*Polski jest niewoli' Gazeta Żołnierza*, 11 July 1945.

82. PISM, A.XII.1/48a, The Intention of the Polish armed forces at the Side of Great Britain, 9 March 1945.

83. PISM, KGA.1g, Commander 2nd Polish Corps, Officers' Order Nr. 10, 11 September 1945.

84. General Sir Mike Jackson, *Soldier. The Autobiography of General Sir Mike Jackson*, London, Bantam Press, 2007, pp. 89–90.

85. PISM, KGA/5a, Lieutenant General W.D. Morgan (Chief of Staff) [Allied Force Headquarters] to Lieutenant General Anders, 25 July 1945.

86. PISM, A.XII.1/48d, The Polish armed forces, 2 Corps in Italy, 1944–1945, Major General Regulski to Major General J.A. Sinclair (WO) 5 February 1945.

87. PISM, A.XII.1/48d, Major General Sinclair to Major General Regulski, 5 March 1945.

88. PISM, KGA/5b, Conversations with the Allies, Minutes of a Meeting between Field Marshal Sir Harold Alexander, Supreme Allied Commander and Lieutenant General W. Anders, Commander 2 Polish Corps, 17 February 1945.

89. Anders, p. 256.

90. Ibid, p. 259. Alan Bullock, p. 484.

91. PISM, KGA/5c, Writings of General Anders, Order of the Day issued by General W. Anders to the men of 2 Polish Corps, 8 July 1945.

92. PISM, KGA/5b, Notes on Meeting between Chief of Staff AFHQ (Allied Forces Headquarters) and Lieutenant General Anders at Caserta, 23 July 1945.

93. PISM, KGA/5b, Notes on Meeting between the SAC (Supreme Allied Commander) and Lieutenant General Anders, Commander 2 Polish Corps, 27 September 1945.

94. PISM, KGA/5b, Minutes of Meeting between Anders and Lieutenant General Sir W. Morgan, Supreme Allied Commander at Caserta, 28 November 1945.

95. PISM, KGA/5c, General Anders to President Raczkiewicz, 21 November 1945.

96. PISM, KGA/5d, Miscellaneous Correspondence, 1945, General Anders to the Soldiers of 2nd (Polish) Corps, July 1945.

97. PISM, KGA/5d, Staff Report, Colonel Józef Skolebski, 16 November 1945.

98. PISM, KGA/13, Notes on a Meeting at 10 Downing Street, 15 March 1946.

99. PISM, C.88/11, 3rd Carpathian Rifle Brigade, Order Nr. 50, 22 December 1945.

100. TNA, KV 4/286, Polish Resettlement Corps, Policy for the Absorption and Control of Polish Forces in the UK, Including Procedure for Discharge and Repatriation, 14 October 1946; 29 October 1946.

101. PISM, KGA/13, Future of the Polish armed forces; Notes of a Conference held in Room 220, The War Office, 23 May 1946; see also Conference at FO, 21 May 1946.

102. PISM, KGA/13, T. Filipowicz to Attlee, 30 May 1946.

103. PISM, KGA/13, Notes on a Meeting between SAC and Lieutenant General Anders at Caserta, 6 June 1946.

104. PISM, C.80/II, *Kronika 5KDP*, Anders, 15 June 1946.

105. PISM, KGA/13, Anders to HE Myron Taylor, Personal Representative of the President of the USA to his Holiness, the Pope, 15 June 1946.

106. PISM, KGA/13, Lieutenant General Sir William Morgan to Lieutenant General Anders, 1 July 1946.

107. PISM, KGA/13, Minutes of a Conference held in the Office of the Supreme Allied Commander, Mediterranean Theatre, 31 July 1946.

108. PISM, KGA. 652, 28 September 1946.

109. Sarner, p. 233.

110. Ibid, pp. 239–240.

Chapter Ten: The End: 1947–1970

1. TNA, FO 371/47661 N 2681, Sir A. Clark–Kerr (Moscow) to Sir Orme Sargent, 12 March 1945.

2. TNA, FO 371/47660 N 279/123/55, Reports on 2 Polish Corps, Major General Beaumont, 16 December 1944.

3. Martin Kitchen, *British Policy towards the Soviet Union During the Second World War*, London, Macmillan, 1986, p. 245.

4. TNA, FO 371/47665 N 6300/G, Colville to Dixon, 31 May 1945; FO 371/47665 N 7260/G, June 1945.

5. PISM, A.XII.1/48a, Lieutenant General Anders to General Sosnkowski, 30 August 1944.

6. PISM, A.XII.1/48a, Memorandum, Polish Embassy, London, 8 September 1944.

7. PISM, A.XII.1/48a, Lieutenant General S. Kopański to Lieutenant General Scobie (RM) undated.

8. TNA, FO 371/47662 N 3103/123/G55, Minute of F. Gatehouse, 6 April 1945.

9. TNA, FO 371/47665 N6300/G, Colville to Dixon, 31 May 1945.

10. TNA, CAB 122, British Joint Staff Mission, Washington, CAB 122/925 COS (45) 323 (0) 'Future of the Polish armed forces'. Note by the Chief of the Imperial General Staff, Minute 2, 9 May 1945.

11. TNA, FO 371/4766 N6918, Captain Addis (War Office) to Allen, (FO) 16 June 1945.

12. McGilvray, *Man of Steel and Honour,* p. 106.

13. TNA, FO 371/47666, Telegram from Mr Broad (Caserta, Italy) 23 June 1945.

14. PISM, PRM 20/26, Conversation between General Sikorski and Ernest Bevin, Minister for Labour, 1 November 1940; PRM 37B/37, Polish Consulate, Istanbul to London, 14 September 1940, re: moving Polish troops to Egypt.

15. PISM, KGA/5a, Memorandum on 2 Polish Corps, 24 August 1945. Anders had resigned as Acting C–in–C Polish Armed Forces during May 1945, TNA, FO 371/47665 N654/G, Anders to Churchill, 28 May 1945.

16. TNA, FO 371/47665 N6545/G, Prime Minister's Personal Minute M.543/5, 31 May 1945.

17. Sarner, pp. 270–272. See also: *The Times* (London) 10–27 February 1960, 1 March 1960.

18. Ibid.

19. Ewa Berberyusz, *Anders Spieszony*, London, Aneks, 1992, p. 9.

20. Ibid, p. 24.

21. Dobbs, pp. 58–60. Boris Johnson, *The Churchill Factor. How One Man Made History*, London, Hodder & Stoughton, 2015, p. 280.

22. Walter Reid, *Churchill, 1940–1945: Under Friendly Fire*, Edinburgh, Birlinn, 2008, p. 279.

23. Sarner, pp. 247–248, 256.

Index